Phantasmatic Death: The Unconscious Shaping of Our End

by

Deivede Eder Ferreira

Does the Unconscious Desire Determine the Way We Die?: The New Theory of Phantasmatic Death

Deivede Eder Ferreira

Published by ABRAFP, 2025.

DOES THE UNCONSCIOUS DESIRE DETERMINE THE WAY WE DIE?: THE NEW THEORY OF PHANTASMATIC DEATH

First edition. November 21, 2025.

ISBN: 979-8232778224

Written by Deivede Eder Ferreira.

Also by Deivede Eder Ferreira

Behind the Theory: The Lives of the Great Psychoanalysts
Freud — The Definitive Biography: The True Story of the Father of Psychoanalysis

Últimos Dias dos Grandes Pensadores
Sócrates: O Último Amanhecer
Platão: Quando o Mestre Silenciou
Aristóteles: O Nascimento do Método

Standalone
Psychoanalysis
The Quantum Switch: How to Shift Your Inner Reality
Does the Unconscious Desire Determine the Way We Die?: The New Theory of Phantasmatic Death
سقراط: الفجر الأخير

Table of Contents

Front Matter

To the silent architects of our inner worlds, the weavers of dreams and the sculptors of dread, whose unconscious visions chart the courses of our lives and, in their final, most profound resonance, the very shape of our endings. This exploration is a testament to the intricate, often hidden, artistry that imbues each human life with its unique signature, a signature that extends even to the ultimate silence. May this work serve as a bridge, illuminating the profound connection between the life lived and the art of dying, acknowledging the persistent whisper of the unconscious in the face of oblivion. For those who wrestle with the shadows, who seek meaning in the face of finitude, and who understand that even in dissolution, there is a profound, often poetic, truth to be found.

The shadow of death looms large in the human psyche, a perennial enigma that has captivated philosophers, artists, and clinicians for millennia. Yet, our understanding of this ultimate frontier often remains tethered to biological finality, a cessation of breath and consciousness. This book ventures into a less charted territory: the unconscious architecture of our dying. It proposes that death, far from being a purely random or determined event, is profoundly shaped by the symbolic narratives woven within the deepest recesses of our minds.

Drawing from the rich theoretical landscapes of psychoanalysis, particularly the seminal insights of Freud and Lacan, alongside the existential currents of philosophy and the evocative power of literary theory, this work posits the existence of a 'phantasmatic signature.' This signature, imprinted by our unconscious desires, fears, and unresolved conflicts, dictates not the timing of our death, but its symbolic form, its aesthetic, and its narrative. It is the unique, often hidden, artistry with which we unconsciously compose our final act.

We will explore how this phantasmatic signature manifests in distinct aesthetic patterns of dying: the quiet erasure of vanishing without a trace, the desperate spectacle of dramatic appearance, the yearning for profound mourning, and the seductive allure of escape from unbearable realities. Furthermore, we will grapple with the insidious realm of 'suicide without suicide,' where indirect self-destructiveness leads to a fatal conclusion without overt suicidal intent, highlighting the intricate and often paradoxical ways the unconscious negotiates with annihilation.

This journey will be illuminated by anonymized clinical vignettes that offer tangible examples of these theoretical constructs, alongside literary and philosophical references that provide broader cultural and symbolic resonance. Our exploration is an invitation to move beyond the biological fact of death and to engage with its psychological and symbolic dimensions, recognizing that in the way we die, we often find the ultimate expression of who we were. This is an endeavor to understand the unconscious as the ultimate author of our endings, transforming the mystery of death into a profound, albeit often spectral, form of life's art.

The human experience is inextricably bound to the awareness of finitude. From the earliest whispers of consciousness, mortality casts its long shadow, shaping our desires, our anxieties, and our very understanding of existence. Yet, the discourse surrounding death often remains confined to the realms of biology, theology, or stark existential dread. This book embarks on a more psychoanalytically informed exploration, proposing that the ultimate event of dying is not merely a biological cessation but a profoundly symbolic act, orchestrated by the unconscious architecture of the self.

We are not suggesting a deterministic blueprint dictating the precise moment of our demise. Rather, we contend that the *manner* of our death, its symbolic form, its narrative texture, and its aesthetic quality, is deeply imbued with the subject's unique unconscious landscape. This is the essence of the 'phantasmatic signature'—a concept that posits that our deepest, often unacknowledged, fantasies, desires, and unresolved conflicts unconsciously shape the symbolic script of our final exit. This signature is not about the cause of death, but the underlying psychic logic that imbues it with its particular resonance and meaning, however obscure.

This psychoanalytic inquiry into the aesthetics of dying draws upon the foundational insights of Freud, particularly his complex formulations of the death drive and repression, and the post-Freudian elaborations of Lacan, with his emphasis on the Real, the Symbolic, and the Imaginary. These theoretical frameworks provide the conceptual tools necessary to dissect the unconscious processes that inform our relationship with mortality, revealing how early life experiences, relational dynamics, and enduring psychic patterns converge to 'write' the narrative of our end. We will examine how death can be understood as the final, potent staging of the unconscious, a singular performance where repressed desires and enduring conflicts find their ultimate, symbolic resolution.

Through this lens, we move beyond a purely biological or existential understanding of death to embrace its rich symbolic dimension. The chapters that follow will systematically unpack various 'aesthetics of dying,' exploring patterns such as the unconscious desire for complete erasure ('vanishing without a trace'), the compelling need for a spectacular exit ('dramatic appearance'), the deep-seated yearning to be mourned, and the seductive flight from unbearable realities ('the aesthetics of escape'). We will also confront the complex phenomenon of 'suicide without suicide,' a testament to the myriad indirect pathways through which unconscious self-destructive impulses can lead to a fatal conclusion. Furthermore, we will trace the origins of these death scripts back to early childhood narratives and explore how the unconscious negotiation with the unsymbolizable 'Real' plays a pivotal role in shaping our ultimate confrontation with finitude. This intricate tapestry of unconscious influence, woven throughout life, culminates in a 'fantasmatic signature' that renders each death a unique, deeply personal, and often poetic expression of the self.

Chapter 1: The Unconscious and the Art of Dying

The biological cessation of life, a moment universally understood as death, is but one facet of a far more intricate phenomenon. Beneath the stark finality of the physical event lies a profound symbolic architecture, meticulously constructed within the unseen chambers of the unconscious. It is this internal edifice, forged by the unique crucible of individual experience, desire, and defense, that imbues our dying with its characteristic form and narrative style. Our central thesis posits that while the precise timing of biological death may elude definitive psychic prediction, its symbolic manifestation—the *how* of our passing—is inextricably shaped by the deepest currents of our unconscious life. This is the realm of **phantasmatic death**: the ultimate, often unacknowledged, expression of our most potent unconscious fantasies and desires, a final act orchestrated by the psyche itself.

To delineate 'phantasmatic death' from mere biological cessation is to recognize the distinction between the brute fact of cessation and the subjective, symbolic meaning that surrounds it. Biological death is the undeniable endpoint of physiological processes. Phantasmatic death, however, is the

script of that ending, the aesthetic and narrative texture with which it is imbued, dictated by the subject's internal world. It is not a question of *if* death will arrive, but of the particular language and imagery through which it will be articulated. This perspective shifts our focus from the clinical inevitability of death to its psychological and symbolic dimensions, framing it not as an alien intrusion upon life, but as its most profound and deeply personal culmination. Every life, in its unique unfolding, is unconsciously preparing the stage for this final scene, drawing upon the enduring patterns, the repressed traumas, and the unfulfilled longings that constitute the individual psychic landscape. This deeply personal narrative, written in the language of the unconscious, sets the stage for a far richer and more nuanced exploration into the aesthetic dimensions of our endings, revealing death not as a void, but as a final, albeit often enigmatic, statement.

The unconscious, a vast and mysterious repository of our psychic history, exerts an almost sovereign influence over the way we approach and experience our final moments. It is the repository of primal drives, the echo chamber of early relational patterns, and the birthplace of our most enduring fantasies. These elements, operating beyond the grasp of conscious awareness, do not merely influence our thoughts or behaviors; they actively shape the symbolic form of our demise. Consider the individual who, throughout life, has grappled with an overwhelming sense of worthlessness, an existential conviction of their own insignificance. This internal narrative, so deeply entrenched in the unconscious, may not lead to a conscious decision to end their life. Instead, it might manifest in a passive surrender, a quiet fading into obscurity, an ending characterized by an absence of any significant mark or memory—a 'vanishing without a trace.' This is not a choice made in the light of day, but a symbolic fulfillment of a deeply held, unconscious belief.

Conversely, the unconscious might harbor a powerful, compensatory fantasy of omnipotence or a desperate need for validation that was never adequately met in life. This potent internal force can manifest in an 'aesthetic of dramatic appearance,' where the individual's death becomes a spectacular, albeit tragic, event. This could involve acts of extreme defiance, a public denunciation, or a final, desperate bid for attention that ensures their name, their story, or their grievance will be remembered. The timing and manner of such an end are not dictated by biological imperatives alone, but by the unconscious need to rewrite a life perceived as overlooked or undervalued into a final, unforgettable act. The unconscious, in its relentless pursuit of symbolic resolution, crafts these narratives of disappearance and spectacle, weaving them into the very fabric of our eventual demise.

The concept of 'phantasmatic death' posits that our unconscious fantasies do not dictate the

when of death, but rather the symbolic *how*. This distinction is crucial. It acknowledges the biological reality of mortality while insisting on the paramount importance of the psyche in shaping the *experience* and *meaning* of that end. For instance, the unconscious fear of abandonment might not lead to a direct suicidal act, but it could shape an individual's final days to be characterized by a desperate, unconscious manipulation of loved ones, ensuring they are surrounded and cared for, thereby symbolically negating the primal fear of being left alone. The death, in this instance, becomes an unconscious 'performance' designed to elicit specific affective responses, fulfilling a deep-seated need for connection and reassurance even in the face of oblivion. The timing is incidental; the symbolic fulfillment is paramount.

The influence of early life narratives cannot be overstated in the construction of this phantasmatic death. The primal experiences of separation from primary caregivers, the anxieties surrounding parental loss, or the early intimations of mortality that a child encounters all contribute to the formation of unconscious 'death scripts.' These scripts are not conscious plans, but deeply embedded emotional and imagistic templates that shape our fundamental understanding of endings. A child who experiences the sudden, unexplained absence of a parent might internalize a fantasy of disintegration or disappearance as the primary mode of loss. This early template can then unconsciously inform their own death narrative, leading to an ending characterized by a profound sense of fading or an inability to articulate the experience of dying, mirroring the unanswered questions and unresolved anxieties of their childhood.

Furthermore, the persistent patterns of our lives, those repetitive behaviors and relational dynamics that we often struggle to consciously alter, are potent signifiers of unconscious forces at play. The compulsion to repeat, a cornerstone of psychoanalytic theory, suggests that we are often driven to re-enact unresolved conflicts, seeking a different outcome or a symbolic resolution that was denied in the past. This compulsion extends to our relationship with death. An individual who has consistently sabotaged their own success, driven by unconscious guilt or a belief in their own unworthiness, may find that this pattern culminates in a fatal self-destructive act that is not overtly suicidal but nonetheless a direct consequence of these deeply ingrained, self-defeating maneuvers. The death, in such cases, becomes the ultimate, albeit tragic, repetition of a lifelong pattern.

This is not to suggest that all deaths are consciously or unconsciously desired. Rather, it is to assert that the

symbolic form of our passing is profoundly influenced by our internal psychic landscape. The unconscious does not necessarily 'choose' death, but it imbues the process with a narrative and an aesthetic that reflect its deepest preoccupations. For some, this might involve a yearning for profound mourning, a desire that their absence be deeply felt, thus validating the significance of their life.

This unconscious need can shape their relationships, their interactions, and their very presentation of self, all with the aim of ensuring that their death will resonate with a significant emotional echo. The death, then, becomes a posthumous fulfillment of a lifelong need for affective recognition.

The aesthetic dimension of death, as shaped by the unconscious, is thus incredibly varied. It can range from the quietude of dissolution to the fanfare of a dramatic exit, from the stark confrontation with the unspeakable 'Real' to the seductive allure of escape. Each of these manifestations is a testament to the psyche's capacity to imbue even the most biological of events with profound symbolic meaning. By introducing the concept of phantasmatic death, we aim to open a conceptual space for understanding these deeply personal and often paradoxical ways in which we navigate our mortality. It is an invitation to look beyond the clinical or biological facts of dying and to consider the rich, symbolic tapestry that the unconscious weaves into our final act, revealing death not merely as an end, but as a profoundly significant, uniquely authored conclusion to the narrative of a life. This approach provides the foundational understanding for exploring the multifaceted aesthetics of human endings, moving towards a more comprehensive psychoanalytic engagement with mortality.

The unconscious mind, a vast and largely uncharted territory, is the architect of our deepest desires, our most guarded fears, and the enduring narratives that shape our perception of reality. It is within this intricate psychic architecture that the blueprint for our death is, in part, drawn. This subsection serves as an introduction to the central thesis that the unconscious profoundly influences the symbolic form and narrative style of our dying, not necessarily its precise timing. We are not suggesting that the unconscious dictates the exact moment of biological cessation, but rather that it imbues the experience of death with a unique aesthetic and a personal narrative, transforming it from a purely biological event into a final, potent expression of our deepest psychic preoccupations. This is the essence of what we term 'phantasmatic death'.

To understand phantasmatic death is to recognize that our biological end is imbued with a symbolic resonance, a quality that reflects the unique contours of our individual psychic landscape. This landscape is sculpted by a confluence of factors: early life experiences, formative relational dynamics, ingrained defense mechanisms, and the persistent echoes of unconscious fantasies. These elements coalesce to create a 'fantasmatic signature'—a distinct, often unconscious, imprint on the style and meaning of our dying. For example, an individual whose life has been characterized by a pervasive sense of guilt may unconsciously structure their death to reflect this internal state, perhaps through a protracted illness that serves as a form of penance, or an ending that leaves behind a legacy of unresolved conflict for their loved ones, a symbolic continuation of their internal burden. The timing of this ending is biological, but its narrative and symbolic texture are undeniably phantasmatic.

The distinction between phantasmatic death and biological cessation is fundamental. Biological death is the undisputed cessation of bodily functions, a physical reality that is universal and irreversible. Phantasmatic death, conversely, is the symbolic culmination of a lifetime of psychic work, the final act in a drama orchestrated by the unconscious. It is the aesthetic, the narrative, the emotional tonality that surrounds and colors the biological event. Consider the difference between the simple fact of a heart stopping and the elaborate, deeply personal, and often unconscious meaning that the individual's psyche assigns to that moment. This symbolic layer is where the unconscious asserts its profound influence, shaping how this ultimate transition is experienced and, often posthumously, understood. The unconscious, in its tireless pursuit of meaning and resolution, imbues our endings with a narrative arc, a characterization, and a final thematic statement.

The aim of conceptualizing phantasmatic death is to frame our endings not as mere biological incidents, but as final, symbolic acts. Each death becomes a testament to the subject's unique psychic journey, a culmination of enduring unconscious patterns that have shaped their desires, their defenses, and their understanding of existence itself. These patterns are not static; they evolve and are reinterpreted throughout life, but their fundamental influence on our ultimate symbolic resolution remains potent. Early childhood narratives of loss, separation, and abandonment, for instance, can lay down powerful templates for how an individual unconsciously anticipates and experiences their own final separation. A childhood marked by a profound sense of being unseen or unheard might unconsciously predispose an individual towards an ending characterized by a quiet disappearance, a fading without recognition, a symbolic echo of their lived experience.

This perspective allows us to move beyond a purely clinical or biological understanding of death and to appreciate its richer, psychological dimensions. It opens up a space for exploring the aesthetic qualities of our endings. Just as a life can be characterized by its artistic style, its dramatic flair, or its quiet introspection, so too can a death possess its own unique aesthetic. This aesthetic is not chosen consciously in the way one might choose an outfit, but rather it emerges organically from the deepest strata of the unconscious. It is the imprint of an individual's internal world upon the universal experience of dying. The 'fantasmatic signature' of death, as we will explore further, is the unique manifestation of this unconscious artistry. It is the distinct style, the recurring motifs, the emotional timbre that makes each death a singular, albeit often unconscious, statement.

The unconscious does not operate in a vacuum; it is in constant dialogue with our lived experiences, our relationships, and our attempts to make sense of the world. The narratives we construct about our lives, the stories we tell ourselves and others, are unconsciously filtered and shaped by these deeper psychic forces. These life narratives, in turn, act as precursors to the narrative of our death. The themes that dominate our conscious and unconscious preoccupation throughout life—themes of struggle, love, loss, ambition, or despair—are likely to find their echo, their symbolic resolution, in the final act. For example, an individual who has spent their life striving for recognition and validation might unconsciously orchestrate their death to be a moment of ultimate, albeit posthumous, triumph or a poignant testament to their unmet needs.

This approach also allows for a more compassionate understanding of certain behaviors that may precede death. The unconscious drive towards self-destruction, often expressed not through overt suicidal intent but through indirect means like reckless behavior, addiction, or chronic neglect of one's health, can be understood as a manifestation of phantasmatic death. In these instances, the unconscious seeks a symbolic resolution that culminates in an end, not necessarily out of a desire for oblivion, but perhaps as a form of punishment, an escape from unbearable psychic pain, or a desperate attempt to exert control in a life that feels overwhelmingly chaotic. The death, in these cases, becomes the final chapter in a long narrative of unconscious self-sabotage, a tragic fulfillment of a deeply ingrained psychic script.

By focusing on the symbolic and narrative dimensions of death, we are not diminishing the reality of biological finality. Instead, we are seeking to understand the profound psychological work that the unconscious undertakes in shaping our experience of that finality. It is an acknowledgment that human beings are not merely biological organisms confronting an inevitable end, but complex psychic entities for whom death is a deeply symbolic event, intricately interwoven with the threads of their personal history and their unconscious desires. This framework sets the stage for a deeper exploration into the aesthetic dimensions of our endings, inviting us to consider the poetry, the drama, and the profound personal meaning that can be found, even in the face of annihilation. The unconscious, in its mysterious ways, ensures that our dying is never merely an end, but a final, uniquely authored testament to a life lived, a final expression of the self in its most symbolic form. This introduction, therefore, lays the groundwork for understanding death not as an arbitrary biological event, but as a deeply personal, psychically constructed narrative, an art form of the unconscious.

The intricate tapestry of human mortality, as we have begun to explore, is not merely a biological countdown but a deeply psychically woven narrative. This narrative is largely orchestrated by the unconscious, a realm that psychoanalytic theory has striven to illuminate. Central to this endeavor are the seminal contributions of Sigmund Freud and Jacques Lacan, whose divergent yet complementary perspectives offer profound insights into the unconscious architecture of our endings. Their conceptual frameworks provide the essential tools for dissecting the 'phantasmatic signature' that characterizes an individual's death, moving beyond mere biological cessation to the symbolic and aesthetic dimensions of our final moments.

Freud's groundbreaking work on the unconscious laid the foundation for understanding repression and the operation of drives that transcend the pleasure principle. His concept of the

Trieb (drive), particularly the death drive (*Thanatos*), introduces a fundamental tension within the psyche. While the life drives (*Eros*) propel us towards connection, growth, and preservation, the death drive, in its most primal form, pushes towards dissolution, a return to an inorganic state. This drive, however, does not manifest as a conscious desire for self-annihilation. Instead, it operates through complex defense mechanisms, manifesting as aggression, masochism, or an unconscious compulsion to repeat traumatic experiences. In the context of dying, the death drive can be seen as the ultimate, albeit often obscured, force pushing towards a cessation, an undoing of the organism's complex organization. However, it is crucial to reiterate that this is not a conscious volition. Rather, it is a deep, instinctual tendency that seeks a return to a primal state of quiescence, a state before the agonizing complexities of conscious existence and desire.

Repression, the cornerstone of Freudian psychoanalysis, plays a critical role in how the unconscious architecture of death is constructed. Experiences, thoughts, and feelings that are too traumatic, too anxiety-provoking, or too socially unacceptable for the conscious ego to bear are relegated to the unconscious. These repressed elements do not disappear; they continue to exert influence, shaping our behavior, our fantasies, and ultimately, our symbolic representation of death. For instance, a profound childhood trauma involving loss or violence might be deeply repressed. The psychic energy invested in maintaining this repression is immense, and it can find an outlet in the symbolic staging of one's death. This could manifest as an unconscious reenactment of the original trauma, a dramatic, albeit non-conscious, return of the repressed, or a subtle yet pervasive sense of impending doom that colours the individual's final days. The repressed thus becomes a hidden architect, dictating the emotional tonality and thematic content of the phantasmatic death.

Furthermore, Freud's exploration of melancholia and mourning provides a crucial lens through which to view the psychological processing of loss, both internal and external. Melancholia, unlike normal mourning, involves an introjection of the lost object, leading to a breakdown of the ego's boundaries and a profound sense of self-recrimination. When this internal dynamic is projected onto the individual's own eventual demise, it can contribute to a death characterized by a sense of desolate emptiness, a profound feeling of worthlessness, or an unconscious self-punishment that mirrors the internalized critique. The phantasmatic signature, in such cases, would be one of profound sadness, a quiet disintegration, or an ending that leaves a legacy of emotional desolation for those left behind, a symbolic extension of the internal melancholic state.

Jacques Lacan, building upon and often diverging from Freud, introduced a tripartite model of the psyche – the Imaginary, the Symbolic, and the Real – that offers a more nuanced understanding of how meaning, language, and the unspeakable coalesce in our experience of life and death. Lacan's framework profoundly reshapes our understanding of the unconscious by emphasizing its structural relationship to language and social order. The unconscious, for Lacan, is not merely a repository of repressed content but is "structured like a language." This means that our deepest desires, fears, and fantasies are articulated and experienced through the symbolic order, the network of language, laws, and social conventions that structure our reality.

The Imaginary order, characterized by identifications and the formation of the ego through narcissistic mirroring, plays a significant role in the early construction of our sense of self. It is within the Imaginary that we develop idealized self-images and engage in the often deceptive play of appearances. In relation to death, the Imaginary might be responsible for the glamorous or heroic fantasies of how one might die, the desire to be remembered as a martyr or a legend. It is the realm of the imagined self, the self we project and wish to be, and this projection can significantly influence the narrative we unconsciously script for our final act. The phantasmatic signature here might involve a desire for a memorable exit, a dramatic flourish, a posthumous validation of the idealized self.

The Symbolic order, on the other hand, is the realm of language, law, and the paternal metaphor that introduces order and meaning into our lives. It is through the Symbolic that we are integrated into the social fabric, given a name, and subjected to the rules of society. Death, in this order, is a universal signifier, a point of passage that is articulated through language and cultural rituals. However, the Symbolic order also introduces alienation, as our entry into language means we can never fully possess or express our being. The unconscious struggle with this fundamental alienation, the gap between our subjective experience and the linguistic signifiers available to us, can significantly shape our phantasmatic death.

Lacan's concept of desire is central here. Desire, for Lacan, is not a simple want but the fundamental lack that structures the human subject. It is an endlessly deferred pursuit, always seeking satisfaction that is perpetually out of reach. This inherent lack, this unfulfillable desire, becomes inextricably bound up with our understanding of death. The unconscious may project this unfulfilled desire onto the very act of dying, transforming it into a symbolic fulfillment or a final attempt to grasp what has always been elusive. This can lead to a death that is driven by an unconscious seeking of ultimate satisfaction or resolution, a final, desperate grasp at meaning. The phantasmatic signature could be one of profound longing, a sense of unfinished business, or an ending that seems to be reaching for something beyond the immediate.

The Real, the third dimension of Lacan's topology, is perhaps the most enigmatic and the most relevant to the experience of death. The Real represents that which lies outside the Symbolic and Imaginary orders, that which is unrepresentable, unsymbolizable, and resistant to language. It is the brute facticity of existence, the primal void, the fundamental trauma that lies at the heart of our being. Death, in its ultimate essence, touches upon the Real. It is the point where the Symbolic order breaks down, where language fails, and where the subject is confronted with the ultimate limit of their existence.

For Lacan, the unconscious is deeply intertwined with the Real, representing the irruption of this unassailable dimension into our otherwise structured psychic lives. In the context of dying, the Real manifests as the sheer terror of annihilation, the unspeakable horror of non-being, the absolute cessation of experience. The phantasmatic signature of a death confronting the Real might be characterized by a profound sense of dread, an encounter with the ineffable, a breakdown of coherent narrative and symbolic meaning. It is the moment where the carefully constructed edifice of the self, built from Imaginary identifications and Symbolic representations, crumbles in the face of a stark, unvarnished reality.

The theory of

objet petit a, Lacan's concept of the elusive object-cause of desire, also sheds light on the unconscious architecture of ending. This object is not a concrete thing but a placeholder for the unattainable, the lost object that fuels our desire. In the context of death, the unconscious might cathect this *objet petit a* onto the very process of dying, imbuing it with a mysterious allure or a profound, albeit often tragic, significance. The death becomes a quest for this ultimate object, a final, desperate attempt to achieve an impossible fulfillment. The phantasmatic signature here would be one of uncanny fascination, a spectral lure, or an ending that seems to be pulled by an invisible, irresistible force.

When considering the 'phantasmatic signature' of an individual's death, Freud and Lacan provide complementary lenses. Freud helps us understand the mechanisms of repression and the influence of primal drives, explaining

how repressed content might find its way into the symbolic staging of death. Lacan, on the other hand, provides the linguistic and structural framework to understand *why* death becomes such a potent site for the articulation of desire, lack, and the confrontation with the Real. Together, their theories illuminate how unconscious processes, operating outside our conscious awareness, weave a complex, symbolic narrative that shapes the aesthetic and emotional texture of our final moments.

For example, consider an individual who has lived with profound, unacknowledged shame stemming from early experiences of perceived failure. Freud's concepts would suggest that this shame is repressed, its psychic energy manifesting in unconscious self-sabotaging behaviors. Lacan's framework would then explain how this repressed shame finds symbolic expression in the death narrative. It might manifest as a death characterized by extreme isolation (a rejection of social recognition, aligning with the Symbolic's demand for integration), or perhaps a death that involves a dramatic, symbolic act of self-abasement or confession (an eruption of the Real into the Symbolic, challenging the idealized self of the Imaginary). The phantasmatic signature here is not one of bravery or peaceful surrender, but one of profound, inescapable shame, a narrative dictated by the unconscious imperative to enact the repressed emotional truth.

Similarly, an individual consumed by a lifelong pursuit of an unattainable ideal – be it love, success, or recognition – embodies Lacan's concept of desire as a fundamental lack. Freud's death drive, in this context, might be understood as a sublimated expression of this ultimate frustration, a yearning for an end to the perpetual striving. The phantasmatic death could then be one of tragic grandeur, a final, desperate attempt to grasp the elusive

objet petit a, leading to an ending that is simultaneously heroic and profoundly melancholic. The signature is one of magnificent failure, a life's narrative culminating in an equally symbolic, albeit fatal, quest. The unconscious, in these instances, utilizes the available symbolic resources, influenced by repressed drives and the fundamental structures of desire, to script an ending that attempts to resolve, or at least dramatically enact, the deepest psychic conflicts.

The interplay between Freud's emphasis on instinctual drives and Lacan's focus on the structural role of language and the Real provides a robust theoretical scaffolding for understanding the unconscious construction of death. It moves us from a simplistic view of death as a biological endpoint to a recognition of its profound symbolic and aesthetic dimensions, shaped by the hidden currents of our psychic lives. These theoretical foundations are not merely academic exercises; they offer a way to conceptualize the deeply personal and often perplexing narratives that emerge at the threshold of existence, underscoring that the 'how' of our dying is an intricate psychodrama, authored in the silent theaters of the unconscious. The phantasmatic signature, therefore, is the unique mark of this unconscious authorship, a testament to the individual's deepest desires, their most profound defenses, and their ultimate encounter with the limits of being.

Death, in its stark biological finality, becomes the ultimate canvas upon which the unconscious paints its most profound and often paradoxical masterpiece. It is not merely an end but a culmination, a final performance where the deeply buried narratives of our lives, the unresolved conflicts, the unacknowledged desires, and the spectral echoes of primal drives are brought to their most potent symbolic resolution. This is the final act of a drama that has been playing out in the hidden theaters of the psyche, a psychodrama scripted by the unconscious, where the dying individual, often unknowingly, embodies their deepest truths and confronts their most fundamental anxieties about existence and its cessation. The concept of death as the final scene of the unconscious posits that even in the face of biological dissolution, a potent symbolic narrative unfolds, an aesthetic quality that reflects the unique unconscious journey of the individual and their most profound wishes or fears concerning disappearance.

The unconscious, as the unseen architect of our psychic lives, leaves its indelible signature on the very process of dying. This signature is not a conscious decision, nor is it necessarily a reflection of the individual's waking beliefs or desires. Instead, it is the emergent property of deeply ingrained patterns, repressed experiences, and the inherent dynamics of the drives. Early childhood experiences, the very bedrock of our psychic formation, play a crucial role in etching these patterns. The relational dynamics established in infancy, the primal bonds and their inevitable ruptures, the initial encounters with loss and separation – these formative moments become the foundational grammar of our unconscious script. The way an infant learns to manage distress, the implicit narratives of safety or abandonment internalized, the primal fears of annihilation and the nascent desires for connection and autonomy – all these early lessons are encoded in the unconscious, waiting to be played out on the grand stage of death. These are not memories in the conventional sense, but rather embodied knowledge, affective imprints that shape our fundamental relationship with vulnerability, dependency, and the inevitable separateness of being.

Consider, for instance, an individual who, in early childhood, experienced profound emotional neglect, where their cries for comfort were consistently met with silence or indifference. This experience, deeply wounding and largely unacknowledged by the conscious mind as it developed its defenses, can imbue the unconscious with a narrative of inherent unworthiness and an expectation of ultimate abandonment. When this individual approaches the end of their life, the unconscious may orchestrate a death that symbolically enacts this primal experience. This might manifest not as a conscious desire to be alone or to punish others, but as a series of circumstances that lead to profound isolation in their final days or hours. They may find themselves estranged from loved ones, or their death may occur in a solitary setting, a silent echo of that early, unanswered plea. The phantasmatic signature here is one of desolation, a quiet fading away that mirrors the internalized sense of being fundamentally alone and unloved. It is the unconscious drive towards a symbolic resolution of that early trauma, a final confirmation of the deeply held, albeit unconscious, belief that in the end, one is truly alone. This is not a rational choice; it is the unconscious compelling the final scene to reflect the most deeply buried emotional truth.

Furthermore, the inherent drives, as conceptualized by Freud, become potent forces in shaping this final performance. While

Eros, the life drives, propel us towards connection, creativity, and the perpetuation of life, *Thanatos*, the death drive, exerts a subtle yet persistent pull towards dissolution, a return to an inorganic state of quiescence. This is not a conscious suicidal impulse but a more fundamental, instinctual tendency towards the undoing of complex organization. In the context of dying, the death drive can manifest as an unconscious acquiescence, a deep weariness with the struggle of being, a subtle yielding to the forces of entropy. It can also fuel a more aggressive or self-destructive trajectory in the dying process itself, as if the organism, driven by an unconscious imperative, is hastening its own dissolution. The phantasmatic signature in such cases might be one of an unusually rapid decline, an inexplicable loss of vitality, or an ending characterized by a profound sense of inertia, a quiet surrender to the forces of disintegration that mirrors the unconscious pull towards the void.

Lacanian psychoanalysis offers a vital perspective on how language and the symbolic order contribute to this final act. The unconscious, structured like a language, means that our deepest conflicts and desires are articulated through signifiers, through the very fabric of meaning we inhabit. Death, as the ultimate signifier of finitude, becomes a potent site for the eruption of these unconscious linguistic dramas. The symbolic order, which provides us with identity, social positioning, and a framework for understanding reality, is profoundly challenged by death. For Lacan, the unconscious is the locus where the Real, that which resists symbolization, irrupts into our symbolic existence. Death is precisely such a point of irruption, where the unspeakable nature of annihilation confronts the subject.

Consider an individual who has built their identity around a carefully crafted image of strength, control, and unwavering competence. This carefully constructed self, deeply rooted in the Imaginary order of idealized self-images, is inherently vulnerable to the uncontrollable and undignified realities of illness and physical decline. The unconscious, recognizing this fragility, may orchestrate a final scene that dramatically confronts this meticulously constructed facade. This could manifest as a death characterized by an extreme loss of control, a descent into a state of profound vulnerability that shatters the lifelong performance of invincibility. The individual might become delirious, their carefully guarded thoughts and repressed fears spilling forth in a torrent of uninhibited speech, revealing the hidden anxieties that lay beneath the polished surface. Alternatively, their death might be protracted and agonizing, a stark contrast to the desired image of a swift, dignified exit. The phantasmatic signature here is one of dramatic collapse, a symbolic undoing of the lifelong ego defenses, revealing the terrifying abyss of the Real that the individual had so desperately sought to keep at bay. The unconscious, in its relentless pursuit of truth, forces the final scene to expose the hidden fragility beneath the carefully constructed persona.

The concept of

objet petit a, Lacan's elusive object-cause of desire, also illuminates the unconscious scripting of death. This object, never fully attainable, represents that which fuels our longing, the lost object that perpetually draws us forward. In the context of death, the unconscious may cathect this *objet petit a* onto the very process of dying, imbuing it with a phantom allure or a tragic significance. The death becomes a final, desperate pursuit of this unattainable object, a symbolic quest for ultimate fulfillment. This can manifest as a dying process driven by an almost feverish intensity, a relentless seeking of something just beyond reach. The individual may express a profound sense of longing, a feeling of unfinished business that transcends any tangible earthly concerns. They might speak of a need to "find" or "reach" something, their gaze fixed on an unseen horizon. The phantasmatic signature here is one of uncanny fascination, a spectral lure that draws the individual towards their end, an ending that is imbued with a sense of mysterious, almost sacred, purpose. It is the unconscious drive to finally grasp, or at least confront, the ultimate object of desire, even if that confrontation leads to oblivion.

The tension between Freud's death drive and Lacan's confrontation with the Real provides a compelling framework for understanding how unconscious conflicts are resolved in the final act. The death drive, in its push towards dissolution, can be seen as the primal force that impels the subject towards the boundary of existence. The Real, on the other hand, represents the terror and the unspeakable nature of that boundary itself. The unconscious, in its complex operations, orchestrates a dialogue between these forces, weaving them into the symbolic narrative of the dying process.

Consider an individual who has harbored a lifelong, unacknowledged rage, perhaps stemming from early experiences of injustice or powerlessness. This rage, repressed by the conscious ego due to its destructive potential and the societal pressures to conform, festers in the unconscious. The death drive, in its aggressive manifestation, can provide an unconscious channel for this pent-up fury. The final scene might then be characterized by a defiant, even angry, passage through death. This could manifest as an acute illness that runs a rapid, aggressive course, as if the body itself is waging a furious battle against its own dissolution. The individual might exhibit a fierce resistance to care, an almost combative attitude towards their own decline, a symbolic enactment of their unexpressed fury. The phantasmatic signature here is one of tempestuous defiance, a death that is not a gentle surrender but a final, powerful assertion of will, a symbolic release of lifelong, repressed anger. It is the unconscious using the death drive to enact the primal rage that could not be expressed in life.

Conversely, the unconscious can also employ the very processes of mourning and melancholia to script the final scene. When an individual has introjected significant losses, turning inward the grief and self-recrimination, their relationship with their own mortality can become deeply colored by a sense of internal devastation. The unconscious may then orchestrate a death that is characterized by a profound sense of emptiness, a profound feeling of worthlessness, or an almost deliberate self-effacement. The phantasmatic signature here is one of desolate quietude, a fading away that mirrors the internalized emptiness. The individual may express a deep sense of resignation, a feeling that their life has amounted to nothing, or that their death is a just consequence of their perceived failings. This is the unconscious enacting the internalized critique, the silent pronouncement of guilt that has been carried for years. The death becomes a final act of self-punishment, a symbolic annihilation that mirrors the psychic devastation of melancholia.

The aesthetic quality of death, therefore, is not an incidental byproduct but an integral component of its unconscious scripting. It is the style, the texture, the emotional resonance of the final moments, a testament to the unique psychic landscape of the individual. This aesthetic can be dramatic or subtle, tragic or serene, violent or peaceful, but it is always meaningful. It is the unconscious's way of giving form to the formless, of articulating the unspeakable, of resolving, or at least dramatically enacting, the deepest conflicts of a lifetime. The phantasmatic signature is the artistic imprint of the unconscious on the canvas of mortality, a final, deeply personal statement that transcends the biological event itself. It is the echo of our deepest selves reverberating in the silence of our passing, a testament to the enduring power of the unconscious to shape even our ultimate disappearance.

The ways in which the unconscious orchestrates this final act are as diverse as humanity itself. It draws from the wellspring of primal fantasies, the enduring patterns of relational dynamics, and the fundamental forces of the drives. It is the unconscious that imbues the dying process with its unique symbolic resonance, transforming a biological endpoint into a profound, albeit often hidden, psychic resolution. Whether it is a death that enacts a lifelong trauma, a final confrontation with repressed desires, or a desperate attempt to grasp the elusive object of longing, the unconscious is the ultimate author of this final, profound scene. It is in these final moments, when the defenses of the ego begin to crumble and the veil between the conscious and the unconscious thins, that the deepest truths of our existence are often most powerfully, and most tragically, revealed. The signature it leaves is the indelible mark of our deepest psychic reality, a testament to the enduring power of the unconscious to shape not only our lives but also the very way in which we cease to be. This is the art of dying, not in the conscious mastery of the process, but in the unconscious performance that defines its ultimate meaning and aesthetic.

This unique imprint, the 'fantasmatic signature,' is more than just a personal quirk; it is the unconscious's final, indelible mark on the tapestry of existence. It is the subtle, often unnoticed, stylistic flourish that distinguishes one person's cessation from another's. We are not speaking here of the medical classification of death—a heart attack, a fall, an illness—but rather of the *how* in a symbolic, deeply psychic sense. It is the unconscious logic that dictates the prevailing mood, the overarching theme, the symbolic resolution that imbues the final moments with a specific, singular resonance. Each of us, through the unique constellation of our psychic history, our core anxieties, our deepest yearnings, and our most persistent internal conflicts, crafts this signature. It is an aesthetic of dying, an unconscious art form that makes each individual's end a singular, irreplicable masterpiece, written in the invisible ink of the psyche.

This signature is not consciously chosen. One does not wake up and decide, "Today, I shall die with a flourish of existential dread," or "My final moments will be imbued with a serene acceptance of the void." Instead, it is the emergent property of a lifetime of unconscious processing. Think of it as the psychic fingerprint left on the act of ceasing to be. It is formed from the residue of our earliest relational experiences, the internalization of primal fantasies, and the ongoing negotiation between the life and death drives. These elements, interwoven and processed in the unique crucible of our unconscious, manifest in the final act, giving it its particular character. It is the unconscious, in its relentless pursuit of symbolic coherence, that orchestrates this final performance, ensuring that the closing scene reflects the deeply embedded narratives of our psychic lives.

Consider, for instance, an individual whose life has been characterized by an unrelenting pursuit of external validation, a constant striving for approval that stems from a deeply ingrained sense of inadequacy. The unconscious might, in its final act, render this striving into a death that is paradoxically marked by profound insignificance. This isn't necessarily a death in obscurity, but one where the individual, in their final moments, feels a crushing lack of recognition, a chilling absence of the affirmation they so desperately craved throughout their life. They might experience a deep, unshakeable feeling that their life has ultimately meant nothing, that their passing is unnoticed and unacknowledged by the world they sought so ardently to impress. The fantasmatic signature here is one of existential emptiness, a void that mirrors the internalized belief in their own worthlessness, a final, stark confirmation of the inadequacy they always suspected lay beneath the surface. It is the unconscious, in its final, cruel stroke, confirming the deepest, most feared truth of the individual's inner world. The

objet petit a, the elusive object-cause of desire, might be intensely cathected onto the very act of being seen and validated, and its ultimate failure to be attained in death, even with the finality of existence, creates this signature of profound lack.

Alternatively, an individual whose life has been a relentless, often aggressive, assertion of control might manifest a death that is characterized by an utter loss of autonomy and a chaotic descent into helplessness. This isn't a matter of medical dependency, but a subjective experience of profound disempowerment, a surrender to forces entirely beyond their command. The unconscious, having spent a lifetime battling against any perceived threat to its sense of mastery, might orchestrate a final scene where this control is utterly obliterated. This could manifest as a rapid physical deterioration that leaves the individual utterly dependent, or a mental disintegration where thoughts and perceptions become fragmented and uncontrollable. The fantasmatic signature is one of overwhelming chaos, a stark and terrifying inversion of a lifelong commitment to order and command. It is the unconscious, in its final, dramatic flourish, forcing a confrontation with the very vulnerability the ego had so strenuously denied. This could be seen as an extreme manifestation of the death drive, not as a simple yielding, but as a furious, chaotic undoing that mirrors the inner turmoil of a self that has spent its existence fighting against dissolution.

The concept of unresolved relational dynamics also plays a crucial role in shaping this signature. For someone who has experienced profound early betrayal, the unconscious might craft a death that symbolically enacts this betrayal. This could manifest not as an overt act of treachery by others, but as a series of seemingly coincidental events that leave the individual feeling utterly abandoned and deceived in their final days. Perhaps loved ones are unexpectedly absent, or crucial support systems crumble at the last moment, leaving the individual isolated and vulnerable. The fantasmatic signature here is one of profound alienation, a final confirmation of a lifelong expectation of being let down. It is the unconscious replaying the original trauma, ensuring that the closing scene mirrors the foundational wounds of the past. This is the Lacanian Real of betrayal, the unsymbolizable terror of abandonment, irrupting into the final act of life.

Conversely, an individual who has dedicated their life to nurturing and caring for others, perhaps sublimating their own unmet needs, might find their death characterized by a peculiar sense of serene detachment, almost as if they are an observer of their own dissolution. The unconscious, having fulfilled its perceived mandate of self-sacrifice, might usher in an end marked by a quiet, almost impersonal, fading away. There is no dramatic struggle, no outcry of unfulfilled desire, but a gentle receding from the world. The fantasmatic signature here is one of profound, almost otherworldly, peace, a testament to a psychic economy that has found its ultimate resolution in the act of release. It is the unconscious enacting a symbolic completion of a life devoted to the needs of others, where the self is finally allowed to recede into a quiet stillness. This could be seen as a manifestation of

Eros finding its ultimate peaceful cessation, a release from the constant striving to give.

The nature of the individual's primary internal conflicts also leaves its mark. For someone whose life has been a constant battle between profound desires and crushing prohibitions, the death might be tinged with a sense of forbidden pleasure or a tragic enactment of frustrated longing. This could manifest as a death that is simultaneously longed for and resisted, a dying process filled with both a sense of release from internal torment and a deep sadness for the unattainable joys that life offered. The fantasmatic signature is one of bittersweet finality, a poignant blend of liberation and regret. It is the unconscious, in its final act, holding up a mirror to the fundamental dialectic of desire and prohibition that has defined the individual's psychic existence. The

objet petit a, in this context, might represent the lost object of desire that can never be fully grasped, making the very act of dying a final confrontation with this perpetual lack.

Consider, too, the impact of unresolved guilt. An individual who has carried a hidden burden of shame or transgression, perhaps stemming from a childhood event or a suppressed action, may experience a death that is symbolically redemptive or, conversely, one that is marked by a profound sense of self-condemnation. The former might involve a death that brings a sense of peace and forgiveness, as if the act of dying somehow expiates the past. The latter might involve a death characterized by suffering, isolation, or a profound sense of unworthiness, as if the individual is enduring a final punishment. The fantasmatic signature here is one of symbolic reckoning, a final accounting of the soul. It is the unconscious ensuring that the ending narrative aligns with the deeply held, often unacknowledged, sense of justice or injustice that has governed the individual's inner life. This is the death drive operating not towards simple dissolution, but towards a form of psychic justice, however harsh.

The literary critic Harold Bloom, in his discussions of "anxiety of influence," spoke of poets wrestling with their predecessors, "slaying the father" to forge their own unique voice. In a similar vein, the fantasmatic signature can be understood as the ultimate manifestation of this individual struggle for psychic autonomy. Each death is a unique inscription, a final, definitive statement that declares, "This is how

I cease to be." It is the unconscious asserting its final, unassailable authorship. This signature is not about the quantity of life lived, but the unique quality of its psychic trajectory. It is the ghost of our deepest selves, leaving its final, artful trace on the silence.

This artistic imprint is not always dramatic or overtly symbolic. Sometimes, the signature is one of quietude, of an almost imperceptible fading. This might be the signature of an individual who, throughout their life, sought to minimize their impact, to avoid drawing attention to themselves. Their death, in such cases, might be characterized by a profound stillness, a lack of fuss, an almost apologetic departure from the world. The unconscious, in its alignment with the conscious ego's lifelong pursuit of invisibility, orchestrates an ending that perfectly mirrors this deeply ingrained desire. The signature is one of subtle erasure, a final act of self-effacement that echoes a lifetime of wanting to be unnoticed.

Conversely, for those whose lives have been marked by a relentless, almost obsessive, pursuit of order and cleanliness, their death might carry a symbolic resonance of purification or cleansing. This is not necessarily a religious connotation, but a psychic one. The dying process itself might be perceived by the individual, or by those close to them, as a purging, a washing away of the perceived impurities of life. The fantasmatic signature is one of final catharsis, a symbolic cleansing that brings a sense of resolution and peace. It is the unconscious enacting a deeply held fantasy of beginning anew, even in the act of ending.

The concept of the fantasmatic signature also accounts for the peculiar, almost magnetic, pull that certain deaths have on those left behind. When a death carries a strong, coherent signature—be it one of tragic beauty, profound peace, or even violent intensity—it tends to lodge itself in the collective memory, resonating with a power that transcends the mere biological event. This resonance stems from the unconscious recognition of a life played out to its symbolic conclusion. The signature, in its uniqueness, touches upon universal themes of life, death, desire, and loss, but it does so with a specific, individual inflection that makes it both relatable and profoundly singular. It is the art of the unconscious, communicating its final message in a language that, while deeply personal, can still be understood on a deeper, more intuitive level by others.

Ultimately, the fantasmatic signature is a testament to the enduring power of the unconscious to imbue even the most final of experiences with meaning and form. It transforms the stark biological reality of death into a profoundly psychic event, a unique culmination of a life's journey. It is the unconscious's final, masterful stroke, an artistic flourish that defines the ineffable quality of an individual's passing, making each death a singular, albeit unconscious, work of art. This signature is the echo of our deepest selves, a final whisper of our most profound truths, imprinted upon the silence of our departure. It is the indelible mark of our unique psychic existence, a testament to the unconscious's role in shaping not just our lives, but the very manner of our ceasing to be.

The cessation of biological function, while undeniably the ultimate determinant of physical death, represents only one facet of this profound human transition. To confine our understanding of dying solely to the physiological mechanics—the failing heart, the compromised lungs, the ceased neural activity—is to overlook the vast, often unmapped, territory of the unconscious. It is within this psychic landscape that the true *experience* of dying is forged, a landscape sculpted by a lifetime of accumulated fantasies, repressed desires, and the deeply ingrained narratives that have shaped our individual realities. This subsection delves into this crucial symbolic dimension, moving beyond the purely biological to explore how our unconscious imbues the final moments with meaning, texture, and a uniquely personal resonance.

Our engagement with death is not merely a passive witnessing of bodily decline; it is an active, albeit often unconscious, psychic elaboration. We don't just die; we die

in a certain way, a way that is dictated by the intricate workings of our inner worlds. This "way" is not a matter of conscious choice but an emergent property of our deepest psychological structures. Cultural anthropologists and depth psychologists have long observed how different societies construct elaborate rituals and belief systems around death, imbuing it with layers of meaning that extend far beyond its biological finality. These cultural frameworks, however, are not external impositions on a neutral biological event; rather, they are the very tools and language through which the unconscious negotiates its own dissolution. The collective narratives of the afterlife, the ancestral realms, or the final judgment become the symbolic canvas upon which the individual unconscious paints its own cessation.

Consider, for instance, the potent symbolism of a "peaceful death." While medically, this might be described as a gradual decline with minimal physical distress, psychologically, it speaks to a deep unconscious yearning for resolution, for an end to internal conflict, or a resolution of unresolved guilt. The individual may have spent a lifetime wrestling with internal demons, with a harsh superego, or with profound anxieties. The peaceful passing, in this context, is not merely the absence of pain but the unconscious achievement of a psychic truce, a final surrender that is experienced as a release from internal warfare. It is as if the psychic apparatus, having fought its battles, finally finds a moment of grace, a quietude that mirrors a long-sought inner harmony. The cultural narrative of a "good death"—one that is serene, surrounded by loved ones, and accepting—provides the symbolic template for this internal psychic resolution. The unconscious seizes upon this template, not as an external mandate, but as the most fitting symbolic representation for its own profound sense of achieved peace.

Conversely, a death characterized by agitation, fear, or a desperate clinging to life, while medically explained by delirium or physiological distress, can also be understood as a powerful manifestation of unconscious drives. For an individual whose life has been marked by a deep-seated fear of annihilation, a profound existential dread that they have managed to suppress or deny, their final moments might become a stark enactment of this primal terror. The unconscious, unable to maintain its defenses any longer, forces a confrontation with the very void it has spent a lifetime evading. This is not a conscious choice to be afraid, but the eruption of an unconscious dread that finds its ultimate, undeniable expression in the biological act of dying. The symbolic meaning here is one of ultimate helplessness, the ego's final capitulation to the overwhelming forces of dissolution.

The concept of the "deathbed confession," a recurring motif in literature and popular culture, also highlights this symbolic dimension. While often dramatized, these confessions speak to a deeper psychological truth: the unconscious desire for resolution, for the unburdening of secrets, and for a symbolic reintegration before the final separation. The individual may have carried the weight of a transgression or a profound regret for years, the unconscious harboring this hidden truth. In the liminal space of dying, where the ego's defenses begin to crumble, this repressed material may surface, seeking a final release. The confession, whether spoken aloud or enacted through symbolic gestures, becomes a psychic act of purification, a desperate attempt to align the internal narrative with a perceived moral or existential order before the ultimate silence. The symbolic meaning is one of seeking absolution, of attempting to settle psychic debts before the final accounting.

Furthermore, our unconscious fantasies about death are not solely personal; they are deeply intertwined with the collective unconscious and the prevailing cultural narratives that surround mortality. Carl Jung's concept of archetypes offers a powerful lens through which to understand these shared symbolic frameworks. The archetype of the Great Mother, for instance, can manifest in death as a return to the womb, a dissolution back into a primal, undifferentiated state. Conversely, the archetype of the Wise Old Man or the divine redeemer can offer a symbolic pathway towards transcendence or spiritual reunion. These archetypes, deeply embedded in the human psyche, provide a symbolic language for the unconscious to articulate its experience of dying. The individual's personal unconscious does not operate in isolation; it draws upon this rich tapestry of collective imagery and meaning, shaping its unique narrative of cessation.

Consider the fantasy of "dying in one's sleep" as a peaceful, almost desirable, end. This fantasy taps into a desire for an effortless transition, a cessation of consciousness without the struggle or terror that the conscious mind might associate with the dying process. The unconscious, in this scenario, crafts an ending that aligns with this idealized vision, a narrative of gentle fading away. It is a psychic sublimation of the potential horrors of dying, replacing them with a comforting image of surrender. This is not to say that such deaths are not genuinely peaceful in their biological manifestation, but that the *meaning* we ascribe to them, the unconscious narrative we construct around them, is deeply influenced by these deeply held fantasies. The unconscious appropriates the biological event and imbues it with a desired symbolic significance.

The symbolic dimension of death also accounts for the profound sense of presence that some individuals report experiencing from those who have passed. This is not merely memory or grief; it is often described as a felt sense of the deceased's continued existence, their "spirit" or essence. Psychologically, this can be understood as the unconscious carrying forward the symbolic imprint, the fantasmatic signature, of the deceased. The unconscious of the mourner continues to engage with the symbolic representation of the deceased, a representation that is shaped by the deceased's own psychic life and their unique way of dying. The unresolved internal dynamics, the core fantasies, and the symbolic resolutions of the deceased continue to resonate within the unconscious of the bereaved, creating a sense of continued, albeit transformed, connection. The death, in this sense, does not entirely sever the psychic bond; it transforms it into a new symbolic configuration.

The role of language in shaping our understanding and experience of death is also paramount. The words we use—"passed away," "lost," "departed," "succumbed"—each carry different symbolic weight and emotional resonance. These linguistic choices are not merely polite euphemisms; they reflect underlying unconscious attitudes and beliefs about what death truly is. A culture that predominantly uses terms like "passed away" suggests an unconscious belief in a continuation, a transition to another state, while terms like "succumbed" emphasize a defeat, a surrender to an overwhelming force. The unconscious absorbs these linguistic cues, integrating them into its own symbolic apprehension of mortality. The very act of naming death, of framing it within a linguistic structure, is a process of psychic elaboration.

The concept of "unfinished business" also speaks to the symbolic nature of dying. This refers to unresolved emotional conflicts, unexpressed feelings, or unmet desires that linger at the end of life. The unconscious, in its drive towards psychic coherence, may even orchestrate events or internal experiences that bring these unfinished matters to the forefront, allowing for a symbolic, if not actual, resolution. This might manifest as a sudden urge to reconnect with a estranged loved one, a dream that clarifies a past trauma, or a profound insight that brings peace regarding a lifelong regret. These are not simply the random occurrences of a failing organism; they are often the unconscious's final attempt to weave a coherent narrative, to bring closure to the psychic dramas that have defined a life.

The aesthetic dimension of death, often overlooked in purely biological or medical discourse, is intrinsically linked to its symbolic nature. Just as artists imbue their work with intention and meaning, the unconscious crafts the experience of dying with a certain symbolic artistry. This artistry is not about beauty in the conventional sense, but about the creation of a coherent, resonant symbolic narrative. The "fantasmatic signature" discussed earlier is a testament to this unconscious aesthetic. It is the unique, symbolic style with which an individual's unconscious orchestrates their final moments, a style that reflects their deepest fears, desires, and internal conflicts. This signature transforms the stark biological event into a moment laden with psychic significance, a final, often unconscious, masterpiece.

The unconscious, in its eternal dance with the drives, particularly the life drive (Eros) and the death drive (Thanatos), plays a pivotal role in shaping this symbolic experience. Eros, the drive towards connection, creativity, and preservation, might manifest in a dying process characterized by a desire for reunion with loved ones, a symbolic return to the maternal source, or a peaceful integration of life experiences. Thanatos, on the other hand, the drive towards dissolution, cessation, and a return to the inorganic, might find expression in a dying process that is experienced as a chaotic undoing, a furious resistance to the inevitable, or a profound sense of alienation and fragmentation. The interplay between these fundamental drives, mediated by the unconscious, creates the unique symbolic texture of each individual's death. It is the unconscious that translates the raw energy of these drives into a symbolic language that the psyche can comprehend.

Furthermore, the cultural reception and interpretation of a death also contribute to its symbolic dimension. The way a society or a community grieves, memorializes, and makes narrative sense of a death can profoundly influence its perceived meaning, both for those who are mourning and, arguably, for the unconscious imprint left behind. A death that is publicly mourned as a tragedy, or celebrated as a heroic sacrifice, gains a symbolic weight that transcends the individual biological event. The unconscious, in its capacity for symbolic resonance, can connect with these shared narratives, weaving them into its own understanding of cessation. This collective symbolic processing can amplify the individual's fantasmatic signature, giving it a broader resonance and a more enduring impact.

Ultimately, to understand death solely as a biological event is to ignore the vast, intricate, and deeply human dimension of its symbolic construction. The unconscious mind, with its rich tapestry of fantasies, desires, conflicts, and narratives, transforms the stark reality of physical cessation into a profoundly meaningful psychic experience. It is within this symbolic arena that we confront our deepest fears, our most cherished hopes, and the ultimate narrative of our existence. This perspective does not diminish the biological reality of dying, but rather enriches our understanding of it, revealing death not just as an end to biological function, but as a final, potent expression of the intricate landscape of the human psyche. It is in this symbolic dimension that the art of dying truly resides.

Chapter 2: The Aesthetics of Disappearance

The allure of absolute oblivion, the fantasy of vanishing without leaving so much as a ripple on the pond of existence, is a potent undercurrent within the human psyche. It is the antithesis of legacy, the antithesis of remembrance, and the ultimate expression of a desire for radical detachment. This aesthetic of disappearance, which we might term the "vanishing act," is not merely about the cessation of life; it is about the cessation of all evidence of that life having ever been. It speaks to a profound yearning for erasure, a wish so complete that it seeks to undo not only the future of one's being but also the past. The unconscious desire for such an obliteration is often rooted in deeply buried feelings of unworthiness, a pervasive sense of shame, or an overwhelming desire to escape the perceived burdens of recognition, accountability, and the very weight of one's own existence.

This aesthetic is not about a dramatic exit, nor a final, defiant statement. On the contrary, it is the quietest of wishes, a whispered plea for ultimate anonymity. It manifests not in grand gestures but in subtle, often unconscious, life choices that steer an individual towards a life lived in the shadows, culminating in an end that is as unremarkable as it is absolute. The individual who embodies this aesthetic may not actively seek death, but they may unconsciously gravitate towards circumstances that ensure their passing goes largely unnoticed. This can be observed in those who systematically dismantle their social networks, who resist forming deep attachments, or who cultivate an existence characterized by extreme solitude. Each act of withdrawal, each severing of a connection, becomes a small step towards the ultimate goal of non-being, a gradual fading from the world's periphery.

The psychological underpinnings of this vanishing desire are complex and often painful. At its core lies a profound sense of self-condemnation. The individual may feel that they are fundamentally flawed, irrevocably damaged, or that their very existence is a burden to themselves and to others. Shame, that corrosive emotion that makes us feel exposed and defective, can be a primary motivator. The fear of being seen, of having one's perceived imperfections laid bare, can lead to a compensatory desire to become invisible, to disappear before the perceived judgment of others can fall. This is not simply shyness or introversion; it is a deep-seated conviction that one's presence is inherently problematic, and that absence is the only true form of redemption. The unconscious logic is stark: if one cannot be good enough, or worthy enough, then the next best thing is to not be at all.

Consider, for example, the life trajectory of someone who deliberately avoids any form of public engagement or social recognition. They might choose professions that are inherently solitary, or they might meticulously curate their online and offline presence to be as minimal as possible. They might resist having their photograph taken, sharing personal details, or even participating in community events. Each of these actions, while seemingly minor in isolation, contributes to a larger pattern of self-effacement. The unconscious mind is actively constructing a narrative of invisibility, preparing the ground for an exit that will leave no trace. The ultimate fantasy is not just death, but a death that occurs as if one never lived, a seamless reintegration into the undifferentiated void. This desire for erasure can be so profound that it can even influence the circumstances of one's demise. A solitary accident, a quiet illness in an isolated dwelling, or even a death that goes undiscovered for some time can all align with this unconscious wish for an unacknowledged end.

This aesthetic of erasure is also deeply entwined with a rejection of the very concept of legacy. For many, the idea of leaving a mark on the world—through children, through work, through contributions to society—is a fundamental aspect of finding meaning in life. But for the individual who yearns to vanish, the very thought of being remembered can be a source of anxiety. To be remembered is to be held accountable, to be judged by future generations, to have one's life evaluated against the standards of time. The desire to disappear is, in this sense, a desire to escape the temporal judgment of history, to opt out of the ongoing narrative of human existence. It is a radical act of rebellion against the imperative to be significant, to matter.

The unconscious wish for obliteration can also be a desperate attempt to escape profound psychic pain. Imagine an individual who has experienced deep trauma, betrayal, or loss. The memory of these experiences can be so unbearable, so corrosive, that the idea of ceasing to exist becomes a welcome release. It is not a morbid fascination with death, but rather an urgent desire to escape the confines of one's own suffering. The unconscious mind, in its desperate bid for survival, might construct this elaborate fantasy of disappearing entirely as a way to conceptualize an end to the torment. The world itself, with all its reminders of past wounds, becomes something to be left behind, to be utterly removed from.

This aesthetic can manifest in seemingly innocuous ways that, upon closer examination, reveal a deeper pattern. It might be the person who always declines invitations to reunions, who never updates their social media, or who consistently opts for the most anonymous forms of travel and accommodation. These are not necessarily signs of social awkwardness; they can be subtle manifestations of an unconscious strategy to minimize one's footprint, to become less visible, and ultimately, to prepare for an unobserved departure. The goal is not to be forgotten, for that implies a prior state of being remembered; it is to never have been significantly perceived in the first place.

The philosophical underpinnings of this desire for erasure are also noteworthy. Existentialist thought, for instance, grapples with the burden of freedom and the inherent meaninglessness that can pervade human existence. For some, the realization of this freedom can be overwhelming, leading to a desire to abdicate responsibility, to cease to be the author of their own actions. The fantasy of vanishing without a trace can be seen as a desire to return to a state of pre-conscious being, to a realm where choice and consequence do not exist, where the burden of existence is lifted entirely. It is a yearning for an absolute freedom from the self, a state of pure non-being that offers an ultimate escape from the existential predicament.

Moreover, societal pressures can inadvertently foster this aesthetic. In a world that often equates worth with visibility, with social media presence, with public achievement, those who do not conform to these metrics can feel increasingly marginalized and insignificant. For individuals who struggle to find their place within these competitive frameworks, the desire to disappear can become a subtle form of resistance, a quiet act of defiance against a system that seems to value only the loudest voices and the brightest spotlights. The unconscious choice to live and die unnoticed becomes a way of reclaiming agency, of refusing to play a game that feels rigged against them.

It is crucial to distinguish this aesthetic of erasure from the more common anxieties surrounding death. While many fear the pain of dying or the loss of loved ones, the individual drawn to this vanishing act fears something else: the very act of being known, of being recorded, of leaving a discernible mark. Their anxiety is not about what they will miss, but about what they will leave behind. The ultimate horror is not the cessation of consciousness, but the enduring evidence of a flawed or burdensome existence.

This unconscious drive for obliteration can also manifest in a passive approach to one's own affairs. It might be seen in individuals who fail to make wills, who do not organize their personal documents, or who make no provisions for their passing. While these actions can stem from procrastination or denial, they can also be interpreted as an unconscious alignment with the fantasy of disappearing without a trace. If one is to vanish, then there is no need for posthumous organization, no need for the administrative tasks that acknowledge and solidify one's existence. The ultimate act of disappearing is to make one's absence as seamless as their presumed presence, leaving no loose ends, no administrative detritus for others to sort through.

The concept of "living like a ghost" can serve as a powerful metaphor for this aesthetic. It describes a way of being in the world where one attempts to minimize their impact, to glide through life without disturbing the status quo, to be present yet unseen. This is not a conscious decision to be manipulative or deceitful, but rather an unconscious orientation towards minimizing one's perceived negative impact. The ultimate expression of this is to carry this ghost-like existence into death itself, to fade out of existence as quietly and as unnoticed as one lived.

The literary and artistic portrayals of characters who seek erasure are often compelling. These figures, driven by a desire to escape their past, their identity, or the consequences of their actions, embody the deep-seated human fascination with the possibility of absolute disappearance. They represent a primal fear and a seductive fantasy: the fear of being trapped by one's own existence, and the fantasy of achieving ultimate freedom through complete annihilation of self and of memory.

In essence, the aesthetic of vanishing without a trace is the ultimate expression of a profound internal narrative of worthlessness or an overwhelming desire for escape. It is a wish for a final, absolute stillness, an end that mirrors a life lived in the quietest of corners. It is the desire to become unwritten, to undo the ink of one's existence, and to return to a state of pure, unadulterated nothingness. This is not a surrender to despair, but a desperate, unconscious attempt to achieve peace through absolute erasure, a peace that can only be found, in the deepest recesses of the psyche, in the profound silence of never having been. The individual who carries this aesthetic within them is not necessarily seeking to inflict pain or create a dramatic void, but rather to dissolve, to dissipate, to become one with the absence that they have unconsciously cultivated throughout their lives. Their passing, when it comes, is not a tragedy to be mourned, but a release to be enacted, a final, silent fulfillment of a lifelong yearning for complete disappearance.

The unconscious drive towards an aesthetic of erasure, a quiet fade rather than a dramatic exit, often finds its most potent expression not in grand philosophical pronouncements but in the lived reality of individual lives. To truly grasp the profound and often subtle workings of this desire, it is essential to move from the theoretical to the tangible, to observe the intricate tapestry of a life woven with the threads of intended invisibility. Such a life, when examined through a psychoanalytic lens, reveals the deep-seated motivations and relational patterns that culminate in an ending designed, however unconsciously, for the ultimate in anonymity.

Consider, for instance, the psychic journey of an individual we might refer to as "Elias" (a pseudonym to protect anonymity, as is standard practice in clinical work). Elias's life was a masterclass in self-effacement, a slow, deliberate withdrawal from the world's attention that seemed to begin in his earliest years. He was not a child who sought the spotlight, nor one who actively courted disapproval. Instead, he cultivated a remarkable capacity for blending into the background, for being present without ever truly occupying space. This was not born of shyness, which often carries a hope for eventual connection, but rather from a deeper, more fundamental inclination to avoid making a discernible impact.

Elias's early family environment was characterized by a pervasive emotional coolness. His parents were not overtly abusive, but they were distant, their interactions often transactional, focused on fulfilling basic needs rather than fostering emotional intimacy. Affection was rarely expressed, and praise for achievement was minimal, often overshadowed by an unspoken expectation of quiet competence. In this emotional vacuum, Elias learned that his presence was best tolerated when it was least demanding. He became adept at anticipating needs without being asked, at performing tasks without seeking acknowledgment, and at retreating to the periphery when social interactions became too intense. This early conditioning laid the groundwork for a lifelong pattern of minimizing his own needs and desires, rendering them almost invisible even to himself.

As Elias entered adolescence and then adulthood, this inclination towards unobtrusiveness manifested in his social and professional life. He chose a career path that was solitary by nature – archival work, where his days were spent in quiet communion with the past, cataloging and organizing the remnants of other lives. He was meticulous, diligent, and utterly unassuming. His colleagues regarded him as reliable, if somewhat unremarkable. He participated in office social events only when absolutely necessary, always positioning himself near the edges of the room, a silent observer rather than an active participant. He never initiated conversations beyond the purely functional, and his responses were typically brief, polite, and devoid of personal revelation.

His relational history mirrored this pattern of avoidance and detachment. Elias engaged in a few romantic relationships, but they were characterized by a remarkable lack of depth. He was a compliant partner, rarely expressing strong opinions or demanding attention. When conflict arose, he tended to withdraw rather than engage, his silence often interpreted by his partners as passive aggression or disinterest. Ultimately, these relationships dissolved not through dramatic breakups, but through a slow, quiet drifting apart, a mutual erosion of connection that Elias never fought to preserve. He did not possess the emotional tools to navigate the complexities of intimacy, and his unconscious fear of being truly seen, of exposing the perceived emptiness within, kept him perpetually at arm's length.

His engagement with the wider world was equally muted. He lived in a small, nondescript apartment, sparsely furnished and impeccably tidy, reflecting his desire for order and lack of personal efflorescence. He had no close friends outside of work, and his family relationships were maintained through infrequent, perfunctory phone calls. He did not participate in hobbies that would draw attention, nor did he engage in any form of activism or community involvement. His consumption habits were minimal; he bought only what was essential, never indulging in luxuries or expressing strong brand loyalties. He was, in essence, a person who occupied very little psychic and social space.

The aesthetic of disappearance, as Elias embodied it, was not an active seeking of death but an unconscious cultivation of a life that would, by its very nature, render his passing unremarkable. He made no significant effort to build a legacy, to leave a lasting impression, or to create a memorial of his existence. His financial affairs were, predictably, unorganized. He never made a will, nor did he meticulously document his assets or wishes. This wasn't necessarily an act of irresponsibility, but rather a consistent manifestation of his lifelong orientation towards minimizing his footprint. If one intended to vanish, the elaborate preparations for remembrance and administration seemed superfluous, even contradictory.

When Elias eventually fell ill, it was with a condition that was insidious and debilitating, yet one that allowed him to maintain a semblance of solitary independence for a considerable time. He managed his own care at home, refusing offers of assistance from acquaintances or distant relatives. He continued his work remotely as much as his health allowed, further blurring the lines between his existence and his profession, both of which were characterized by quiet diligence. The progression of his illness was private, his suffering unseen, his decline a solitary affair.

His death, when it came, was discovered only when he failed to respond to automated welfare checks initiated by his employer, who had grown concerned about his uncharacteristic silence. The authorities found him in his apartment, peacefully, it seemed, in his bed. There were no witnesses to his final moments, no dramatic pleas or final pronouncements. His passing was an anticlimax to a life that had been lived largely as an omission. The scene was one of quietude, the only evidence of his prolonged absence being the stillness of the air and the faint scent of disuse.

The ensuing process of settling Elias's affairs was, as anticipated, complicated by the absence of any formal arrangements. The discovery of his solitary existence, devoid of close personal connections, meant that the responsibility fell to distant, vaguely aware relatives and the state. There were no immediate mourners, no outpouring of grief. His passing was noted, documented, and processed with a bureaucratic efficiency that mirrored the unobtrusive nature of his life. A small obituary, written with minimal detail and no personal anecdotes, appeared in a local paper, its brief mention a testament to his success in remaining largely unperceived.

From a psychoanalytic perspective, Elias's trajectory illustrates the profound impact of early object relations on the development of self-representation and the subsequent shaping of one's life course. The lack of consistent emotional mirroring and validation in his formative years led to a fragile sense of self-worth. He internalized the implicit message that his existence was best served by being inconspicuous, by not demanding too much attention or emotional investment. This created a powerful unconscious defense mechanism: the suppression of his own needs and desires to avoid perceived rejection or overwhelming responsibility. The act of disappearing became, for Elias, a form of survival, a way to navigate a world that felt, from his earliest experiences, potentially engulfing or indifferent.

His choice of profession as an archivist further speaks to this internal landscape. He found solace and a sense of purpose in dealing with the remnants of lives, with objects and documents that had already completed their active trajectory. This allowed him to engage with the past without the risk of intense interpersonal engagement. The quiet, ordered world of the archive provided a contained environment where he could exercise his meticulousness and diligence, qualities that were valued, even if they did not translate into social recognition or personal connection. It was a professional manifestation of his personal aesthetic: engaging with that which is already fading, contributing to its preservation without drawing attention to his own role in the process.

The absence of a significant will or any preparatory arrangements for his death is not to be interpreted merely as negligence. It is, in this context, deeply symbolic. It signifies an unconscious alignment with the fantasy of complete dissolution, of leaving no lingering traces or burdens for others. The administrative tasks associated with death – legal documents, funeral arrangements, bequests – are all acts that affirm one's existence and its impact. By eschewing these, Elias was, in his unconscious way, enacting the final phase of his lifelong project of erasure. He sought not to be remembered, not even through the practicalities of his passing, but to simply cease.

The "quiet fade" is, therefore, not a failure of living, but a testament to a deeply ingrained psychic defense and a powerfully felt, albeit unconscious, aesthetic. Elias's life demonstrates how the desire for erasure, rooted in early relational dynamics and reinforced by habitual patterns, can shape the entirety of an individual's existence, culminating in an end that is as deliberate in its anonymity as the life that preceded it. His story serves as a poignant reminder that the deepest desires of the psyche often manifest not in grand declarations, but in the subtlest, most pervasive currents of daily life, guiding the individual towards a final, unobserved dissolution. He did not just die; he dissolved, a process of unmaking that had been underway for decades, culminating in an ending that was the ultimate expression of a life lived in the quietest of whispers.

The narrative of Elias offers a tangible illustration of the "vanishing act" aesthetic. His life trajectory was not marked by dramatic events or profound personal revelations that would necessitate, from an external perspective, a significant degree of remembrance. Instead, his existence was characterized by a consistent, almost artful, avoidance of the very things that typically anchor a person's memory in the minds of others: deep relationships, public contributions, passionate pursuits, or even significant personal struggles that resonate with shared human experience. His withdrawal was not a singular event but a pervasive mode of being, cultivated over a lifetime, which ultimately dictated the nature of his end.

The early relational dynamics are crucial here. In the absence of consistent emotional attunement from his primary caregivers, Elias learned to regulate his internal state and manage his needs through self-minimization. The implicit message he received, or perhaps the interpretation he made of his environment, was that his needs were burdensome, his desires disruptive. Consequently, he developed a finely tuned sensitivity to cues of discomfort or burden in others, and his default response was to recede. This pattern, established in the nursery, became the foundational architecture of his social interactions and his self-perception. It is a classic defense mechanism against anticipated rejection or the overwhelming feeling of being a burden, a defense so deeply ingrained that it became his primary mode of existence.

His professional choices further reinforced this aesthetic. The archival profession, by its very nature, involves dealing with the past rather than shaping the future, with preserving the traces of others rather than forging one's own mark. It is a field that rewards quiet diligence, meticulousness, and a detached engagement with historical narratives. Elias's proficiency in this domain was not merely a matter of skill but a profound alignment with his internal disposition. He was not merely cataloging documents; he was, in a sense, practicing the art of unobtrusive engagement, of working with that which already exists in a state of fading, without adding to its visibility.

His romantic relationships, or rather his limited encounters with intimacy, were similarly structured. The tendency to withdraw during conflict, to offer silence rather than direct emotional engagement, prevented the development of the robust, reciprocal bonds that typically form the bedrock of lasting connections. His partners likely experienced this as a lack of commitment or emotional availability, leading to the gradual erosion of the relationship. Elias, however, may have perceived his compliance and avoidance of confrontation as a way to maintain peace, a misguided attempt to avoid becoming a source of distress for another, thereby inadvertently ensuring his own isolation.

The concept of "living like a ghost," as previously explored, resonates deeply with Elias's existence. He inhabited the world with a minimal impact, present but rarely perceived, engaged but never truly entangled. This spectral existence extended into his personal affairs. The lack of a will, the absence of organized personal documentation, and the minimal engagement with the practicalities of life beyond immediate necessity all speak to a person who was psychologically preparing for an unobserved departure. These are not merely oversights; they are, in this context, manifestations of a deeply held unconscious belief that such preparations are ultimately irrelevant if one's aim is to become entirely absent.

Elias's illness and eventual death provided the final, and most complete, expression of his lifelong aesthetic. His solitary management of his own decline, his refusal of external assistance, and the unobtrusive nature of his passing all align with the unconscious desire to leave no ripple. The discovery of his death by employers, rather than by loved ones, underscores the profound isolation he had cultivated. It was the system, the administrative machinery of life, that ultimately registered his absence, not the intimate network of personal relationships that typically marks a life's end.

The clinical vignette of Elias, therefore, serves as a powerful counterpoint to more dramatic narratives of disappearance. It highlights how the aesthetic of erasure can be a quiet, insidious force, shaping a life from its earliest moments to its final breath. His story is a testament to the unconscious motivations that can drive individuals towards a life of minimal visibility, culminating in a death that is, for all intents and purposes, an act of final, unobserved dissolution. It is a stark reminder that the human psyche, in its complex dance between presence and absence, can indeed orchestrate a fading so complete that it mirrors the void itself, a testament to a life lived as a whisper in the vast expanse of existence. His end was not a tragedy in the conventional sense, but a quiet, almost natural, conclusion to a life meticulously curated for invisibility.

Literature, in its profound capacity to mirror the human psyche, has long served as a fertile ground for exploring the elusive aesthetic of disappearance. Across genres and eras, authors have crafted narratives that delve into the intricate tapestry of lives lived with an almost deliberate desire for oblivion, for an ending that leaves no discernible trace. These literary representations offer invaluable insights into the unconscious motivations, the psychological landscapes, and the profound yearning for an unobserved fade that resonates deeply with our exploration of the aesthetics of disappearance. Unlike the dramatic exits of tragic heroes or the violent disappearances that punctuate conventional narratives, these literary figures often seek a quieter, more insidious form of vanishing, an erasure that is less a violent severing and more a gentle dissolution into the ether.

One potent example can be found in the works of authors who explore the existential ennui and the search for meaning in a seemingly indifferent universe. Consider, for instance, the literary tradition that grapples with the protagonist who, disillusioned with the clamor and superficiality of modern existence, consciously withdraws from societal engagement. These characters often retreat into solitude, their lives becoming increasingly circumscribed until they are little more than whispers in the grand narrative of human experience. Their disappearance is not a sudden event but a gradual erosion, a slow fading into the background that mirrors the concept of an aesthetic of erasure. The author's technique here is often to render the character's internal world with meticulous detail, contrasting the rich, albeit perhaps troubled, inner landscape with the increasingly sparse external manifestations of their life. The reader is privy to the character's thoughts, their anxieties, their rationalizations for withdrawal, and their profound sense of alienation, even as the world outside barely registers their presence.

Within this vein, one might examine narratives where characters actively construct a life of minimal impact. They might eschew the accumulation of possessions, the pursuit of conventional markers of success, or the cultivation of deep interpersonal connections. Instead, they might dedicate themselves to solitary pursuits –

becoming recluses in remote locations, engrossed in esoteric studies, or simply existing in a state of quiet contemplation. The narrative often emphasizes the mundane, the repetitive, and the uneventful aspects of their existence. The author's skill lies in imbuing these seemingly unremarkable details with a profound psychological weight, revealing the character's deep-seated desire to become invisible, to shrink their footprint on the world until it is imperceptible. The climax of such a narrative might not be a dramatic event but the discovery of the character's absence, their body found after a considerable period, the scene itself underscoring the extent of their successful erasure.

Furthermore, literary works frequently explore the theme of a character who, having lived a life that was already characterized by unobtrusiveness, enacts their final disappearance with a similar lack of fanfare. These are individuals who have, perhaps unconsciously, cultivated an existence that lends itself to being overlooked. They may have held jobs that kept them in the background, formed relationships that were functional rather than deeply intimate, and pursued hobbies that were solitary and quiet. When such a character passes, their absence is noted, but the ripples of their departure are minimal. The literary portrayal here often focuses on the mundane details of the aftermath: the administrative tasks of settling affairs, the brief mention in a local newspaper, the faint sense of bewilderment among acquaintances who realize they knew so little about the deceased. The author's achievement lies in conveying the profound pathos of a life that, by its very design, was intended to fade without a ripple, a life that achieved its ultimate aesthetic goal in its own quiet passing.

Consider also the literary trope of the self-effacing artist or intellectual. These characters, often consumed by their creative or intellectual pursuits, may neglect their personal lives, their relationships, and their public presence. They find their fulfillment and sense of self in their work, which often deals with themes of transience, memory, and the ephemeral nature of existence. Their eventual disappearance, whether through death or deliberate withdrawal from public life, can feel like a natural extension of their lifelong preoccupation with the transient. The narrative might highlight the posthumous discovery of their significant body of work, a body of work that, ironically, ensures their lasting legacy even as their physical presence faded into obscurity during their lifetime. The author uses this contrast to explore the complex relationship between presence and absence, between the tangible individual and the intangible impact of their creations.

The theme of erasure also appears in narratives where characters attempt to escape their past or a perceived identity that has become burdensome. These individuals might adopt new names, relocate to unknown places, and meticulously construct new lives characterized by anonymity. Their goal is not necessarily to achieve fame or fortune, but to shed the weight of their former selves, to become someone new, or perhaps, to become no one at all. The literary exploration of such journeys often involves a suspenseful unfolding of the character's attempts to maintain their facade of invisibility, the constant threat of discovery looming over them. The resolution might involve their ultimate success in disappearing, their past remaining buried, or it might involve the inevitable unraveling of their constructed identity, leading to a different kind of disappearance – one that is forced and perhaps more dramatic. In either case, the narrative delves into the psychological cost of such an undertaking, the internal tension and isolation that accompany a life lived in constant vigilance against exposure.

Moreover, literary representations of erasure often engage with the concept of memory itself. Characters who seek to disappear may be acutely aware of the way memory can be both a burden and a prison. They may fear the judgment of others, the weight of past mistakes, or the relentless intrusion of recollections. Their desire for oblivion, therefore, is a desire to escape the confines of memory, both their own and that of others. The author might employ fragmented narratives, unreliable narrators, or shifts in perspective to mirror this fragmentation of memory and identity. The reader is left to piece together the character's story, much like an archaeologist excavating fragments of a lost civilization, a process that underscores the very theme of disappearance and the difficulty of truly knowing another's lived experience.

The aesthetic of disappearance can also be found in narratives that explore the relationship between individual lives and the larger historical or societal forces that threaten to obliterate them. Characters who find themselves marginalized, persecuted, or erased by dominant powers may develop an unconscious or conscious desire to fade away, to become too insignificant to be targeted. Their act of disappearing, in this context, can be seen as a form of passive resistance, a refusal to be fully captured or defined by oppressive structures. The literary depiction might focus on the individual's internal struggle for survival and dignity in the face of overwhelming external forces, their quiet acts of defiance, and their ultimate retreat into a space where they can exist on their own terms, even if that existence is one of near invisibility.

The exploration of non-Western literary traditions also reveals fascinating dimensions of this aesthetic. In cultures where collective identity often holds greater sway than individualistic pursuits, the concept of a solitary, unobserved disappearance might be viewed differently. However, the underlying human impulse to retreat, to find peace in oblivion, and to avoid the burden of a life that feels overwhelming, is a universal theme. These narratives might frame disappearance not as an act of personal failure or isolation, but as a spiritual quest, a return to a primordial state of oneness, or a dignified withdrawal from a world perceived as corrupt or transient. The literary techniques employed might involve allegory, symbolism, and a deep connection to nature, imbuing the act of fading with a sense of cosmic order or spiritual transcendence.

For example, consider narratives from philosophical traditions that emphasize detachment and non-attachment. Characters who have achieved a profound level of equanimity might, upon the natural conclusion of their earthly journey, choose to depart with minimal fuss, their lives having already been stripped of superfluous desires and worldly entanglements. Their passing would be marked by a sense of natural completion, like a leaf falling from a tree, an event that is observed and acknowledged but does not disrupt the fundamental order of things. The literature here would likely focus on the spiritual or philosophical underpinnings of such a departure, framing it as the ultimate expression of inner peace and a life well-lived in accordance with profound existential principles.

Furthermore, the literary genre of magical realism often plays with the concept of disappearance, blurring the lines between the literal and the metaphorical. Characters might literally vanish into thin air, their absence leaving behind a lingering mystery or a profound sense of loss that is nonetheless imbued with a certain fantastical beauty. These disappearances are often not tragic but are presented as natural, albeit extraordinary, occurrences within the fabric of the narrative. The author uses these fantastical elements to explore deeper truths about existence, loss, and the ephemeral nature of reality. The aesthetic here is one of wonder and contemplation, where the act of disappearing becomes a catalyst for exploring the profound mysteries of life and death.

The enduring power of these literary representations lies in their ability to tap into a fundamental human experience: the desire for peace, for respite from the demands of existence, and for an end that is as gentle as the beginning. By portraying characters who embody the aesthetic of disappearance, authors offer readers a lens through which to examine their own anxieties about mortality, legacy, and the meaning of a life lived. These narratives, whether they depict a gradual fading, a deliberate retreat, or a mystical vanishing, all speak to the profound psychological weight of leaving and the intricate ways in which we seek to navigate our own eventual absence from the world. They remind us that the grand narrative of human existence is not solely composed of loud pronouncements and dramatic interventions, but also of the quiet echoes of those who chose to fade, leaving behind not a void, but a space for contemplation, a testament to the quiet poetry of unmaking. The psychological depth of these characters, the authors' masterful use of language and narrative structure to convey their internal states, and the universal resonance of their quests for oblivion, all contribute to a rich and multifaceted literary exploration of this compelling aesthetic.

The very notion of enacting a complete cessation, of achieving a state of utter non-existence, is an inherently paradoxical pursuit. It is akin to a philosopher attempting to meticulously erase every single thought from their mind, or an artist striving to create a painting so perfect in its void that it ceases to be a painting at all. The desire for absolute erasure, for a dissolution so profound that not even a whisper of one's presence remains, runs headlong into the fundamental nature of being, which, by its very definition, is an engagement with existence, however minimal. How can one, as a conscious agent, orchestrate their own annihilation in a way that is itself an act of agency, a deliberate *doing* that aims for a state of ultimate *undoing*? This is where the aesthetic of disappearance encounters its most profound philosophical quandary, revealing not a neat conclusion, but a knot of psychic complexity.

The unconscious, in its labyrinthine workings, often harbors desires that are inherently contradictory. The wish to disappear completely, to become utterly non-existent, is one such potent example. It is a wish that, in its very articulation, betrays its impossibility. For to

wish for something is to be a subject who desires, and subjectivity, by its nature, implies a form of existence. Even the most ardent yearning for oblivion is a psychic phenomenon, a testament to the enduring operation of the mind, however much it may seek its own silence. It is the mind, in its capacity for self-reflection and self-negation, that conjures the image of its own absence. Thus, the very act of desiring non-existence is, paradoxically, an affirmation of existence, albeit an existence defined by its yearning for its own dissolution. This creates a feedback loop: the more one desires to disappear, the more they must, by definition, exist as the desiring subject.

Consider, for instance, the internal narrative of an individual deeply invested in the idea of leaving no trace. Their meticulous planning, their careful selection of a secluded location, their deliberate avoidance of personal connections – these are not passive occurrences. They are active choices, driven by a complex calculus of fear, exhaustion, or a profound disillusionment with the perceived noise and demands of life. The individual might spend years cultivating a life of extreme simplicity, shedding possessions, minimizing social interactions, and even consciously altering their speech patterns to become less noticeable. This deliberate effort to become invisible is, in itself, a profound expenditure of psychic energy. It requires a constant, albeit perhaps unconscious, vigilance, a sustained engagement with the world in order to effectively disengage from it. The sheer effort involved in orchestrating such an erasure is a testament to the persistence of the individual's will, a will that, even in its aim for annihilation, is still asserting itself.

The philosophical underpinnings of this paradox can be traced through various schools of thought. Existentialism, with its emphasis on radical freedom and responsibility, highlights the burden of choice. Even the choice to negate oneself, to opt out of the human condition, is an act of profound self-definition. The individual who seeks to disappear is still grappling with the "condemnation to be free," as Sartre put it. Their disappearance is not an escape from this freedom, but rather a final, desperate exercise of it. They are choosing their own erasure, and in doing so, they are inscribing their own definitive narrative, albeit a narrative that concludes with a blank page. The very act of striving for an unwritten ending is, in a curious way, a statement about the writer.

Moreover, psychoanalytic theory offers compelling insights into the unconscious motivations behind such a desire. Freud's concept of the death drive, the "instinct toward the inorganic," hints at a deep-seated urge towards a state of no excitation, a return to an inanimate peace. However, even this drive is mediated through the psyche. It is not a simple dissolution but a complex psychic process, often manifesting as a yearning for stillness, for a reduction of internal tension. The individual who seeks to disappear may be unconsciously driven by an overwhelming sense of guilt, a desire for self-punishment, or a profound weariness that surpasses even the will to live. These unconscious forces, while aiming for ultimate cessation, are nevertheless active psychic forces. They shape the individual's perception of reality and their behavior within it, leading them towards the very act of disappearing that they so ardently desire.

The paradox intensifies when we consider the symbolic residue that even the most successful disappearance inevitably leaves. A life lived in deliberate obscurity might conclude with a rediscovered journal, a forgotten letter, or a solitary dwelling that, upon discovery, speaks volumes about the person who inhabited it. These remnants, however small, act as breadcrumbs, leading back to a presence that was meant to be eradicated. This is the ghostly imprint of the self, an echo that resounds even in the intended silence. The aesthetic achievement of complete erasure is thus often marred by the unconscious or accidental leaving behind of these fragments, which, in their very discreteness, highlight the profound difficulty of achieving absolute oblivion. The more one tries to erase their footprint, the more their attempts themselves become a narrative, a story of deliberate vanishing.

Furthermore, the very concept of "non-existence" is itself a human construct, a philosophical abstraction. From a purely materialist perspective, existence is merely a state of being within the universe, and cessation of life is simply a return to fundamental elements. However, the human psyche, with its capacity for consciousness, meaning-making, and the creation of internal worlds, cannot easily divest itself of its own being. The desire for non-existence, therefore, is not a literal desire to become a stone or a gas, but a deeply psychological yearning for a release from the burdens of consciousness, identity, and the perceived obligations of life. This abstract desire, when pursued with the intent of literal erasure, creates a profound internal conflict. The individual is trying to achieve a state that is, by its very nature, beyond the capacity of a conscious agent to fully grasp or enact.

The futility of this pursuit highlights the resilience of the ego and the persistent presence of the self, even in its most self-negating forms. The unconscious mind, even when striving for dissolution, employs the very mechanisms of existence – thought, desire, intention – to achieve its goal. It is a testament to the intricate, often contradictory, nature of psychic life. The individual who seeks to disappear is, in a sense, trapped in a Sisyphean task: they labor tirelessly to achieve a state of ultimate passivity, but the very act of laboring is a testament to their active, striving existence. The aesthetic of disappearance, in this light, is not about achieving a true void, but about the profound and often tragic performance of trying to do so. It is the ultimate act of self-consciousness, paradoxically aimed at its own annihilation.

This leads to a deeper understanding of the psychological mechanisms at play. The desire for complete erasure might be a defense against overwhelming feelings of shame, inadequacy, or a sense of having caused irreparable harm. By wishing to disappear entirely, the individual attempts to extinguish not only their own presence but also the potential for further transgressions or for the perpetuation of suffering. It is a radical form of atonement, an attempt to achieve a state of purity through absolute negation. However, this act, while stemming from a desire for peace, is itself a deeply disruptive psychic event, a violent disruption of the individual's own being that seeks to mimic a non-event. The paradox lies in the fact that the most extreme attempt to stop being is, in its very intensity, an intensely felt experience of being.

The literary and artistic expressions of this paradox often revolve around the theme of the ghost, the lingering presence of someone who is no longer physically there. While these figures may represent a form of "afterlife," their lingering often stems from unresolved issues, unfinished business, or an unfulfilled desire – ironically, often a desire for recognition or connection, the very things the individual seeking erasure aims to avoid. This speaks to the idea that even in death, or in the pursuit of it, a form of presence can persist, an echo of the self that refuses to be entirely silenced. The aesthetic of disappearance, therefore, is less about achieving a perfect void and more about the complex, often melancholic, interplay between presence and absence, between the desire for oblivion and the persistent traces of a life lived. It is a constant negotiation with the impossible, a performance of non-being that, by its very nature, affirms the enduring reality of the performer.

The intricate dance between individual psychic desire and collective societal experience is a fertile ground for exploring the aesthetic of disappearance. While the previous discourse has delved into the personal, often unconscious, yearning for erasure, it is crucial to expand this inquiry to the broader social fabric. For the fantasy of vanishing, so potent on an individual level, finds its disquieting echoes in the very way societies organize themselves, the stories they choose to tell, and, perhaps more significantly, the narratives they allow to fade into oblivion. These societal echoes are not mere reflections; they are active manifestations of similar underlying impulses, revealing how the desire for erasure can become a shared, albeit often unacknowledged, cultural phenomenon.

Consider, for instance, the spectral presence of forgotten historical figures. History, as it is commonly taught and remembered, is a curated narrative, an edited version of the past. Certain individuals, movements, or entire communities can, over time, slip from collective memory. They are not actively erased in a malicious sense, but rather they fade, their contributions becoming footnotes, their very existence relegated to the dusty archives of obscure research. These are the individuals who may have been revolutionaries whose ideas were co-opted and diluted, artists whose groundbreaking work was unrecognized in their time, or thinkers whose perspectives were too radical to be assimilated. Their disappearance from the forefront of our historical consciousness is not always the result of a deliberate act of silencing, but rather a gradual erosion, a consequence of shifting societal interests, evolving dominant ideologies, or simply the sheer volume of new narratives that vie for our attention. The aesthetic of their vanishing lies in the poignant sense of a life, a struggle, a contribution, that has ceased to resonate, a story that has been meticulously unwritten by the passage of time and the selective memory of humankind. It is a disappearance that occurs not with a bang, but with a whimper of forgotten significance.

This societal amnesia is not merely an unfortunate byproduct of historical processes; it can, in some instances, reflect a more active devaluation of certain lives and experiences. The anonymous victims of natural disasters, such as earthquakes, floods, or famines, often become statistics, their individual stories subsumed by the overwhelming scale of the catastrophe. While humanitarian efforts may acknowledge their plight, the sheer number of lives lost can render individual identities almost impossible to track or memorialize. The names, faces, and personal narratives of thousands can be lost to the rubble, the rising waters, or the ravages of disease. What remains is a collective tragedy, a number that represents an incalculable sum of individual vanishings. The aesthetic here is one of profound, almost unbearable, anonymity. It is the aesthetic of a mass erasure, where the very magnitude of loss renders the individual presence too fragmented, too scattered, to be reconstituted. These are lives that were extinguished without the comfort of individual remembrance, their endings marked not by personal farewells, but by the impersonal force of overwhelming circumstance. Their disappearance is a stark reminder of how easily individual existence can be dissolved within larger, impersonal forces.

Furthermore, the concept of individuals falling through societal safety nets represents a more insidious form of vanishing. These are the individuals who, for a myriad of reasons – economic hardship, mental illness, addiction, or social isolation – become invisible to the systems designed to support them. They are the homeless who are overlooked on street corners, the undocumented migrants who fear any interaction with authority, or the individuals struggling with severe mental health issues who have lost contact with family and friends. Their lives may continue in a precarious state, but they cease to register in the official records, the social consciousness, or the communal awareness. They become statistical ghosts, their existence a matter of conjecture rather than established fact. The aesthetic of their disappearance is one of profound neglect, a quiet fading away that speaks to a society's failure to acknowledge or engage with its most vulnerable members. It is the aesthetic of being present yet entirely unseen, of existing on the margins of perception until even those margins cease to hold them. Their vanishing is not an act of will, but a slow dissolution born of societal indifference.

These collective instances of vanishing, whether of forgotten historical figures, anonymous disaster victims, or individuals lost to societal neglect, profoundly echo the individual unconscious desire for erasure. The impulse to disappear, to cease to be perceived or to carry the burden of existence, is mirrored in the way communities and cultures allow certain lives and narratives to fade. This is not to suggest that these societal phenomena are conscious enactments of a desire for oblivion; rather, they reveal a collective tendency towards a form of societal self-negation, a willingness to overlook, to forget, or to devalue those elements that do not fit neatly into dominant narratives or that prove too burdensome to acknowledge.

The devaluation of certain lives, in particular, is a potent driver of societal disappearance. When entire groups of people are systematically marginalized, oppressed, or rendered subordinate, their very existence can become diminished in the collective imagination. The stories of enslaved peoples, indigenous populations dispossessed of their lands, or minority groups facing discrimination are often relegated to the periphery of historical accounts, their experiences rendered secondary to those of the dominant culture. Their suffering may be acknowledged in passing, but the depth of their loss, the richness of their lost traditions, and the enduring impact of their subjugation are often glossed over. This selective amnesia serves to reinforce existing power structures and to maintain a comfortable narrative for the privileged. The aesthetic of disappearance in such cases is one of imposed invisibility, where lives are systematically rendered less significant, their absence from the historical record a testament to their perceived lack of value.

Moreover, the modern phenomenon of rapid technological advancement and the relentless pace of information flow can contribute to a new form of societal disappearance. In a world saturated with fleeting trends, viral content, and ephemeral digital identities, what is deemed significant today can be utterly forgotten tomorrow. This constant churn creates a culture where long-term impact and enduring legacy can be difficult to achieve. Individuals and their contributions can be easily eclipsed by the next wave of digital noise. The digital footprint, while seemingly permanent, can also be remarkably fragile, subject to platform obsolescence, data loss, or the simple act of being buried beneath an avalanche of new content. This creates an aesthetic of rapid obsolescence, where disappearance is not a slow fading but a swift, almost instantaneous, plunge into digital irrelevance. Lives lived and contributions made can vanish from immediate public consciousness with alarming speed.

The connection between the individual psychic fantasy of erasure and these broader societal patterns is a complex but crucial one. The unconscious desire to escape the burdens of consciousness, identity, and responsibility finds a macrocosmic parallel in societies that, consciously or unconsciously, choose to divest themselves of difficult histories, marginalized populations, or inconvenient truths. The psychic comfort derived from a simplified, less challenging narrative mirrors the societal tendency to curate a more palatable version of reality. Just as an individual might repress traumatic memories to maintain psychological equilibrium, a society might collectively forget or downplay traumatic events to preserve its self-image or avoid confronting uncomfortable ethical questions.

The aesthetic of disappearance, therefore, extends beyond the individual's desire for oblivion; it permeates the very fabric of our collective memory and cultural narrative. It is present in the quiet fading of certain professions rendered obsolete by automation, the erasure of linguistic diversity as global languages dominate, or the homogenizing effects of mass consumer culture that can diminish unique cultural expressions. Each of these instances, in its own way, represents a form of vanishing, a loss of what once was, that resonates with the individual yearning to shed the weight of existence.

The persistence of these societal echoes of disappearance also raises questions about what it means to be truly remembered. Is remembrance a passive state, or does it require an active engagement, a conscious effort to maintain the presence of the past? The aesthetic of disappearance suggests that without such active engagement, all but the most dominant narratives are susceptible to fading. The forgotten figures, the anonymous victims, the marginalized communities – their stories linger in the potentiality of remembrance, but without continued societal effort, they remain in a state of spectral existence, a testament to the fragility of memory.

This contemplation of societal echoes brings us back to the inherent paradox of disappearance. Even when a society seemingly erases certain histories or populations, traces often remain. The scars of injustice, the demographic shifts caused by historical events, the subtle cultural influences of marginalized groups – these are all whispers of a past that refuses to be entirely silenced. These lingering remnants are the societal equivalent of the individual's dropped journal or forgotten letter, providing fragmented evidence of a presence that was meant to be eradicated. The aesthetic of societal disappearance, therefore, is not one of absolute void but of persistent, often disquieting, echoes that challenge the neatness of erasure. It reveals that the act of forgetting, like the act of disappearing, is a complex performance, one that is never entirely complete and often carries its own spectral weight. The more a society attempts to consign certain aspects of its past or certain groups of its population to oblivion, the more these very acts of exclusion and erasure can leave indelible marks, shaping the present in ways that are often unintended and deeply revealing. The aesthetic of disappearance, in its societal manifestation, becomes a commentary on what a culture chooses to value, what it is willing to discard, and the often-unseen consequences of such choices. It highlights that even in the grand theatre of collective human experience, the desire for oblivion, or the consequence of being rendered forgotten, casts a long and enduring shadow. The silence that follows a societal vanishing is rarely absolute; it is often filled with the murmurs of what has been suppressed, the ghost notes of lives that, though erased from the score, still resonate in the background.

Chapter 3: The Aesthetics of Dramatic Appearance

The preceding exploration has illuminated the subtle, often quiet, retreat from existence, the aesthetic of disappearance where the unconscious impulse towards erasure finds its expression. Now, we turn our gaze towards a diametrically opposed, yet equally potent, manifestation of this impulse: the aesthetic of the grand exit. If disappearance is the fading echo, the whispered adieu, then the grand exit is the shattering crescendo, the unforgettable spectacle that demands an audience, even if that audience is comprised solely of those who remain to witness the aftermath. This is not a gentle melting into the ether, but a defiant, often violent, assertion of presence at the very moment of perceived absence. It is the death that writhes with an unconscious need to be seen, to be acknowledged, to leave an indelible scar upon the consciousness of the living.

The unconscious drive behind such a dramatic departure is often rooted in a profound, existential sense of insignificance. For the individual who has felt unseen, unheard, or undervalued throughout their life, the moment of death can become the ultimate, albeit tragic, opportunity to command attention. It is a desperate, often unconscious, bid to rewrite a narrative of overlooked existence into one of undeniable impact. The life that may have been perceived as a muted hum is, in its final moments, amplified into a deafening roar. This is not about a conscious desire for notoriety in life, but rather a posthumous assertion of worth, a final, desperate plea for recognition etched in the very manner of one's demise. The individual, unable to secure validation during their living hours, seeks it through the sheer force of their final act. The death becomes a performance, meticulously (though unconsciously) crafted to resonate long after the performer has exited the stage.

Consider the historical archetypes that embody this aesthetic. The figure who chooses a public, almost theatrical, self-immolation, or the individual who orchestrates a suicide that implicates others, thereby ensuring their story will be dissected and debated. These are not merely acts of desperation; they are, from a psychoanalytic perspective, carefully staged finales. The unconscious logic at play suggests a desperate recalibration of power. When power is felt to be absent in life – the power to control one's destiny, to influence others, to simply be

seen – the moment of death becomes the ultimate equalizer. It is the one moment where the individual can exert absolute, albeit final, control over how they are perceived. The spectacle of their ending becomes a testament to their power, however morbid, to disrupt, to shock, and to imprint themselves upon the collective memory. The helplessness experienced in life is transmuted into a potent, terrifying agency in death.

This aesthetic is deeply intertwined with a fantasy of control. When the threads of one's life feel frayed, uncontrollable, or simply insignificant, the moment of death offers a perverse opportunity to seize the reins. The unconscious mind, grappling with feelings of powerlessness, may engineer an exit that is so striking, so shocking, that it cannot be ignored. It is as if the individual is saying, "If you didn't see me when I was alive, you will certainly see me now. My absence will be more potent than my presence ever was." This is not a reasoned decision; it is a deep-seated psychic imperative, a desperate attempt to imbue a life that felt devoid of meaning with a final, overwhelming significance. The death itself becomes the masterpiece, the magnum opus of an artist who felt their earlier works were ignored.

The unconscious need for validation fuels this dramatic exit. For individuals who have lived with a chronic sense of inadequacy, who have constantly sought external approval and found it wanting, the grand exit offers a guaranteed, albeit grim, form of affirmation. The shock and awe of their final act will undoubtedly elicit reactions: grief, horror, pity, perhaps even a grudging admiration for the audacity of it all. These reactions, however negative, are still forms of attention, confirmations that the individual

mattered, even if only in their spectacular demise. The void left by their departure will be palpable, a tangible absence that forces those left behind to confront the gravity of their exit. This is the unconscious fulfillment of a lifelong hunger: to be truly seen, to be profoundly acknowledged, even if only through the lens of tragedy.

The desire to leave an indelible mark is another crucial component of the grand exit. Life can feel ephemeral, a fleeting moment in the vast expanse of time. For those who fear being forgotten, whose greatest dread is to have lived and died without leaving any trace, the dramatic death serves as an ultimate inscription. It is a way of carving their name, however tragically, into the stone of history. The more spectacular the exit, the more enduring the memory. The unconscious mind, in its pursuit of permanence, opts for a death that is so striking, so unforgettable, that it cannot possibly fade into the background. It is a desperate act of defiance against the inevitability of oblivion, a final, powerful declaration of "I was here."

This aesthetic also plays out in the realm of power dynamics. When an individual feels systematically disempowered, marginalized, or oppressed, their final act can become a potent, albeit distorted, expression of agency. The grand exit can be an unconscious attempt to reclaim a sense of control, to disrupt the established order, and to impose their will, even in death. It is a final act of rebellion, a refusal to go quietly into the night. The sheer audacity of a dramatic death can serve as a powerful statement, a shockwave that reverberates through the lives of those perceived as having held power over them. The helplessness of their living circumstances is subverted by the terrifying power they wield in their final, spectacular withdrawal.

Furthermore, the grand exit can be an attempt to manipulate the narrative surrounding one's life. If a life has been perceived as mundane, ordinary, or even a disappointment, a dramatic death can serve to reframe the entire story. It becomes a tragedy of epic proportions, a tale of a life cut short by circumstances, or a noble sacrifice. This unconscious rewriting of a life's trajectory through its ending is a powerful psychological defense mechanism. It allows the individual, and often those who survive them, to construct a more palatable and memorable narrative, transforming perceived failures into elements of a grand, albeit tragic, drama. The death becomes the definitive plot twist, redeeming what might have been seen as a less compelling storyline.

The unconscious projection of this aesthetic can be seen in the cultural narratives we consume and create. The romanticized suicides in literature and film, the tragic figures who meet their end in a blaze of glory, often tap into this primal human need for a significant, memorable departure. These stories, while often tragic, speak to a part of our collective psyche that yearns for lives lived with intense passion, even if that passion ultimately leads to destruction. They offer a vicarious experience of confronting mortality with dramatic flair, a testament to the enduring human fascination with the spectacle of death as a final, defining act. These narratives, in turn, can reinforce the unconscious drive for such dramatic exits in individuals who feel their own lives lack that perceived intensity or significance.

It is crucial to distinguish this aesthetic from a conscious desire for martyrdom or a deliberate act of self-destruction for a specific, external goal. The grand exit operates on a deeper, unconscious level. It is not necessarily about sending a message, but about an internal, psychic imperative to

be remembered, to *be seen*, to *assert power* in the face of perceived oblivion. The individual may not even be fully aware of the magnitude of the performance they are orchestrating. It is a deeply ingrained pattern, a compulsion born from the profound fear of an insignificant existence. The death becomes a surrogate for a life that felt perpetually unheard, a final, desperate act of self-creation through self-destruction. The aesthetic lies in the very unreasonableness of it all, the sheer, unadulterated impact of an ending that refuses to be quiet or overlooked. It is the dramatic flourish that eclipses the entire performance of life, ensuring that the curtain falls not with a sigh, but with a thunderous, unforgettable crash. The void left behind is not merely an absence; it is a statement, a monument to a life that, in its final act, demanded to be acknowledged in the most profound and terrifying way.

The theatre of the self, when its performances become too painful to bear in silence, often seeks its final, indelible act upon the stage of existence itself. This is not the quiet fading into the wings, but a final, explosive entrance into the consciousness of others, a desperate bid to ensure the play, and its protagonist, are never forgotten. We turn now to a clinical exploration, a anonymized distillation of a life that embodied this aesthetic of the dramatic appearance, a life that culminated not in a whisper, but in a thunderous, unforgettable crescendo. This is the story of an individual whose very being seemed attuned to the dramatic, whose unconscious tapestry was woven with threads of spectacle, and whose end became the ultimate, albeit tragic, performance.

The individual, let us call them Alex, presented a life characterized by a relentless pursuit of intensity. From early adulthood, Alex's relationships were marked by a volatile ebb and flow, a dramatic oscillation between adulation and condemnation. Conversations often felt like monologues, punctuated by Alex's impassioned pronouncements, sweeping gestures, and an almost palpable need for their emotional state to be mirrored and validated by those around them. There was a pervasive sense of being on display, even in the most intimate of settings. Friendships, romantic partnerships, and even casual acquaintances were subject to Alex's elaborate emotional narratives, replete with exaggerated joys and profound sorrows, all delivered with a rhetorical flourish that suggested an awareness, however unconscious, of an audience. This was not simply about expressing feelings; it was about

performing them, about orchestrating a symphony of emotional experience that demanded rapt attention.

In therapeutic sessions, Alex's narrative was consistently framed with a theatrical bent. Every setback was a crushing injustice, every small triumph a heroic victory against overwhelming odds. The language used was elevated, often drawing on archetypal themes of betrayal, sacrifice, and misunderstood genius. There was a profound difficulty in acknowledging mundane realities or accepting responsibility for ordinary failures. Instead, events were re-framed through a lens of dramatic conflict, where Alex was invariably cast as the noble victim or the embattled hero. This created a feedback loop: the more intensely Alex performed these roles, the more the people in their life either became entangled in the drama or, more often, withdrew, further fueling Alex's sense of isolation and reinforcing the narrative of being uniquely misunderstood and wronged.

Unconscious fantasies of omnipotence and profound significance played a crucial role in Alex's internal world. There was a deep-seated belief that they were destined for something extraordinary, a conviction that set them apart from the perceived mediocrity of others. This grandiosity, however, was constantly undermined by an equally powerful undercurrent of insecurity and worthlessness. The dramatic displays served as a defense against this terrifying inner void. By commanding such intense emotional reactions from others, Alex sought to solidify their own sense of existence, to prove to themselves and to the world that they were not invisible, not insignificant. The more extreme the emotional output, the more potent the perceived affirmation. This was a desperate, unconscious strategy to fill an existential emptiness with the potent, albeit fleeting, energy of dramatic engagement.

The interpersonal dynamics were particularly telling. Alex's relationships often became arenas for a reenactment of early, unresolved relational patterns. There was a tendency to provoke strong emotional responses, often through acts of defiance, public criticism, or dramatic declarations of loyalty followed by equally dramatic pronouncements of betrayal. The pattern was repetitive: Alex would invest intensely in a relationship, then engineer a crisis that would force the other person to respond with overwhelming emotion – anger, distress, or passionate defense. This intense emotional engagement, however negative, was experienced by Alex as a form of connection, a confirmation that they were perceived, and therefore real. When these relationships inevitably faltered, Alex would often embark on a cycle of lamentation and accusation, painting themselves as the wronged party, the victim of cruelty or misunderstanding. This served to both garner sympathy and subtly punish the perceived transgressor, ensuring that their departure from Alex's life was anything but quiet.

Alex's life was a series of carefully orchestrated "moments." These were not necessarily planned events in the conventional sense, but rather instances where Alex seemed to instinctively seize an opportunity to elevate the emotional stakes. A casual gathering could transform into a platform for Alex's impassioned defense of a controversial idea, delivered with tears or righteous anger. A minor disagreement could escalate into a dramatic denunciation, often involving invoking past grievances and painting a picture of long-standing persecution. The unconscious goal was always the same: to create an unforgettable impression, to inject a potent dose of drama into the mundane, and to ensure that their presence, or indeed their absence, would be profoundly felt.

Consider a specific, recurring pattern: Alex's tendency to create "scenes" when feeling overlooked or slighted. If a friend cancelled plans, Alex might respond with a theatrical display of grief and despair, perhaps even hinting at self-harm, thereby compelling the friend to rush back, filled with guilt and concern. This was not about genuine suicidal ideation in the moment, but rather a manipulative tactic born from the unconscious fantasy that only extreme emotional distress could elicit the attention and care Alex craved. The "threat" of dramatic suffering was wielded as a tool to ensure connection, a desperate bargain for recognition. When challenged, Alex would retreat into a posture of wounded victimhood, reinforcing the narrative of being unfairly judged and incapable of receiving genuine empathy.

This aesthetic of dramatic appearance also manifested in Alex's professional life, albeit with more covert strategies. While direct outbursts were less common in formal settings, Alex had a talent for subtly sabotaging situations or creating interpersonal tensions that would erupt into dramatic confrontations. This might involve misinterpreting instructions to cause a project delay, subtly pitting colleagues against each other through carefully placed remarks, or using emotional appeals to manipulate superiors into granting special concessions. The goal was not necessarily to achieve professional success, but to remain the center of attention, to be the subject of gossip and speculation, and to ensure that their presence was always felt, even if it was through creating discord. The unconscious drive was to be seen as a powerful, if problematic, force, rather than an easily dismissible employee.

The unconscious fantasies at play were complex, often contradictory. On one hand, there was the omnipotent fantasy of being a central, powerful figure, capable of shaping the emotional landscape around them. On the other hand, there was the deeply entrenched fantasy of the victim, the misunderstood soul destined for suffering, whose dramatic pronouncements were the only recourse against a cruel and indifferent world. These two fantasies, rather than being mutually exclusive, coexisted and fueled each other. The grandiosity provided the motivation for dramatic displays, while the victimhood narrative offered a ready-made explanation and justification for the intensity of those displays. The theatricality was the bridge between these two poles, allowing Alex to embody both the powerful manipulator and the tragically suffering soul, depending on the perceived needs of the audience.

The concept of "heroic sacrifice" also played a significant role in Alex's internal landscape, particularly as the end of life approached. There was a growing narrative that Alex was suffering immensely, bearing burdens no one else could comprehend, and that their life was a noble struggle against insurmountable odds. This narrative, while containing elements of genuine distress, was also heavily infused with the aesthetic of dramatic appearance. Alex began to speak of making a "final statement," of ensuring that their suffering would not be in vain, and that their life would serve as a lesson to others. This was not necessarily a conscious plan for suicide, but rather a growing articulation of a life story that demanded a grand, conclusive ending. The unconscious was gearing up for a final, definitive performance that would cement Alex's place in the narrative of those who had suffered greatly, but heroically.

When Alex's life finally drew to a close, it was not in a quiet, unassuming manner. The circumstances surrounding Alex's death were, in keeping with the lifelong aesthetic, dramatic and profoundly impactful. While respecting the anonymization and sensitivity required, it is important to note that the exit was a spectacle, a deliberate and unforgettable event that left an indelible mark on all who were aware of it. It was a culmination of years of unconscious maneuvering, of a life lived in the shadow of a profound need to be seen and acknowledged. The final act was not an aberration, but the logical, albeit tragic, conclusion of a deeply ingrained pattern of dramatic appearance. Alex's death was not merely an end; it was a statement, a final, powerful performance that ensured the protagonist would indeed be remembered, their story echoing long after the curtain fell. This theatrical demise, born from a desperate unconscious yearning for significance, serves as a stark illustration of how the aesthetic of dramatic appearance can shape not only how we live, but how we choose, in our final moments, to exit the stage. The need to be seen, to be felt, to leave a mark, can manifest in the most profound and self-destructive ways, turning life into a rehearsal for a final, unforgettable bow.

The theatre of the self, when its performances become too painful to bear in silence, often seeks its final, indelible act upon the stage of existence itself. This is not the quiet fading into the wings, but a final, explosive entrance into the consciousness of others, a desperate bid to ensure the play, and its protagonist, are never forgotten. We turn now to a clinical exploration, a anonymized distillation of a life that embodied this aesthetic of the dramatic appearance, a life that culminated not in a whisper, but in a thunderous, unforgettable crescendo. This is the story of an individual whose very being seemed attuned to the dramatic, whose unconscious tapestry was woven with threads of spectacle, and whose end became the ultimate, albeit tragic, performance.

The individual, let us call them Alex, presented a life characterized by a relentless pursuit of intensity. From early adulthood, Alex's relationships were marked by a volatile ebb and flow, a dramatic oscillation between adulation and condemnation. Conversations often felt like monologues, punctuated by Alex's impassioned pronouncements, sweeping gestures, and an almost palpable need for their emotional state to be mirrored and validated by those around them. There was a pervasive sense of being on display, even in the most intimate of settings. Friendships, romantic partnerships, and even casual acquaintances were subject to Alex's elaborate emotional narratives, replete with exaggerated joys and profound sorrows, all delivered with a rhetorical flourish that suggested an awareness, however unconscious, of an audience. This was not simply about expressing feelings; it was about

performing them, about orchestrating a symphony of emotional experience that demanded rapt attention.

In therapeutic sessions, Alex's narrative was consistently framed with a theatrical bent. Every setback was a crushing injustice, every small triumph a heroic victory against overwhelming odds. The language used was elevated, often drawing on archetypal themes of betrayal, sacrifice, and misunderstood genius. There was a profound difficulty in acknowledging mundane realities or accepting responsibility for ordinary failures. Instead, events were re-framed through a lens of dramatic conflict, where Alex was invariably cast as the noble victim or the embattled hero. This created a feedback loop: the more intensely Alex performed these roles, the more the people in their life either became entangled in the drama or, more often, withdrew, further fueling Alex's sense of isolation and reinforcing the narrative of being uniquely misunderstood and wronged.

Unconscious fantasies of omnipotence and profound significance played a crucial role in Alex's internal world. There was a deep-seated belief that they were destined for something extraordinary, a conviction that set them apart from the perceived mediocrity of others. This grandiosity, however, was constantly undermined by an equally powerful undercurrent of insecurity and worthlessness. The dramatic displays served as a defense against this terrifying inner void. By commanding such intense emotional reactions from others, Alex sought to solidify their own sense of existence, to prove to themselves and to the world that they were not invisible, not insignificant. The more extreme the emotional output, the more potent the perceived affirmation. This was a desperate, unconscious strategy to fill an existential emptiness with the potent, albeit fleeting, energy of dramatic engagement.

The interpersonal dynamics were particularly telling. Alex's relationships often became arenas for a reenactment of early, unresolved relational patterns. There was a tendency to provoke strong emotional responses, often through acts of defiance, public criticism, or dramatic declarations of loyalty followed by equally dramatic pronouncements of betrayal. The pattern was repetitive: Alex would invest intensely in a relationship, then engineer a crisis that would force the other person to respond with overwhelming emotion – anger, distress, or passionate defense. This intense emotional engagement, however negative, was experienced by Alex as a form of connection, a confirmation that they were perceived, and therefore real. When these relationships inevitably faltered, Alex would often embark on a cycle of lamentation and accusation, painting themselves as the wronged party, the victim of cruelty or misunderstanding. This served to both garner sympathy and subtly punish the perceived transgressor, ensuring that their departure from Alex's life was anything but quiet.

Alex's life was a series of carefully orchestrated "moments." These were not necessarily planned events in the conventional sense, but rather instances where Alex seemed to instinctively seize an opportunity to elevate the emotional stakes. A casual gathering could transform into a platform for Alex's impassioned defense of a controversial idea, delivered with tears or righteous anger. A minor disagreement could escalate into a dramatic denunciation, often involving invoking past grievances and painting a picture of long-standing persecution. The unconscious goal was always the same: to create an unforgettable impression, to inject a potent dose of drama into the mundane, and to ensure that their presence, or indeed their absence, would be profoundly felt.

Consider a specific, recurring pattern: Alex's tendency to create "scenes" when feeling overlooked or slighted. If a friend cancelled plans, Alex might respond with a theatrical display of grief and despair, perhaps even hinting at self-harm, thereby compelling the friend to rush back, filled with guilt and concern. This was not about genuine suicidal ideation in the moment, but rather a manipulative tactic born from the unconscious fantasy that only extreme emotional distress could elicit the attention and care Alex craved. The "threat" of dramatic suffering was wielded as a tool to ensure connection, a desperate bargain for recognition. When challenged, Alex would retreat into a posture of wounded victimhood, reinforcing the narrative of being unfairly judged and incapable of receiving genuine empathy.

This aesthetic of dramatic appearance also manifested in Alex's professional life, albeit with more covert strategies. While direct outbursts were less common in formal settings, Alex had a talent for subtly sabotaging situations or creating interpersonal tensions that would erupt into dramatic confrontations. This might involve misinterpreting instructions to cause a project delay, subtly pitting colleagues against each other through carefully placed remarks, or using emotional appeals to manipulate superiors into granting special concessions. The goal was not necessarily to achieve professional success, but to remain the center of attention, to be the subject of gossip and speculation, and to ensure that their presence was always felt, even if it was through creating discord. The unconscious drive was to be seen as a powerful, if problematic, force, rather than an easily dismissible employee.

The unconscious fantasies at play were complex, often contradictory. On one hand, there was the omnipotent fantasy of being a central, powerful figure, capable of shaping the emotional landscape around them. On the other hand, there was the deeply entrenched fantasy of the victim, the misunderstood soul destined for suffering, whose dramatic pronouncements were the only recourse against a cruel and indifferent world. These two fantasies, rather than being mutually exclusive, coexisted and fueled each other. The grandiosity provided the motivation for dramatic displays, while the victimhood narrative offered a ready-made explanation and justification for the intensity of those displays. The theatricality was the bridge between these two poles, allowing Alex to embody both the powerful manipulator and the tragically suffering soul, depending on the perceived needs of the audience.

The concept of "heroic sacrifice" also played a significant role in Alex's internal landscape, particularly as the end of life approached. There was a growing narrative that Alex was suffering immensely, bearing burdens no one else could comprehend, and that their life was a noble struggle against insurmountable odds. This narrative, while containing elements of genuine distress, was also heavily infused with the aesthetic of dramatic appearance. Alex began to speak of making a "final statement," of ensuring that their suffering would not be in vain, and that their life would serve as a lesson to others. This was not necessarily a conscious plan for suicide, but rather a growing articulation of a life story that demanded a grand, conclusive ending. The unconscious was gearing up for a final, definitive performance that would cement Alex's place in the narrative of those who had suffered greatly, but heroically.

When Alex's life finally drew to a close, it was not in a quiet, unassuming manner. The circumstances surrounding Alex's death were, in keeping with the lifelong aesthetic, dramatic and profoundly impactful. While respecting the anonymization and sensitivity required, it is important to note that the exit was a spectacle, a deliberate and unforgettable event that left an indelible mark on all who were aware of it. It was a culmination of years of unconscious maneuvering, of a life lived in the shadow of a profound need to be seen and acknowledged. The final act was not an aberration, but the logical, albeit tragic, conclusion of a deeply ingrained pattern of dramatic appearance. Alex's death was not merely an end; it was a statement, a final, powerful performance that ensured the protagonist would indeed be remembered, their story echoing long after the curtain fell. This theatrical demise, born from a desperate unconscious yearning for significance, serves as a stark illustration of how the aesthetic of dramatic appearance can shape not only how we live, but how we choose, in our final moments, to exit the stage. The need to be seen, to be felt, to leave a mark, can manifest in the most profound and self-destructive ways, turning life into a rehearsal for a final, unforgettable bow.

Beyond the clinical individual, the annals of cultural history are replete with figures whose departures from this world were not mere biological events but carefully or instinctively curated spectacles. These are individuals who, consciously or unconsciously, understood the potent power of an ending, and whose final acts reverberated through collective consciousness, shaping legacies and solidifying their place in the pantheon of the memorable. These "spectacle deaths" often transcend personal tragedy to become cultural touchstones, imbued with layers of meaning that speak to deeper societal anxieties, aspirations, and the enduring human fascination with the dramatic.

Consider the enduring mythos surrounding Marilyn Monroe. Her death, officially ruled an overdose of barbiturates, became instantly iconic, a tragic tableau that cemented her image as the ultimate femme fatale, a fragile beauty consumed by her own fame and the pressures of Hollywood. The narrative that emerged was one of a woman desperately seeking genuine connection and validation, adrift in a world that only appreciated her image. The details surrounding her passing – the empty pill bottles, the disarray of her apartment, the lingering questions about whether it was accidental, intentional, or even a result of foul play – all contributed to an atmosphere of mystery and drama, amplifying the sense of a life that burned too brightly to last. Her death was not simply an end to her existence; it was the final, devastating act in a lifelong performance of vulnerability and allure, a performance that continued to captivate and haunt the public imagination. The unconscious desires at play here are manifold: the public's yearning for a tangible symbol of Hollywood's destructive glamour, a projection of their own fears about fame and beauty, and perhaps a collective mourning for a perceived lost innocence. Monroe's demise became a cautionary tale, a poignant illustration of the destructive potential of living under an unrelenting spotlight, and in its spectacular finality, it ensured her immortality in a way that a quiet passing never could.

Similarly, the death of Jimi Hendrix, a revolutionary guitarist and cultural icon, became another indelible moment in the tapestry of the 1960s. His passing, attributed to a barbiturate overdose and asphyxiation on his own vomit, was as unconventional and dramatic as his stage presence. Hendrix, known for his virtuosic guitar playing, his psychedelic performances, and his counter-cultural appeal, died young, at the age of 27, a fate shared by several prominent musicians of that era, thus contributing to the morbid mythology of the "27 Club." His death was perceived not just as a personal tragedy but as a symbolic loss for the psychedelic movement and a generation seeking to break free from societal constraints. The narrative surrounding his death often emphasized the excesses of the rock and roll lifestyle, the intense pressure of superstardom, and the spiritual quests that characterized his artistic journey. The very manner of his death, messy and seemingly uncontrolled, resonated with the raw, untamed energy that defined his music and his public persona. It was a dramatic exit for a man who embodied raw creative power and rebellion. The unconscious elements here might include a collective desire to see the radical icon meet a radical end, a confirmation of the destructive allure of the bohemian lifestyle, and a yearning to understand the price of unparalleled artistic genius. Hendrix's death, like Monroe's, was not merely an end; it was a spectacle that amplified his legend, making him a permanent fixture in the cultural firmament.

These are not isolated incidents. Throughout history, artists, revolutionaries, and public figures have, through deliberate action or by succumbing to circumstances that amplified their existing personas, orchestrated endings that served as final, dramatic statements. The unconscious desire for legacy, for notoriety, or even for a form of symbolic revenge against a world perceived as unforgiving, can drive individuals towards such spectacular finales. These deaths become potent myths, endlessly reinterpreted and imbued with meaning, far beyond the biological cessation of life. They are performances, in the most profound and often tragic sense, that ensure the protagonist is never forgotten, their final act indelibly etched into the collective imagination. The allure of such dramatic deaths lies in their ability to crystallize complex narratives, to offer catharsis, and to provide a final, powerful expression of the forces that shaped a life, transforming mortality into a testament. The aesthetics of dramatic appearance, therefore, do not cease with life itself; they find their ultimate, and often most haunting, expression in the manner of one's departure. The spectacle of a cultural icon's death is, in essence, the final, unmissable performance in a life lived under the gaze of an eager, and often unforgiving, public. It is in these moments of ultimate dramatic exit that the line between individual consciousness and collective narrative blurs, leaving behind an enduring legacy that transcends the limitations of a finite existence. The unconscious imperative to be remembered, to leave an indelible mark, finds its most potent expression in the carefully (or instinctively) constructed drama of a final bow, transforming death into an enduring cultural text.

The echo of a life lived intensely often finds its most profound resonance not in its quiet conclusion, but in a final, dramatic pronouncement. This is particularly true for those whose unconscious landscape is governed by a potent, often paradoxical, imperative: the need to be remembered. When the fear of insignificance gnaws at the very core of one's being, the prospect of fading into obscurity becomes a fate more terrifying than death itself. This dread can transmute into an almost alchemical pursuit of a spectacular exit, a final, unforgettable performance that guarantees a place, however infamously, in the annals of consciousness. The very act of dying, for such individuals, can become imbued with an unconscious logic that transforms it from a biological endpoint into a climactic artistic statement, a testament to a life felt so acutely that its cessation must, by necessity, be equally impactful.

This drive towards a dramatic death is not merely a morbid fascination; it is deeply rooted in the unconscious desire for validation and the profound terror of existential insignificance. For some, the fear of a life unacknowledged, a whisper lost in the cacophony of existence, is an unbearable burden. Fame, even infamy, offers a potent antidote. It signifies that one has, at the very least, been seen, has registered on the collective consciousness. A spectacular death, therefore, can be unconsciously perceived as the ultimate form of recognition, a final, undeniable proof of one's existence and impact. It is a way of imposing one's narrative onto the world with an irreversible force, ensuring that the story, however tragic, cannot be silenced or forgotten. This is the psychological mechanism by which the ultimate failure – the loss of life – can be unconsciously reframed as the ultimate achievement – the ultimate act of self-creation and legacy-building.

The unconscious mind, in its intricate and often bewildering logic, can equate a dramatic end with a powerful affirmation of self. This is not to suggest a rational calculus, but rather a deep-seated, instinctual drive that operates on symbolic and archetypal levels. A life lived with a sense of grandiosity or profound suffering can find its ultimate expression in an equally grand or suffering-laden death. The drama of the end mirrors the perceived drama of the life, creating a narrative coherence that is deeply satisfying on an unconscious level. The greater the spectacle, the more profound the perceived significance. Think of the ancient tragedians, whose heroes often met their demise in acts of epic self-sacrifice or divine retribution. These narratives, woven into the fabric of human culture, suggest a primal understanding that a life's meaning can be profoundly amplified, even solidified, by the manner of its conclusion. The fear is not of ending, but of ending without having truly

lived in a way that is perceived, both internally and externally, as significant.

This dynamic is intricately linked to the concept of the "unlived life" and the unconscious yearning to compensate for perceived failures or missed opportunities. If an individual feels their life has been constrained, misunderstood, or denied its full potential, a dramatic death can offer a posthumous vindication. It is a way of reclaiming agency, of asserting control over one's narrative when it felt lost during life. The spectacular nature of the exit becomes a testament to the suppressed power and brilliance that the world failed to recognize. It is a posthumous declaration: "See what you have lost. See the magnitude of what you overlooked." The unconscious logic here is one of extreme compensation, where the ultimate price – life itself – is paid to secure a legacy that perhaps felt unattainable during the living years. The infamy that might accompany such an exit is often a secondary concern, a price willingly paid for the assurance of being remembered.

Consider the inherent theatricality of human existence. We are, in many ways, performers on the stage of life. For some, this performance is so deeply ingrained, so intrinsically linked to their sense of self, that even the final act must adhere to this aesthetic. The unconscious mind, accustomed to crafting dramatic narratives, may struggle to conceive of an ending that is quiet, mundane, or simply ordinary. The desire for a memorable exit becomes an extension of the lifelong drive to maintain a certain persona, to fulfill a certain narrative arc. The fear of breaking character, of ending the performance with a whimper rather than a bang, can be a powerful unconscious motivator towards a more dramatic conclusion. This is especially true for individuals who have historically used dramatic appearance as a primary mode of relating to the world and asserting their presence.

The cultural amplification of certain deaths further fuels this unconscious imperative. Media saturation, the posthumous creation of legends, and the enduring fascination with the lives and deaths of iconic figures all contribute to a collective understanding of what constitutes a "memorable" end. When the lives of artists, musicians, or public figures are dissected and mythologized, their deaths often become pivotal chapters in their stories. These narratives, consciously or unconsciously absorbed, can shape an individual's perception of what a "significant" death looks like. The unconscious mind may then internalize these cultural scripts, leading to an aspiration, however veiled, towards a similar dramatic final act. The desire to become a part of this cultural pantheon, even through tragedy, can be a powerful, albeit unconscious, influence.

The aesthetic of dramatic appearance, therefore, does not necessarily cease with biological death. Instead, it can find its ultimate, and often most haunting, expression in the manner of one's departure. The unconscious drive for recognition, amplified by the fear of insignificance and the cultural valorization of dramatic endings, can conspire to transform a final breath into a powerful, unforgettable statement. This is the dark allure of infamy, the potent compensation for a life unacknowledged, and the final, defiant act of a self that demands to be seen, even in its ultimate undoing. The spectacle of a dramatic death, for those compelled by such unconscious forces, is not an aberration but the logical, albeit tragic, culmination of a life lived with an unshakeable need for an indelible mark. It is the final performance in a lifelong play, ensuring that the protagonist, no matter the cost, will never truly leave the stage.

Furthermore, the unconscious equation of a dramatic death with a form of ultimate achievement or validation is deeply intertwined with archetypal narratives of martyrdom and sacrifice. Throughout history, individuals have been revered not only for their lives but for the manner of their deaths, often framed as profound sacrifices for a greater cause, a belief, or an ideal. While these instances are often heroic, the unconscious mind can, in its desperate search for significance, co-opt these archetypes in a more personal and often distorted manner. The individual who feels overlooked or undervalued in life might unconsciously perceive their own death, particularly if it is dramatic and draws significant attention, as a supreme act of sacrifice. This sacrifice, in their internal logic, validates their suffering, elevates their perceived importance, and posthumously grants them the recognition they felt was denied during their lifetime.

This psychic mechanism can be understood as a desperate attempt to exert control over one's own narrative when life has felt largely uncontrollable. The fear of insignificance is not just the fear of being forgotten, but the fear of one's life having lacked agency, of having been passively swept along by circumstances. A dramatic death, especially one that is perceived as having a clear cause or consequence, can offer a sense of ultimate control. It is the final, decisive act that shapes how one is remembered, imposing a specific interpretation on one's life. This is particularly potent when individuals feel they have been wronged, misunderstood, or unfairly treated. The dramatic death becomes a powerful, silent accusation against the world, a testament to the unbearable burdens they carried.

Consider the concept of "going out with a bang" as a colloquial expression, yet one that taps into a deep-seated psychological phenomenon. The unconscious mind, seeking to maximize impact and ensure a lasting impression, may gravitate towards actions that generate maximum emotional response and attention. A spectacular death, by its very nature, elicits intense emotions – shock, grief, horror, fascination, pity. For someone whose internal world is structured around dramatic appearance, this outward display of intense emotion can be unconsciously interpreted as a confirmation of their significance. It is a visceral, undeniable proof that they have touched others profoundly, even if that touch is one of tragedy. The infamy, in this context, can be seen as a byproduct of this profound impact, a testament to the power of their presence, however destructive its end.

The allure of a dramatic death is also amplified by the very human fascination with the liminal, the moment of transition where life meets its end. There is an inherent drama in the unknown, in the boundary between existence and non-existence. For those who are drawn to the aesthetic of dramatic appearance, this liminal space becomes the ultimate stage. It is the final frontier of performance, where the stakes are highest and the potential for impact is immense. The unconscious drive to push boundaries, to explore the extremities of experience, can lead to an unconscious attraction to a death that is itself an extreme event. This is not about a conscious desire to die, but about an unconscious allure to the *spectacle* of dying in a way that guarantees it will be remembered.

The concept of a "legacy" is deeply intertwined with this phenomenon. While often associated with positive achievements, a legacy can also be forged through notoriety. For individuals who feel their life's achievements have been insufficient or unacknowledged, the prospect of leaving a powerful, albeit infamous, legacy can become an unconscious compensation. The dramatic death ensures that their name will be spoken, their story will be told, and their life will be dissected for generations. It is a way of ensuring that their existence, however flawed or tragic, will have a lasting impact on the collective consciousness. The fear of being forgotten is, in this sense, the fear of a nullified existence, and a dramatic death offers the ultimate, albeit dark, guarantee against such oblivion.

Ultimately, the unconscious logic of fame and infamy in the context of dramatic death is a complex interplay of the fear of insignificance, the yearning for recognition, the adoption of cultural narratives, and the inherent human fascination with the dramatic. It is a testament to the profound power of the unconscious mind to shape not only our lives but our very understanding of death, transforming it from a biological event into a final, potent performance. The desire to be remembered, to have made an indelible mark, can drive individuals towards endings that are not merely conclusions, but powerful statements, ensuring that their story, no matter how tragic, will be told, and retold, long after the curtain has fallen. This drives the exploration of how this unconscious imperative can manifest in ways that blur the lines between self-destruction and self-creation, between ultimate failure and ultimate legacy. The dramatic exit becomes the ultimate affirmation of a life perceived as extraordinary, even if that extraordinariness is only fully realized in its tragic conclusion.

The compulsion towards a dramatic appearance, when it reaches its apex, often finds its most potent expression on the razor's edge of annihilation. This is not always a direct, consciously sought suicide, but rather a complex psychological dance with mortality, a performance choreographed on the brink of utter dissolution. The unconscious mind, in its relentless pursuit of an unforgettable presence, can transmute the primal fear of death into an almost perverse fascination with its proximity. Life-threatening behaviors become not merely reckless acts, but potential stagecraft for a final, magnificent act, a dazzling display of defiance against the inevitable fade. The individual, trapped in the grip of this imperative, may engage in activities that court disaster, not with the explicit aim of self-annihilation, but with an implicit, often unconscious, fantasy of controlling their end through a spectacular, ultimately fatal, demonstration of their power, brilliance, or defiance.

Consider the realm of extreme sports, where individuals willingly place themselves in situations that defy the natural order of survival. The adrenaline-fueled ascent up a sheer rock face, the plummeting descent into the abyss on a wingsuit, the daring surf of a colossal wave – these are not simply athletic pursuits. For some, they represent a profound engagement with the sublime, a conscious confrontation with the forces that threaten to obliterate them. The unconscious fantasy here can be one of absolute mastery, of bending the very laws of physics and nature to their will, even if only for fleeting moments. The dramatic appearance is achieved not through words or artistry in the conventional sense, but through the sheer audacity of their actions, a visceral performance of human will against the indifferent, often brutal, forces of the natural world. The ultimate risk, the flirtation with obliteration, becomes the ultimate stage. The mind can conjure an image of a final, breathtaking maneuver, a moment of unparalleled grace or power just before the inevitable, a spectacular swan dive into the void that guarantees their legend, their remembrance, even in the face of their physical demise. It is the unconscious projection of a god-like ability to transcend limitations, to dance with death and, for a glorious instant, appear to win. The risk is calculated not in terms of survival, but in terms of spectacle, the potential for a truly awe-inspiring, unforgettable exit.

This phenomenon extends beyond the arena of physical danger into the volatile arenas of politics and social activism. Individuals driven by a deep-seated need for dramatic appearance may engage in radical political actions, confrontational stances, or acts of defiance that place them squarely in the crosshairs of powerful forces. The intent may not be to provoke their own demise, but to orchestrate a moment of profound, unforgettable impact. A hunger strike that pushes the body to its absolute limit, a defiant stand against an overwhelming authority that courts imprisonment or worse, a public denouncement that guarantees ostracization and reprisal – these acts, while possessing a political or social dimension, can also serve as unconscious vehicles for a dramatic exit. The individual imagines their sacrifice, their unwavering conviction in the face of persecution, as the ultimate testament to their principles, their power, their very being. The suffering they endure, the risks they take, are reframed in their internal landscape as a noble prelude to a grand finale, a final act of martyrdom that will etch their name into history. They are not merely advocating for a cause; they are curating their own legend, using their life and potential death as the ultimate form of persuasive rhetoric. The unconscious fantasy is one of apotheosis through suffering, of achieving a status beyond the mundane by embracing the extreme, by allowing their life's narrative to culminate in a moment of profound, unforgettable sacrifice.

The artistic sphere, too, offers fertile ground for this intersection of dramatic appearance, risk, and the brink of annihilation. Avant-garde performers, conceptual artists, and boundary-pushing musicians have, throughout history, employed tactics that deliberately court danger and provoke extreme reactions. Performances that involve self-mutilation, dangerous stunts, or the confrontation with hostile audiences can be viewed through this lens. The artist, in such instances, may not consciously desire to die, but they consciously embrace the possibility as an inherent part of their artistic expression. The performance becomes a ritualistic engagement with the destructive impulse, a controlled descent into chaos designed to elicit a powerful emotional response from the audience and, perhaps more importantly, from themselves. The unconscious fantasy is of an art so potent, so transformative, that it can only be fully realized through an act of ultimate surrender, a dissolution of the self into the work itself. The artwork becomes inseparable from the artist's being, and its completion necessitates a form of annihilation, a shedding of the mundane self to achieve a higher, more impactful artistic truth. The performance is the ultimate expression of their vision, and if that vision demands the ultimate price, then so be it. The risk is not just to their physical well-being, but to their very identity, a willingness to dissolve into their creation, to become one with the spectacle they have orchestrated.

The conscious choice to engage in such high-stakes behavior, even without explicit suicidal intent, speaks to a profound internal narrative where control over one's ending is paramount. It is the unconscious belief that a life lived on the edge, a life that consistently flirts with obliteration, can be crowned with a final, glorious act of self-determination. The individual, feeling perhaps powerless in other aspects of their life, finds agency in their ability to deliberately court danger, to make choices that bring them to the precipice. This is not about impulsivity; it is about a carefully crafted performance of daring. The fantasy is not of being consumed by fate, but of mastering it, of choosing the moment and the manner of one's departure, even if that departure is not overtly chosen as a final act of suicide. It is the unconscious equation of extreme risk with ultimate freedom, the belief that in confronting the void, one can achieve a profound sense of selfhood and leave an indelible, unforgettable mark. The performance on the brink is a way of asserting one's existence with a power that transcends mere survival.

This intricate interplay between risk and dramatic appearance can be observed in various historical and cultural contexts. Consider figures who have engaged in audacious acts of rebellion, knowing full well the lethal consequences. Their actions are often remembered not just for their political or social impact, but for their sheer audacity, their willingness to stand against overwhelming odds, to embrace a fate that was almost certain. The unconscious narrative at play is one of transformation through sacrifice, of becoming an immortal legend by embracing mortality with a flourish. The individual may not have consciously sought death, but they consciously embraced a path where death was a highly probable, even sought-after, consequence, because that path offered the greatest potential for a dramatic, unforgettable appearance. The very act of courting annihilation becomes the ultimate act of self-creation, a final, powerful statement of defiance against the constraints of existence.

The internal logic often involves a process of "burning brightly" rather than "fading away." For individuals who are deeply invested in the aesthetics of dramatic appearance, the idea of a quiet, unassuming end is anathema. It represents a failure to live up to the internal imperative, a letting down of the persona that has been meticulously crafted throughout their lives. Thus, the brink of annihilation becomes not a threat to be avoided, but a stage to be commanded. The individual navigates these dangerous waters with a conscious or unconscious belief that their final moments, their ultimate act of defiance or brilliance, will be the most potent and memorable. They are not necessarily seeking to end their life, but to end their performance in a way that guarantees it will be remembered for eternity, a final, incandescent flash before the darkness. This is the ultimate expression of control, the ultimate dramatic flourish, the final act of a life lived with the unwavering conviction that its ending must be as spectacular as its perceived, or desired, essence. The risk is the ink with which they write their final, unforgettable chapter, the ultimate manifestation of their aesthetic imperative.

Chapter 4: The Desire to Be Mourned

The profound desire for one's passing to be met with deep and resonant mourning speaks to a fundamental human need: the yearning to be seen, to be known, and to have one's existence affirmed in the eyes of others. This is not merely a superficial wish for attention, but a deeply embedded psychic imperative that touches upon our most primal fears and our most cherished aspirations. At its core, the aesthetic of dying as profoundly mourned is a testament to the deeply relational nature of our being. We do not exist in a vacuum; our identities are forged and sustained through our connections with others. Consequently, the manner in which our absence is registered, the depth of the sorrow we leave behind, becomes a crucial measure of our life's significance. To be mourned deeply is, in essence, to have one's life validated, to have its impact acknowledged, and to be assured that one's absence will leave a palpable void.

This unconscious yearning for heartfelt grief is intricately linked to the existential dread of insignificance, of a life lived and departed without leaving a trace, without having truly touched the lives of others. It is the fear of a quiet disappearance, of being forgotten before one has even truly been remembered. This phantom of oblivion can drive individuals, often without their conscious awareness, to cultivate relationships and life circumstances that promise a more emotionally charged departure. The unconscious mind, ever seeking to preemptively assuage this dread, can subtly steer individuals towards situations and connections that will, upon their death, guarantee a visceral outpouring of sorrow. It is as if, from within the depths of the psyche, a narrative is being constructed, a final act being rehearsed, where the crescendo of grief from those left behind serves as the ultimate validation of a life well-lived, or at least, a life profoundly felt.

Consider the individual who, throughout their life, meticulously cultivates a circle of dependents, individuals whose emotional and material well-being is inextricably bound to their presence. This might manifest as the archetypal matriarch or patriarch who, through acts of both genuine care and subtle manipulation, ensures that their children and grandchildren revolve around them. The unconscious motive here is not necessarily a conscious desire for control in life, but a premonition of the significance of their absence. The hope, woven into the fabric of their being, is that the disruption and pain caused by their departure will be so profound, so widespread, that their mourning will be extensive and deeply felt. The sacrifices they have made, the guidance they have offered, the very fabric of their being interwoven with the lives of others, becomes the foundation upon which a significant and deeply felt grief will be built. Their death, in this scenario, is not an ending so much as a dramatic unveiling of their indispensable role in the lives of those they have touched, a final, irrefutable testament to their importance.

This aesthetic also finds expression in the realm of romantic relationships, particularly those characterized by an intense, almost theatrical, emotional dynamic. The individual who feels they have poured their entire being into a partnership, who believes they have loved with an unparalleled intensity, may unconsciously anticipate that their death will shatter their beloved, plunging them into a state of inconsolable grief. The unspoken fantasy is that the depth of their beloved's sorrow will be a direct reflection of the magnitude of their love and their own intrinsic worth. The tears shed, the wails of anguish, the sheer desolation expressed by the surviving partner, become the ultimate proof that they were, indeed, irreplaceable. This is not about wishing harm upon another, but about a deep-seated need for their own life's significance to be mirrored in the profound emotional devastation of another. The mourning becomes a measure of their love, a testament to the unique and powerful bond they shared, and a guarantee that their memory will be kept alive through the echoes of profound heartbreak.

In a broader social context, this desire can manifest in individuals who dedicate their lives to causes or communities, investing themselves so fully that their departure is felt as a collective loss. The beloved teacher, the tireless community organizer, the devoted caregiver – these are individuals whose identities are deeply entwined with the welfare and emotional landscape of others. Their unconscious motivation for such profound dedication might be partly fueled by a subconscious anticipation of the void their absence will create. They are not necessarily seeking to orchestrate their own death, but they are, perhaps, unconsciously tending the garden of their legacy, ensuring that when they are gone, the fruits of their labor, and the love they have sown, will result in a harvest of sincere and widespread grief. The mourning of many becomes the ultimate affirmation of a life lived in service, a life that has demonstrably made a difference. Their passing, therefore, is not an isolated event but a communal reckoning with the loss of someone who was, in essence, a pillar of the community.

The phenomenon can also be observed in individuals who consciously foster an image of themselves as indispensable or as a source of unique emotional comfort and support. They might be the confidante, the emotional anchor, the one who always knows what to say or do to ease the suffering of others. The unconscious calculation at play is that the more others have come to rely on them, the more profound their absence will be. This reliance, cultivated over years, becomes the fertile ground upon which a deep and lasting grief can grow. The fear of dying alone or unloved is a powerful motivator, and for these individuals, ensuring that their death will trigger a significant emotional response becomes a way of preemptively securing their place in the hearts and memories of those around them. They are, in a sense, investing in their own posthumous emotional significance, ensuring that their memory will be kept alive through the palpable pain of loss experienced by those they have so carefully integrated into their lives.

The unconscious yearning for deep mourning is also fueled by a desire for one's narrative to be complete, for the story of one's life to have a powerful and memorable conclusion. A quiet fading away, while perhaps peaceful, can feel like an unfinished sentence, an incomplete symphony. A death that elicits profound grief, conversely, suggests a life that was intensely lived, deeply felt, and significantly impactful. The mourning itself becomes part of the narrative, a dramatic final chapter that solidifies the protagonist's importance. This is particularly true for individuals who have perhaps felt overlooked or unappreciated during their lives. The intense grief of others can serve as a corrective, a posthumous acknowledgment of their worth that was perhaps lacking in their living years. The tears of their loved ones become a balm for old wounds, a final, potent validation that their existence truly mattered.

Furthermore, this aesthetic of dying is intrinsically tied to the human capacity for empathy. We are wired to feel the pain of others, and when someone we have loved or depended on is lost, that pain can be immense. For those who unconsciously seek profound mourning, there is an implicit understanding of this capacity. They may have, perhaps through their own life experiences, developed a keen awareness of how deeply humans can grieve. Their unconscious desire, then, is to tap into this profound wellspring of human emotion, to evoke a response that mirrors the depth of the connection they have fostered or the impact they believe they have had. It is a testament to the power of human connection, a belief that a life well-lived will inevitably leave its imprint on the hearts of others, an imprint that will be deeply felt and expressed upon their passing.

This yearning can also be a way of asserting control over one's legacy in the face of mortality's ultimate lack of control. While one cannot control the fact of death, one can, perhaps unconsciously, influence the emotional aftermath. By cultivating deep connections and investing emotionally in others, an individual can, in a sense, lay the groundwork for a future where their absence will be acutely felt. The profound mourning becomes a posthumous expression of agency, a final act of self-determination in shaping how one will be remembered. It is a way of ensuring that one's departure is not simply an event, but a significant emotional happening, a moment that reverberates through the lives of those left behind. The sheer weight of their grief becomes a monument to the deceased, a living testament to their impact and their significance.

The contemplation of this aesthetic also brings to the fore the darker, perhaps more uncomfortable, aspects of human desire. It touches upon a need for validation that, when unconscious, can be insatiable. The individual may be driven by a deep-seated insecurity, a fear that without the outward demonstration of grief from others, their life was, in some fundamental way, a failure. This is not to judge, but to understand the complex interplay of needs and defenses that shape our inner lives. The unconscious mind, in its pursuit of security and affirmation, can devise intricate strategies, and the desire to be profoundly mourned is one of the most poignant and powerful of these strategies. It speaks to a fundamental human longing to matter, to be cherished, and to leave behind a legacy of love and remembrance that transcends the finality of death. The sorrow of others, in this context, is not a morbid wish but a desired confirmation of a life's enduring value.

The unconscious desire to be mourned can manifest in profoundly intricate and often deeply personal ways, shaping the very fabric of an individual's life and their relationships. While the previous chapters have explored the theoretical underpinnings of this yearning – its roots in existential dread, the need for validation, and the aesthetic of a life's conclusion – this section delves into a specific, albeit anonymized, clinical observation that brings these abstract concepts into sharp, human focus. This case study serves not as a generalization, but as an illustration of how these deep-seated psychological currents can play out, guiding actions and influencing relational dynamics with the unspoken aim of orchestrating a meaningful and deeply felt absence.

Consider, for instance, an individual we will refer to as "Alex." Alex presented in therapy not with overt complaints about grief, but with a subtle, pervasive anxiety surrounding endings and a preoccupation with the perceived fragility of their relationships. Throughout their life, Alex had a remarkable, almost preternatural ability to foster intense emotional bonds. These were not superficial acquaintances; Alex cultivated deep, almost symbiotic connections with a select few individuals. These relationships were characterized by an extraordinary level of mutual dependence, where Alex provided unwavering emotional support, often to the point of self-neglect, and in return, received an equally profound, though sometimes anxious, devotion.

From a psychoanalytic perspective, Alex's patterns suggested an early attachment history marked by a perceived scarcity of consistent emotional availability. The unconscious mind, in its adaptive drive to secure attachment, may have learned that the most effective way to ensure one's continued presence in the emotional landscape of others was to become indispensable. This was not a conscious strategy of manipulation, but a deeply ingrained relational schema. Alex's unconscious calculus seemed to be: "If I am the sole source of comfort, the only one who truly understands, then my absence will be unbearable." This created a precarious equilibrium within their relationships, where Alex's well-being was inextricably linked to the emotional stability of those they were close to.

A closer examination of Alex's behavior revealed symbolic gestures that, in retrospect, appear to have been preparations for a significant departure. There were instances of meticulously documenting personal histories, not for posterity in a public sense, but for specific individuals. Alex would share detailed anecdotes, sometimes tinged with melancholy, about their childhood or past experiences, framing them not as simple reminiscences, but as crucial pieces of a narrative that

needed to be understood. These were akin to bequeathing fragments of their soul, ensuring that the essence of their being would be held and preserved by those left behind. The unconscious intention was to provide the raw material for an elaborate tapestry of memory, a rich source from which profound grief could draw its sustenance.

Furthermore, Alex possessed a singular talent for creating moments of heightened emotional significance. These weren't necessarily dramatic outbursts, but rather carefully orchestrated instances of vulnerability or profound connection. There were times when Alex would confide in a loved one about a deep-seated fear or a cherished dream, articulating it with an intensity that left the listener breathless, imbued with a sense of bearing a sacred trust. These were not simply intimate disclosures; they were acts of emotional endowment, designed to create indelible impressions, to carve a place in the listener's heart that would ache with emptiness upon Alex's eventual absence. The unconscious desire was to create emotional anchors, points of intense feeling that would serve as touchstones for remembrance and mourning.

The concept of "leaving a void" was central to Alex's unconscious narrative. They often spoke, in therapy, about the fear of "fading away," of becoming a "ghost in the machine" of life. This abstract anxiety coalesced into a concrete, albeit unconscious, goal: to ensure that their departure would not be a quiet dissolution, but a seismic event within the emotional lives of their loved ones. This ambition wasn't born of a desire for power or control in a narcissistic sense, but from a fundamental need to ascertain their own significance. If their absence could provoke profound sorrow, if their departure could disrupt the lives of those they cherished, then it stood as irrefutable proof that their life had mattered, that they had indeed left an indelible mark.

This quest for validation through grief was particularly evident in Alex's interactions with their partner. Alex would often express a deep-seated fear of their partner "moving on too easily" after their death. This was not a reflection of a lack of trust in their partner's love, but a profound existential anxiety. The unconscious thought process seemed to be: "If my passing causes immense, prolonged pain, then my partner will never forget me. My existence will be permanently etched into their life narrative." Alex would sometimes subtly encourage expressions of deep affection and reliance, not to bind their partner in life, but to lay the groundwork for the depth of sorrow they hoped to inspire in death. It was a form of posthumous insurance against oblivion, a guarantee that their memory would be kept alive through the very language of heartbreak.

The relationships Alex cultivated were, therefore, not merely social connections but carefully tended gardens, where the seeds of profound grief were sown with the unconscious intention of a bountiful harvest upon their departure. This involved a delicate dance between offering genuine love and support, and subtly fostering a level of dependency that would ensure a visceral response to their absence. It was a testament to Alex's deep understanding of human attachment, and an unconscious manipulation of those very bonds to fulfill a deep-seated existential need. The intensity of the mourning was to be the ultimate measure of the intensity of their life and love.

This pattern also extended to Alex's professional life. While outwardly they maintained a professional demeanor, there were subtle indicators of a similar underlying drive. Alex was known for being an exceptionally dedicated colleague, someone who would go above and beyond, often at personal cost, to support team projects or mentor junior staff. While this could be attributed to altruism, in Alex's case, it also seemed to serve a secondary, unconscious purpose: to embed themselves so deeply into the operational and emotional fabric of their workplace that their departure would create a tangible disruption. The hope was that the collective sense of loss, the shared acknowledgement of their indispensable contributions, would translate into a potent and widely felt grief among their colleagues. This was about ensuring that their legacy was not just professional achievement, but an emotional imprint on the collective consciousness of their work environment.

The unconscious mind is a master architect of self-preservation, and for individuals like Alex, the fear of non-existence can be a powerful motivator. The desire to be mourned is, in essence, a desperate plea for continued existence, albeit in an altered form. It is the unconscious belief that if one's absence can evoke profound sadness, then one has, in a very real sense, continued to exist within the emotional and psychological lives of others. The tears shed, the stories told, the pangs of regret – these become the posthumous echoes of a life lived, a testament that the individual mattered, that their journey through existence was significant enough to leave a lasting ache.

This case study of Alex underscores the profound interplay between attachment, loss, and the human need for existential validation. Alex's life was a carefully orchestrated performance, not for an audience in the present, but for the mourners of the future. Every deep connection forged, every moment of vulnerability shared, every act of selfless dedication, can be understood, in part, as laying the groundwork for a profound and deeply felt absence. The unconscious desire to be mourned, therefore, is not merely a morbid fascination with death, but a complex and often poignant manifestation of our deepest need to be seen, to be valued, and to know that our existence has left an indelible mark on the world and on the hearts of those we leave behind. The intensity of the grief we inspire becomes, in this unconscious calculus, the ultimate proof of our own enduring significance.

The narrative of Alex's life, as observed through their therapeutic journey, reveals a consistent and deeply embedded pattern: the cultivation of relationships that would guarantee a significant emotional aftermath. This wasn't about seeking attention in life, but about pre-emptively securing a legacy of emotional resonance. The intensity of the anticipated grief became the unconscious metric by which Alex measured their own worth and the impact of their life. Their existence was, in a sense, a prelude to their absence, and the quality of that absence was to be the final, definitive statement of their life's significance. This unconscious drive is not inherently pathological, but it speaks to a profound human vulnerability: the fear that without the tangible evidence of sorrow from others, one's life may have passed unacknowledged, unloved, and ultimately, insignificant. The mourning, then, becomes a form of posthumous immortality, a guarantee that the self, in some enduring way, will continue to exist within the hearts and memories of others.

Consider the specific ways Alex managed their relational landscape. They were the confidante who absorbed the anxieties of friends, the colleague who shouldered the burdens of difficult projects, the partner who offered an almost unnerving level of emotional availability. These were not simply acts of kindness; they were strategic investments in future emotional capital. Alex's unconscious mind understood that deep emotional entanglement, particularly when accompanied by a sense of indispensability, was the fertile ground from which profound grief would bloom. They were, in essence, meticulously laying the emotional foundations for a dramatic and deeply felt departure. The shared secrets, the reliance, the mutual vulnerability – all served to weave a tapestry of connection so intricate that its unraveling, upon Alex's death, would inevitably cause widespread and profound sorrow.

This deeply ingrained desire for a significant mourning experience also had a palliative effect on Alex's own existential anxieties. The constant, underlying fear of oblivion was, perhaps, assuaged by the ongoing efforts to create bonds of such intensity that they could not be easily broken. Each moment of deepened connection, each instance of being relied upon, served as a temporary reassurance that Alex was indeed significant, that their existence was meaningful to others. This created a dynamic where Alex's life was, in a sense, a continuous rehearsal for their death, with each relationship serving as a testament to the anticipated depth of sorrow that their eventual passing would evoke. The unconscious drive was to transform the inevitability of death into a profound affirmation of life.

The symbolic actions Alex undertook were often subtle but potent. There were instances of leaving behind specific objects – a worn book with a passage underlined, a piece of jewelry given with a whispered story, a letter carefully preserved. These were not grand bequests, but intimate tokens designed to evoke potent emotional memories. Each object was imbued with a narrative, a fragment of

Alex's lived experience, intended to serve as a catalyst for grief and remembrance. The unconscious aim was to provide tangible anchors for the intangible: the emotional bonds and the profound sense of loss. These objects were to be the physical manifestations of an emotional legacy, ensuring that even in absence, Alex's presence would continue to be felt.

Moreover, Alex's approach to relationships was marked by a profound understanding of human vulnerability. They seemed to intuitively grasp the ways in which individuals seek solace and validation in connection. By positioning themselves as a constant source of emotional support, Alex was, in essence, creating a dependency that would ensure their memory would be cherished. This wasn't about manipulation for personal gain in life, but about a deep-seated, albeit unconscious, conviction that the most potent way to ensure one's legacy was to become so intertwined with the emotional lives of others that their absence would be felt as a gaping wound. The depth of the wound would, in turn, be the measure of Alex's significance.

The internal world of Alex was a complex interplay of love, fear, and an almost artistic drive to shape the narrative of their own ending. The desire to be mourned was not a simple wish for attention; it was a fundamental psychological imperative, a way of negotiating the profound terror of insignificance. By fostering such intense emotional bonds, and by subtly encouraging a reliance that bordered on indispensability, Alex was, in essence, building a monument to their own existence. This monument was to be constructed not from stone or steel, but from the tears and the profound sorrow of those they left behind. The collective grief of their loved ones would stand as irrefutable proof that Alex's life had been deeply felt, intensely lived, and ultimately, profoundly significant.

This case study serves as a powerful illustration of the complex and often unconscious motivations that can drive our relational patterns and our views of life and death. Alex's journey highlights how the yearning for validation, the fear of insignificance, and the aesthetic of a meaningful ending can converge, shaping a life in pursuit of a deeply felt absence. The intensity of the grief that surrounds a death is, for some, the ultimate testament to a life's worth, a final, poignant affirmation that one truly mattered.

The yearning for a meaningful absence, for a death that reverberates with profound sorrow, finds its most poignant expression not merely in theoretical constructs or clinical vignettes, but in the indelible biographical narratives of those who have left an extraordinary void. These are individuals whose very departure has become a testament to the intensity of their lives, whose mourning is not a quiet reflection but a resounding echo. Examining these lives allows us to understand the intricate interplay between a person's internal psychic landscape and the collective emotional response to their passing, revealing how a conscious or unconscious desire to be mourned can profoundly shape both the living and the posthumous narrative.

Consider, for instance, the impact of figures like Virginia Woolf. Her life was a tumultuous navigation of profound creativity and debilitating mental illness. Her literary output, marked by stream-of-consciousness narratives that plumbed the depths of the human psyche, offered readers an unprecedented immersion into subjective experience. This very intensity, this unflinching exploration of the inner world, created a powerful connection with her audience. Woolf's suicide, a deliberate act born from the crushing weight of her struggles, was met with widespread grief, not only from her intimate circle but from the literary world and countless readers who felt a deep kinship with her explorations of consciousness, vulnerability, and the fragility of the mind. Her death was not an end to her influence, but a tragic culmination that amplified her legacy, cementing her as a figure whose life and death were intrinsically linked to the profound experiences of human existence. The mourning she inspired was a complex tapestry woven from admiration for her genius, empathy for her suffering, and a collective sense of loss for the worlds she might still have created. Her carefully chosen final act, leaving notes for her husband and sister, can be seen as an attempt to manage the aftermath, to offer some measure of explanation and comfort, while simultaneously acknowledging the profound impact her absence would have. This was not about seeking attention in life, but about ensuring that her final act, like her writing, would leave a profound, albeit sorrowful, impression.

Similarly, the charismatic leadership of figures like Martin Luther King Jr. exemplifies how a life dedicated to a powerful cause can forge bonds so strong that their severing unleashes immense collective grief. King's unwavering commitment to civil rights, articulated through eloquent speeches that stirred the conscience of a nation and galvanized a movement, created a profound sense of shared purpose and hope. His assassination was a shockwave that reverberated globally, igniting outrage and sorrow. The mourning for King was not confined to his family and close associates; it was a mass outpouring of grief from millions who saw in him a symbol of justice, courage, and the enduring human aspiration for equality. His death, tragically premature, served to underscore the immense value of his life and the urgency of the cause for which he stood.

The enduring legacy of his work, fueled in part by the profound sorrow his absence evoked, continues to inspire generations. The very intensity of the mourning for King cemented his martyrdom and amplified the moral imperative of the movement he led, demonstrating how a life lived with such conviction can elicit a collective mourning that transcends personal loss.

The lives of influential mentors and teachers also offer compelling examples. Consider the impact of educators who possess an almost alchemical ability to ignite passion and unlock potential in their students. These individuals often become central figures in the lives of those they guide, offering not just knowledge but wisdom, encouragement, and a belief in their students' inherent worth. When such a mentor passes away, the grief experienced by their former students can be profound and deeply personal. The loss is not just of a teacher, but of a guide, a confidante, and a source of unwavering support. The carefully curated memories of their words of wisdom, their patient guidance, and their belief in their students' potential become treasured remnants, fueling a remembrance that keeps their spirit alive. The narrative of their life becomes intertwined with the success stories of those they mentored, a testament to their enduring influence. The mourning is a collective acknowledgment of the seeds they planted, the futures they helped shape, and the indelible mark they left on countless individual lives. This form of remembrance often manifests as a desire to carry forward the mentor's legacy, to embody the values they espoused, thereby ensuring that their influence continues, even in their absence.

The artist Sylvia Plath's life and death, much like Woolf's, are inextricably linked. Her intensely personal and emotionally charged poetry, exploring themes of identity, death, and alienation, resonated deeply with readers who felt a profound connection to her raw vulnerability. Her suicide, occurring at a young age and leaving behind two children, was met with shock and sorrow. The ensuing posthumous recognition of her literary genius, coupled with the tragic circumstances of her death, created a powerful narrative that continues to captivate and move audiences. Her work is often viewed through the lens of her life's struggles, with her death becoming a somber coda that amplishes the emotional weight of her poetry. The intense interest and emotional investment from readers can be seen as a form of collective mourning, a desire to connect with and understand the tormented beauty of her artistic expression. This intense engagement with her work, often tinged with a sense of tragic inevitability, speaks to a deep-seated fascination with lives that burn brightly before being tragically extinguished, and the profound emotional resonance such lives can evoke.

Even in figures known for their more public personas, such as charismatic political leaders or activists, the desire to be mourned can be subtly woven into the fabric of their lives and deaths. The way they conduct themselves, the relationships they cultivate, and the causes they champion can all be seen as contributing to a legacy that anticipates and, perhaps, even orchestrates a profound emotional aftermath. This is not necessarily a conscious, calculated manipulation, but a deep-seated psychological drive to matter, to leave an impact that transcends mere existence. The intensity of the mourning that follows their passing becomes, in this framework, a testament to the significance they held, a posthumous validation of their life's work and their personal impact.

The biographical accounts of these individuals offer a rich tapestry for understanding the multifaceted nature of the desire to be mourned. It is a desire that can manifest in diverse ways, from the artist who pours their soul into their work, creating an emotional connection that outlives them, to the leader who inspires a movement, forging a collective identity that grieves their loss deeply. In each case, the life lived, with its unique struggles, triumphs, and contributions, lays the groundwork for the mourning that follows. The intensity and nature of that mourning are not random; they are, in part, a reflection of the individual's psychic landscape, their relationships, and the profound impact they had on the world around them. The biographical narrative, therefore, becomes a crucial lens through which to examine how the living can shape their own posthumous remembrance, consciously or unconsciously, by the very way they engage with life and with others. This desire to be mourned, in its most profound sense, is the ultimate affirmation of existence, a testament that one's life, in its ephemeral passage, has left an enduring and deeply felt imprint.

The deliberate cultivation of impact can be observed in the way certain individuals shape their public image and their personal relationships. This is not solely about seeking fame or adoration while alive, but about ensuring that their absence will be keenly felt. Think of a writer who meticulously crafts their authorial persona, or a philosopher whose teachings are infused with a personal conviction that draws disciples. Their intellectual or artistic contributions, when coupled with a powerful personal presence, create a reservoir of emotional attachment. When they die, the grief that arises is not just for the loss of their work, but for the loss of the person who embodied those ideas, who inspired such devotion. The biographical accounts often focus on these interpersonal connections, detailing the mentorships, the deep friendships, and the profound influence they exerted. These relationships become the conduits through which the desire to be mourned is fulfilled, as those who were touched by them carry forward their memory, articulate their significance, and express the depth of their sorrow. The shared experiences, the personal anecdotes, the echoes of their wisdom – these form the bedrock of a remembrance that is both intellectual and deeply emotional.

Furthermore, the very act of leaving a legacy, whether material or symbolic, can be viewed as an extension of this desire. While often framed as an act of generosity or foresight, it can also be understood as a strategy for ensuring continued relevance and remembrance. A philanthropist who establishes foundations, an inventor whose creations transform industries, or an activist who dedicates their life to a cause – these individuals are, in a sense, building monuments to their own existence. The ongoing work of these institutions, the continued use of their inventions, or the advancement of their causes all serve to keep their memory alive. The mourning that accompanies their passing is amplified by the tangible evidence of their impact, the enduring structures they built, and the lasting effects of their endeavors. This provides a concrete basis for collective remembrance, transforming personal grief into a broader acknowledgment of their significant contributions. The narratives that surround these figures often highlight their vision, their dedication, and their foresight, framing their lives as purposeful endeavors designed to leave a lasting mark.

In examining these biographical narratives, it becomes clear that the desire to be mourned is not a singular or simple impulse. It is a complex psychological phenomenon that can manifest through creative expression, charismatic leadership, devoted mentorship, and the purposeful shaping of one's legacy. These individuals, through their lives, create the conditions for a profound and enduring sense of loss in others. Their deaths, therefore, become not just an end, but a culmination that amplifies their significance. The intensity of the mourning they inspire serves as a posthumous testament to their impact, a powerful affirmation that their lives mattered, that their presence was deeply felt, and that their absence leaves an indelible void. The stories we tell about them, the memories we cherish, and the sorrow we express are all part of an ongoing dialogue with their legacy, a continuous affirmation of their existence and their enduring significance in the tapestry of human experience. The biographical accounts, in this light, are not merely historical records; they are profound explorations of how lives are lived in anticipation of how they will be remembered, and how the profound impact of an absence can be the ultimate measure of a life's significance.

This unconscious economy of affect, this intricate system of emotional valuation and expenditure, is the very bedrock upon which psychic existence is built. It is a realm where feelings are not merely incidental but are the primary currency, shaping our perceptions, our motivations, and our very sense of self. The desire to be mourned, in this context, emerges not as a vain plea for attention, but as a profound, often unacknowledged, strategy for ensuring the enduring significance of one's psychic investment. It is an attempt to secure a form of immortality, not through grand monuments or lasting achievements in the external world, but through the indelible imprint left upon the emotional landscapes of others. This is the psychological equivalent of planting seeds in the hearts and minds of those we encounter, with the unspoken hope that their eventual grief will be a testament to the fertility of our presence.

Consider the way individuals unconsciously 'invest' in relationships. This investment is not simply about sharing time or resources; it is fundamentally an emotional cathexis, a pouring of psychic energy into another person with the implicit expectation of a return. This return, however, is not always about reciprocity in the present moment. It can be a future-oriented strategy, a way of ensuring that, should the investment be terminated by death, the ensuing sorrow will be a direct reflection of the depth and intensity of that initial investment. The individual, in essence, seeks to engender a profound outpouring of grief, a collective lamentation that serves as irrefutable evidence of their worth and significance. This is not necessarily a conscious calculation; more often, it operates at a pre-verbal, instinctual level, a deep-seated need for emotional validation that seeks its ultimate confirmation in the sorrow of others. The intensity of the mourning becomes the ultimate measure, the final accounting of one's psychic value.

This mechanism can be observed in the seemingly simple acts of forming bonds. When we invest love, care, and attention into friendships, family ties, or romantic partnerships, we are not just building connections; we are, in a sense, creating a future audience for our own absence. The more deeply we are loved, the more profound the potential for grief. This is not to suggest that genuine affection is performed with the ulterior motive of ensuring future sorrow, but rather that the psychic architecture of our emotional lives unconsciously anticipates this possibility. The desire to be deeply loved is, in part, a desire to be deeply mourned. It is a yearning to leave a mark that cannot be easily erased, a void that cannot be readily filled. The tears shed for us, the stories told, the memories invoked – these are the posthumous affirmations of our existence, the tangible proof that we mattered, that our presence was not in vain.

The unconscious economy of affect also highlights how individuals might actively, though not always consciously, cultivate the conditions for such profound mourning. This can manifest in various ways. Some may adopt a persona of indispensability, making themselves so central to the lives of others that their absence would create an almost unbearable disruption. Others might foster an aura of enigmatic complexity, drawing others into a constant effort to understand them, thus ensuring that their departure leaves a lingering sense of unfinished business, a mournful contemplation of the unanswered questions. Still others might channel their energy into creative endeavors or acts of profound kindness, creating a legacy of beauty or benevolence that guarantees an enduring appreciation and a deep sense of loss when that source of inspiration or comfort is extinguished. In each case, the aim, however unconscious, is to make one's absence a palpable, deeply felt event, an emotional vacuum that speaks volumes about the significance of the presence that once filled it.

This psychic economy is particularly evident in how we perceive and process loss. When someone we deeply cherished dies, our grief is not solely a response to their physical absence; it is also a reaction to the devaluation of our own emotional investments. The sorrow we experience is, in part, a lament for the loss of the recipient of our love, our care, our energy. But it is also, and perhaps more profoundly, a mourning for the diminished capacity to continue those investments, for the silencing of the dialogues, the cessation of the shared experiences, the end of the potential for future emotional exchanges. The intensity of our grief, therefore, is a direct indicator of the psychic value we had assigned to the relationship, a testament to the depth of our unconscious investment.

The desire to be mourned, understood through this lens of the unconscious economy of affect, is not about a narcissistic craving for adoration. It is a fundamental expression of the human need for meaning and connection. It is the recognition that our existence gains its ultimate validation not just through our own self-awareness, but through the emotional resonance we have with others. To be mourned deeply is to be recognized as having touched lives, as having made a difference, as having occupied a unique and irreplaceable space in the emotional universe of others. It is a posthumous affirmation of love received and love given, a testament to the enduring power of human connection, even in the face of ultimate separation. The emotional legacy we leave behind is, in this sense, our true inheritance, the most enduring form of immortality we can achieve.

This unconscious valuation process extends to our perception of ourselves. We often gauge our own worth by the emotional responses we evoke in others. A positive response – love, admiration, gratitude – reinforces our sense of self-esteem. However, the desire to be mourned taps into a more primal, perhaps even existential, validation. It suggests a need to be remembered not just as someone who was liked, but as someone who was profoundly significant, whose absence creates a palpable ache. This ache, this void, is the psychic confirmation that our lives were not merely lived, but deeply felt. The emotional expenditure we have made, the psychic energy we have invested, finds its ultimate return in the sorrow that acknowledges the magnitude of that investment.

Consider the subtle ways in which individuals might curate their relationships to ensure such an outcome. This is not about manipulation in a vulgar sense, but about a profound, often unconscious, understanding of what fosters deep emotional bonds. It involves vulnerability, authenticity, and a willingness to invest fully. When an individual is perceived as genuine, as someone who has truly given of themselves, their eventual passing is likely to elicit a more profound and sustained grief. The mourning, in this scenario, is not just a reaction to loss; it is a response to the perceived sacrifice, the emotional generosity, the deep connection that has been severed. The unconscious economy of affect dictates that such profound investments are worthy of profound emotional returns.

Furthermore, this desire to be mourned speaks to a fundamental human fear of insignificance. The prospect of disappearing without a trace, of one's life leaving no discernible impact, can be a source of profound anxiety. The unconscious drive to be mourned can be seen as a defense mechanism against this fear, a way of asserting one's existence and its inherent value. The sorrow of others serves as a bulwark against oblivion, a living testament to the fact that one's life mattered, that one's passage through the world left an indelible mark. This mark is not necessarily one of achievement or fame, but of emotional resonance, of having been a cherished presence in the lives of others.

The intensity of our mourning for another is, therefore, a complex interplay of love, loss, and the unconscious validation of our own emotional capacity. When we grieve deeply, we are not only mourning the deceased; we are also affirming the depth of our own ability to love, to connect, and to feel. The sorrow we experience is a testament to the richness of our own emotional lives, to the investments we have made and the value we have placed upon them. In this sense, the desire to be mourned is not solely about the deceased; it is also about the living, about their capacity to feel, to remember, and to carry forward the emotional legacy of those who have passed.

This unconscious economy also influences how we construct our own narratives of self. We often choose to highlight those aspects of our lives that are most likely to elicit strong emotional responses from others. This can involve emphasizing acts of kindness, moments of profound connection, or instances where we have been a source of support or inspiration. By foregrounding these elements, we are, in essence, shaping the narrative that will be remembered, ensuring that our posthumous story will be one that resonates emotionally, thus laying the groundwork for a meaningful mourning. It is a form of self-archaeing, an unconscious curation of the emotional heritage we wish to leave behind.

The very nature of memory plays a crucial role in this economy. Our memories are not objective records; they are imbued with emotion, shaped by our subjective experiences. When we remember someone, we are not merely recalling facts; we are re-experiencing the emotions associated with them. The more potent the emotional charge of those memories, the more likely they are to be recalled and cherished. The unconscious desire to be mourned, therefore, is a drive to create memories that are so emotionally potent that they will continue to exert an influence long after our physical presence has ceased. These are the memories that will sustain the mourning, that will keep the absent presence alive in the hearts and minds of the living.

In essence, the unconscious economy of affect suggests that our emotional lives are not simply passive responses to external stimuli, but active forces that shape our sense of self, our relationships, and our ultimate legacy. The desire to be mourned is a profound manifestation of this, a deep-seated yearning for our lives to have had a significant emotional impact, a testament to the enduring power of human connection and the indelible mark we can leave upon the psychic landscape of others. It is the ultimate affirmation of existence, a posthumous echo that declares: "I was here, and I mattered."

The profound act of mourning, often perceived solely as a somber reaction to absence, can be more aptly understood as a vital process of psychic reparation. It is not merely a passive acknowledgment of a void, but an active, often unconscious, engagement with the meaning of a life that has passed. In this intricate psychic economy, mourning serves a dual purpose: it mends the fractured emotional landscape of the bereaved, and, in a more subtle, pre-emptive manner, it fulfills a deep-seated, often unarticulated, need within the deceased themselves. The desire to be mourned, therefore, transforms the ultimate cessation of life into a catalyst for this essential psychic work in others, thereby securing an enduring validation of the deceased's existence.

For those left behind, mourning is a necessary rite of passage, a complex negotiation with absence that seeks to re-establish a sense of equilibrium. The intensity of grief is often a direct reflection of the emotional investments made, and the process of mourning is, in essence, the slow, arduous work of disentangling oneself from those investments while simultaneously preserving their value. It is akin to painstakingly salvaging precious artifacts from a collapsed structure, not to rebuild what was, but to create a memorial, a testament to the original edifice. The tears shed, the stories recounted, the memories replayed – these are not simply expressions of sadness, but the building blocks of this psychic reconstruction. Each shared anecdote, each tearful remembrance, reinforces the significance of the lost individual, weaving a new tapestry of meaning that incorporates their absence. This process affirms that the life lived was not ephemeral, that it left an imprint that is worthy of prolonged contemplation and emotional engagement. The mourner, in the act of grieving, is therefore engaged in a form of emotional archaeology, unearthing the layers of connection and meaning that constituted the relationship, and in doing so, they reaffirm the intrinsic value of both the departed and their own capacity for deep emotional engagement. This reaffirms the self, too, by demonstrating the depth of one's own love and the capacity to feel loss acutely, thereby validating one's own emotional existence.

The deceased, though physically absent, remains an active participant in this psychic drama. The unconscious desire to be mourned is a profound expression of a need for existential continuity, a yearning for one's life to have had an impact that transcends mortality. Death, in this context, becomes the ultimate opportunity for this impact to be recognized and ratified. The ensuing grief of loved ones acts as a posthumous confirmation of worth, a tangible demonstration that the life lived was not in vain, that it resonated deeply within the emotional lives of others. This is not a conscious pact between the living and the dead, but an unconscious psychic mechanism where the intensity of the grief signals the magnitude of the investment made by the deceased in their own life and in their relationships. The profound sorrow experienced by the mourners serves as irrefutable evidence that the deceased occupied a significant psychic space, that their absence creates a palpable void that speaks to the fullness of their presence. This fulfills an unconscious need for a sense of completion, a psychic closure where the narrative of a life is affirmed by the emotional response it elicits at its end.

This concept of mourning as psychic reparation can be observed in the way cultures construct rituals and ceremonies around death. These practices are not merely symbolic gestures; they are potent mechanisms for facilitating the work of grief. The funeral, the wake, the memorial services – these communal acts provide a sanctioned space for the expression of sorrow, allowing individuals to collectively engage in the process of psychic reparation. The shared experience of mourning amplifies the sense of connection and mutual support, reinforcing the idea that the loss is significant and that the life of the deceased was valued by a community. The recounting of eulogies, the sharing of memories, and the communal expression of sadness all contribute to the reaffirmation of the deceased's life and the validation of the mourners' feelings. In this shared space, the fractured psyche of the individual mourner begins to mend, supported by the collective endeavor of acknowledging and processing the loss. This collective reparation strengthens the social fabric, demonstrating how individual lives are woven into the larger tapestry of human experience.

Furthermore, the very act of remembering and recounting stories about the deceased is a form of psychic repair. Each narrative shared is a deliberate effort to keep the essence of the individual alive, to reanimate their spirit through memory. These stories are not just factual accounts; they are imbued with the emotional residue of lived experience, serving as conduits for the feelings that were once directed towards the living person. When a loved one recounts a humorous anecdote, a moment of profound kindness, or a shared struggle, they are not merely reminiscing; they are actively engaging in the re-creation of the deceased's psychic presence. This re-creation, while tinged with the sadness of absence, also serves to solidify the enduring significance of the individual, acting as a bulwark against the finality of oblivion. The repeated telling and retelling of these stories are essential in maintaining the emotional connection, allowing the mourner to gradually integrate the loss into their ongoing narrative of self. This ongoing engagement with the memory of the deceased allows for a gradual psychic readjustment, where the pain of absence is tempered by the enduring warmth of remembrance.

The desire to be mourned, when viewed through the lens of psychic reparation, also highlights the profound human need for continuity and legacy. The unconscious drive to be mourned is, in essence, a desire for one's life story to continue to have meaning and resonance even after physical death. The grief of others is the ultimate testament to this continuation, a living echo of the impact one has had. It suggests that the individual has successfully "invested" their psychic energy in a way that ensures its future return, not in tangible assets, but in the emotional currency of remembrance and sorrow. This return is crucial for the unconscious psychic economy of the deceased, as it provides a sense of completion and validation. The profound emotional outpouring of grief signifies that the life was lived fully, that connections were forged deeply, and that the absence is therefore deeply felt. This provides an unconscious reassurance that their existence was not a fleeting moment but an enduring presence that has left an indelible mark.

The concept of reparation in mourning is also deeply entwined with the notion of making amends, both for the mourner and, in a symbolic sense, for the deceased. For the mourner, the process of grieving can involve coming to terms with unresolved issues, forgiving perceived wrongs, or offering unspoken apologies. This internal psychic work helps to alleviate guilt and regret, contributing to a sense of peace and acceptance. In this way, mourning becomes a form of self-expiation, a way of rectifying perceived deficiencies in the past relationship. For the deceased, the mourning by others can be seen as an unconscious attempt by the living to "repair" the relationship in the absence of the individual. By focusing on the positive aspects of the deceased's life, by offering forgiveness for any perceived flaws, and by cherishing their memory, the mourners are, in a sense, completing the psychic narrative of the deceased in a way that brings solace and closure. This completed narrative, shaped by the love and understanding of the mourners, serves as a final act of affirmation for the deceased.

This dynamic of psychic reparation through mourning is particularly evident when considering the grief experienced for individuals who died prematurely or under tragic circumstances. The shock and disbelief that often accompany such losses can heighten the sense of unfinished business and the need for emotional closure. The intense grief in these situations can be seen as a desperate attempt to make sense of the senseless, to find meaning in the abrupt cessation of a life. The mourning process then becomes a crucial avenue for psychic reparation, not only for the survivors but also, unconsciously, for the individual whose life was cut short. The collective sorrow and remembrance can provide a sense of peace for the deceased, a posthumous acknowledgment that their potential was recognized and their loss deeply felt, thereby offering a form of psychic completion that was denied by their untimely death. This collective mourning can assuage the survivor's guilt and despair, transforming it into a meaningful tribute that honors the lost potential and affirms the value of the life that was lived, however briefly.

The desire to be mourned, in its deepest sense, is a yearning for one's life to be understood as a valuable contribution, a psychic investment that yielded significant emotional returns. The act of mourning by others is the ultimate realization of this desire, a posthumous affirmation that the life was not merely lived, but profoundly felt. This process of reparation, where the living engage with the memory and impact of the deceased, serves to mend the fractured emotional landscape of the mourners and, in an unconscious dialogue with the past, provides a sense of completion and validation for the departed. Death, through the powerful mechanism of mourning, thus becomes a catalyst for a profound psychic work that underscores the enduring significance of human connection and the indelible mark that each life leaves upon the emotional tapestry of the world. The intensity of sorrow is, in this light, not merely a measure of loss, but a profound testament to the enduring power of love and the essential human drive for meaning.

Chapter 5: The Aesthetics of Escape

The human psyche, in its relentless pursuit of equilibrium, often seeks avenues of escape when confronted with realities too painful to bear. This leads us to the fourth aesthetic of dying, one that eschews the stoic acceptance of finitude or the defiant struggle against it, and instead embarks on a subtle, yet profound, flight from the very fabric of existence as we know it. This is the "aesthetics of escape," a surrender not to oblivion, but to a perceived transcendence, a dreamlike departure from the harsh contours of the real. It is born from an unconscious fantasy that the unbearable weight of existence – be it the gnawing emptiness of trauma, the suffocating confines of societal expectation, or the sheer existential dread of finitude – can be shed, dissolved, or outmaneuvered. This is not a conscious decision to die, but a pervasive psychic drift, an unconscious yearning for a state of being where the sharp edges of pain are dulled, where the insistent demands of consciousness are silenced, and where the perceived limitations of the physical and emotional self are dissolved.

This yearning for escape often manifests as a seductive allure, a siren song promising release from the burdens of selfhood and the relentless pressure of reality. The individual, caught in the undertow of unbearable psychic pain, begins to develop an unconscious fantasy of transcending their current state, of slipping into an alternative reality that offers solace and relief. This isn't necessarily a desire for annihilation, but rather a profound longing to escape the confines of a suffering consciousness. It is the unconscious wish to be somewhere

else, to be *someone else*, or to simply *not be* in the way one currently is. This aesthetic of escape can be understood as a powerful, albeit often destructive, manifestation of the death drive, not as a straightforward impulse towards self-destruction, but as a complex negotiation with the unbearable aspects of life. The drive is towards a cessation of suffering, a dissolution of the self that is mired in pain, and a movement towards a state of peace that is imagined to exist beyond the confines of the present reality.

The pathways to this aesthetic escape are varied and often insidious. Addiction, in its myriad forms, stands as a primary conduit. Whether it be the numbing embrace of chemical substances, the compulsive pursuit of fleeting pleasures, or the obsessive engagement with digital worlds, addiction offers a temporary reprieve from the demanding presence of reality. The substance, the activity, the virtual space – these become the liminal zones, the imagined "other" realms where the ego's defenses are lowered, and the insistent demands of the real are momentarily suspended. In the state of altered consciousness induced by drugs or alcohol, the boundaries of the self blur, and the overwhelming pressures of everyday life seem to recede. Similarly, the dopamine rush of compulsive behaviors, from gambling to excessive consumption, provides a temporary distraction, a flight from the emptiness or anxiety that lies beneath. In these instances, the individual is not confronting their pain; they are seductively sidetracked from it, creating an illusion of escape that ultimately traps them more profoundly. The unconscious fantasy here is that by losing oneself in the intoxicating haze of addiction, one can transcend the limitations of a suffering existence.

Dissociation is another potent manifestation of this escape aesthetic. This is a profound detachment from one's immediate surroundings, one's body, or one's sense of self. It can range from mild depersonalization, where one feels like an observer of their own life, to more severe dissociative states where memories are fragmented, and personal identity becomes unstable. In dissociative states, the individual's consciousness seems to splinter, allowing parts of the psyche to withdraw from overwhelming experiences. The traumatic event, the unbearable stress, is experienced as if happening to someone else, or as if it is a bad dream from which one can eventually wake up. This psychic splitting is an unconscious defense mechanism, a desperate attempt to compartmentalize and distance oneself from an overwhelming reality. The fantasy is that by detaching from the immediate experience, by becoming a spectator rather than a participant, the pain can be rendered less potent, less real. This detachment, while providing a temporary psychic shield, ultimately leads to a profound alienation from oneself and the world.

Beyond addiction and dissociation, the retreat into fantasy offers a less overtly pathological, yet equally significant, avenue of escape. This is not simply daydreaming; it is a deep immersion in an imagined world, a private universe where the rules of reality are suspended and the individual can enact fantasies of power, control, or idealized connection. For some, this might involve an obsessive engagement with fictional narratives, role-playing games, or elaborate internal daydreams. The allure lies in the ability to create a reality that is more palatable, more fulfilling, or simply less painful than the one being experienced. This can become a self-sustaining illusion, where the individual invests more psychic energy in their imagined world than in their actual life, gradually withdrawing from social engagement and personal responsibility. The unconscious fantasy is that by constructing a superior reality, one can escape the perceived deficiencies and suffering of the actual world. This can lead to a slow erosion of one's engagement with life, a gradual fading away as the individual becomes more invested in the ghost of a life than in its lived reality.

The aesthetic of escape is often characterized by a seductive passivity. Unlike the active struggle against death or the profound engagement with grief, this aesthetic involves a gentle slipping away, a gradual detachment from the moorings of reality. It is a retreat into a state of altered consciousness, whether induced by external agents or internal psychic processes, that offers the promise of peace. The individual may not actively seek death, but they actively seek a state of being that is divorced from the pain of living. This is why the concept of "escape" is so central. It is not about confronting the darkness, but about finding a hidden door that leads to a different, less threatening, landscape. This imagined landscape can be one of blissful ignorance, where the complexities and suffering of the world are simply not perceived, or it can be a realm of heightened, albeit illusory, sensory experience that masks an underlying void.

This unconscious fantasy of transcendence, of slipping beyond the pain, can also manifest in a form of passive resignation. When individuals feel utterly trapped, when all avenues of perceived agency seem to be blocked, the psyche may construct a fantasy of escaping the situation by withdrawing from consciousness itself. This isn't a conscious suicidal ideation, but a pervasive psychic wish for oblivion, for a cessation of the relentless pressure. It is the unconscious belief that if one can just cease to be aware, if one can just "check out," the suffering will cease. This can lead to a gradual disengagement from life, a slow fading of interest, energy, and will. The individual may appear physically present but psychically absent, their internal world having become a desolate landscape of withdrawal. The seductive aspect here is the promise of ultimate peace, a peace that is imagined to be attainable only by ceasing to engage with the relentless demands of existence.

The allure of this aesthetic lies in its promise of effortless release. Unlike the hard work of mourning or the arduous task of rebuilding one's life after trauma, escape offers a seemingly effortless dissolution of suffering. It is the fantasy that one can simply shed their pain like an old coat, leaving it behind as one drifts into a state of altered being. This is particularly potent when individuals feel overwhelmed by forces beyond their control. The feeling of helplessness can breed a profound desire to escape the confines of one's own agency, to simply float away from the unbearable burdens of responsibility and consequence. The unconscious mind, in its relentless quest for self-preservation, can interpret this surrender to a less conscious state as a form of survival, a way to endure when direct confrontation seems impossible.

The aesthetic of escape, therefore, represents a profound turning inward, not in contemplation or self-discovery, but in a desperate attempt to find refuge from the external world. It is a retreat into an imagined interiority, a psychic sanctuary where the harsh realities of existence cannot penetrate. This can be a dangerous fantasy, for while it may offer temporary relief, it ultimately leads to a profound disconnect from life. The individual who has perfected the art of escaping reality risks becoming a phantom in their own existence, their life reduced to a series of fleeting moments of altered consciousness rather than a coherent narrative of lived experience. The ultimate tragedy of this aesthetic is that the escape it offers is an illusion, a temporary reprieve that ultimately leads to a deeper form of confinement, trapped within the self-imposed boundaries of an unlived life. The unconscious fantasy of transcending the real, while born from a desire to alleviate suffering, can ultimately lead to a profound existential diminishment, where the richness and complexity of life are sacrificed for a fleeting sense of peace. This aesthetic, therefore, highlights the complex and often paradoxical ways in which the human psyche grapples with pain, seeking not necessarily to overcome it, but sometimes, to simply outrun it, to slip away into the seductive promise of a world unbound by its cruelties.

The case of "Elias," a pseudonym adopted to veil a profoundly personal narrative, offers a poignant, albeit disturbing, illustration of the aesthetics of escape in its most attenuated and deeply etched form. Elias's life trajectory was not one of grand gestures or explosive confrontations with pain; rather, it was characterized by a pervasive, almost imperceptible drift away from the anchor points of lived experience. From his earliest years, Elias demonstrated an unusual capacity for detachment. Not the intellectual detachment of a scholar or the artistic detachment of an observer, but a visceral, almost somatic unmooring from the present moment. This was not a deliberate withdrawal, but an unconscious maneuver, a sophisticated defense mechanism born from an early environment that offered little safety or predictability.

His childhood was a tapestry woven with threads of neglect and subtle emotional abuse. His parents, themselves wounded individuals, were largely preoccupied with their own internal struggles, leaving Elias to navigate the emotional landscape of his home with an unreliable compass. Experiences that should have fostered a secure attachment instead generated a profound sense of existential uncertainty. The inconsistent presence of maternal comfort, the unpredictable outbursts of paternal anger – these were not just events, but erosions of the very ground upon which a stable sense of self could be built. In response, Elias's psyche began to develop its elaborate architecture of escape. He learned to be elsewhere, even when physically present. His attention would drift, his gaze would become unfocused, and the vibrant, often chaotic, demands of his surroundings would recede, replaced by a more manageable, internally generated world. This was the nascent stage of his dissociative fade, a slow, unconscious shedding of the immediate, the real, in favor of a less threatening internal simulacrum.

These early dissociative experiences were not mere daydreaming. They were profound shifts in consciousness, moments where the solidity of the world seemed to dissolve, and Elias could observe his own life as if from a great distance. He recounted, in later therapy, how the sting of a reprimand or the sting of a perceived rejection would feel not like a wound inflicted upon him, but like an event observed in a film, affecting a character with whom he shared a vague resemblance. This capacity for psychic distance, honed in childhood as a survival mechanism, became the bedrock of his later life, shaping his relationships, his career, and ultimately, his relationship with existence itself. The unconscious fantasy that fueled this mechanism was simple yet devastating: that by not fully inhabiting his own life, by remaining perpetually on the periphery of his own experience, he could shield himself from the pain that seemed to be an inherent part of it.

As Elias entered adolescence and young adulthood, the patterns of dissociation became more pronounced and sophisticated. He found solace not in overt rebellion or dramatic outbursts, but in subtle forms of withdrawal. Social gatherings were endured, not experienced. Conversations were listened to, but rarely fully engaged with. He developed a remarkable ability to present an image of participation while his mind drifted, sometimes into intricate imagined scenarios, other times into a blank, placid mental space. This was not a conscious choice to be disengaged; it was an automatic pilot, a learned response to stimuli that threatened to breach the carefully constructed defenses around his vulnerable inner core. The unconscious fantasy here was that by maintaining this psychic distance, he could avoid the messy, unpredictable, and often painful entanglements of human connection. He could observe love, friendship, and conflict from a safe remove, experiencing only pale imitations of the emotional intensity that others seemed to navigate.

This aesthetic of escape manifested itself in his pursuit of work as well. He gravitated towards professions that allowed for a degree of autonomy and provided opportunities for deep immersion in tasks that could absorb his attention without demanding significant emotional investment. He excelled in fields that involved meticulous detail, pattern recognition, and solitary focus. In these environments, his dissociative tendencies could be perceived as advantageous – a sign of concentration, of deep thought. Yet, beneath the surface of competence, the fundamental mechanism remained. The work became an anchor, not because he was deeply passionate about it, but because it provided a structured space where his dissociative tendencies could be indulged without significant social reperception. He could disappear into his tasks, the boundaries of self blurring with the demands of the project, all while preserving a core of himself that remained untouched, unengaged, and ultimately, un-lived.

His romantic relationships followed a similar pattern. Elias was capable of forming connections, but these were often characterized by a peculiar emotional distance. He could be attentive, even affectionate, but there was always a sense of him being just out of reach. Partners would often describe him as "dreamy" or "somewhat detached," mistaking his dissociative states for introversion or artistic temperament. The unconscious fantasy at play was the desire to experience intimacy without the vulnerability that true emotional closeness entails. He could approximate the behaviors of a loving partner, but the core of his emotional being remained guarded, a sanctuary from which he could observe the relationship unfold, rather than fully participate in its dynamic ebb and flow. When conflict arose, or when the demands of intimacy grew too intense, his dissociative defenses would automatically engage, creating a chasm between him and his partner, a chasm that would often prove too wide to bridge. The relationship would then fade, not with a bang, but with a quiet implosion, mirroring the slow erosion of Elias's own engagement with life.

The critical turning point, or rather, the slow unraveling that characterized Elias's decline, was not marked by a single traumatic event, but by a gradual erosion of the psychic structures that had, for so long, served him. As he aged, the world's insistent demands began to wear down the subtle defenses he had so carefully erected. The repetitive nature of his dissociative escape, while offering temporary relief, offered no genuine resolution. Instead, it created a cumulative effect, a psychic exhaustion. His ability to engage, even superficially, began to diminish. The internal worlds he retreated into became less vivid, less comforting, and increasingly populated by a sense of vague unease. The unconscious fantasy of escaping pain through detachment began to falter, as the very act of detachment itself started to feel like a form of suffering.

This period of decline was marked by an increasing passivity. Elias became less engaged with his work, less responsive in his relationships, and increasingly withdrawn from the external world. It was as if the energy required to maintain the façade of presence had finally been depleted. The subtle fading became more pronounced. He began to miss appointments, to forget commitments, not out of malice or intentional neglect, but because the psychic energy required to orient himself to these external demands had waned. His world shrank, becoming a more circumscribed space, primarily his home, and within that, his room.

The aesthetic of escape, in Elias's case, culminated not in a dramatic act, but in a profound, almost imperceptible diffusion of consciousness. He did not seek death actively; rather, he seemed to drift away from life. His interactions became fewer and farther between, his responses monosyllabic, his presence increasingly spectral. It was as if the very fabric of his being was becoming less cohesive, less anchored to reality. The unconscious fantasy of "not-being-in-the-way-one-currently-is" had, in a perverse fulfillment, begun to manifest as a literal withdrawal from being.

In his final years, Elias became a figure of quiet dissolution. His family, who had long struggled to penetrate his defenses, found themselves increasingly unable to reach him. He was physically present, but psychically absent, lost in a fog of disengagement. This was not a coma, nor a severe illness, but a profound dissociative withdrawal, a state where the self, having for so long sought refuge from the harshness of reality, finally surrendered to the illusion of unreality altogether. The unconscious fantasy that had propelled him through life – the fantasy of escape – had led him to a state of being where the distinction between existence and non-existence had become blurred. He had, in essence, achieved a form of transcendence, not into a realm of peace or fulfillment, but into a state of profound psychic diffusion, a quiet fading from the world that mirrored the slow, almost imperceptible erosion of his own sense of self.

The tragedy of Elias's case lies in the insidious nature of his escape. There were no dramatic confrontations, no clear moments of crisis that might have offered a pathway to intervention. Instead, it was a slow, almost invisible retreat, a life lived on the margins of consciousness, until consciousness itself began to unravel. His story serves as a stark reminder that the aesthetics of escape, when deeply ingrained as a primary defense mechanism, can lead not to a dramatic finale, but to a profound and heartbreaking diminishment of life, a fading away that is as silent as it is complete. The unconscious mind, in its desperate attempt to shield itself from unbearable pain, can construct pathways that lead not to healing, but to a gradual erasure of the self, leaving behind only the faintest of echoes. Elias's life became an elegy to the unlived, a testament to the devastating consequences of seeking refuge in the very mechanisms that prevent us from truly living. His ending was not a cessation of life, but a cessation of

being alive, a final, complete immersion into the dreamlike state from which he had, for so long, sought solace. This dissociative fade, this gradual erosion of psychic presence, represents one of the most profound and sorrowful manifestations of the aesthetics of escape, where the ultimate flight is not from a specific pain, but from the very engagement with existence that defines us.

Addiction, in its myriad forms, represents perhaps the most visceral and tragically potent manifestation of the aesthetics of escape. It is a flight not merely from specific difficulties or pains, but from the very existential condition of being alive. The unconscious fantasy that underpins addictive behavior is a profound yearning to negate the burdens of consciousness, to dissolve the sharp edges of a reality that feels overwhelming, or, in its most extreme formulation, to achieve a state of blissful non-being. This is not simply about avoiding discomfort; it is about seeking an absolute escape, a cessation of the self as it is known and experienced.

The allure of addiction lies in its promise of altered states. Whether through the chemical oblivion offered by substances, the compulsive repetition of behaviors, or the immersive depths of virtual worlds, the addict seeks a radical departure from the mundane, the painful, the merely

real. This pursuit can be understood as a desperate attempt to outrun the demands of the id, the ego, and the superego, those internal forces that perpetually wrestle with desires, realities, and moral imperatives. In the intoxicating haze of an altered state, these internal conflicts can temporarily cease. The sharp edges of guilt, shame, anxiety, and existential dread are softened, blurred, or obliterated. The overwhelming pressure to *be*—to choose, to feel, to act, to suffer—is momentarily lifted.

Consider the alcoholic who, night after night, seeks solace in the bottle. The initial drink is a ritualistic offering to the gods of oblivion. It promises to silence the nagging voices of self-recrimination, to numb the ache of loneliness, to blur the harsh lines of a life that feels unmanageable. Each swallow is a step away from the precipice of conscious experience, a plunge into a warmer, fuzzier, less demanding reality. The fantasy is not merely to forget, but to

cease to feel the sting of memory, the weight of responsibility, the gnawing emptiness that lurks in the quiet hours. The drink becomes a surrogate for a lost mother's embrace, a phantom limb that promises comfort, or, more disturbingly, a liquid shroud that offers temporary respite from the agony of self-awareness.

Similarly, the compulsive gambler chases not just the thrill of the win, but the exhilarating void that opens up when the stakes are highest. In those moments of intense anticipation, the world outside the casino, the bills unpaid, the relationships strained, all fade into irrelevance. The focus narrows to the roll of the dice, the turn of the card, the spin of the wheel. This intense concentration, this immersion in a singular, high-stakes moment, is a form of escape. It offers a temporary reprieve from the vast, often daunting landscape of the gambler's own life. The fantasy here is to transcend the ordinary consequences of actions, to achieve a state where chance dictates fate, and the burden of decision-making is temporarily abdicated. Yet, this escape is a precarious one, always teetering on the brink of ruin, a testament to the destructive potential of seeking refuge in pure contingency.

Behavioral addictions, such as those involving sex, shopping, or technology, operate on similar principles. They offer a readily accessible means of self-soothing, a way to artificially regulate mood and escape from unwanted emotional states. The dopamine rush associated with these activities can mimic the experience of pleasure, but it is a hollow imitation, a fleeting distraction from underlying pain. The unconscious fantasy is that by repeatedly engaging in these compulsive behaviors, the individual can somehow fill the void within, or outrun the feelings that make them feel incomplete or inadequate. The repetitive nature of the act itself becomes a form of dissociation, a way to detach from the self and its attendant suffering.

The ultimate trajectory of addiction, viewed through the lens of the aesthetics of escape, is a tragic fulfillment of the desire for non-being.

It is not necessarily a conscious wish for death, but a profound yearning to cease to be

in the way one currently is. The substance or behavior becomes a vehicle for this ultimate escape, offering a gradual dissolution of the self, a progressive erasure of personal history, responsibility, and connection. The individual, caught in the seductive spiral of addiction, becomes increasingly disconnected from the world and from themselves. Their consciousness, once a source of pain, becomes a prison from which they desperately seek release.

This journey into non-being is often marked by a profound loss of aesthetic sensibility in the conventional sense. The rich tapestry of human experience, with its capacity for beauty, joy, and profound connection, is sacrificed for the monotonous, albeit seductive, grayness of oblivion. The world loses its color, its texture, its meaning. Yet, paradoxically, there can be a perverse aesthetic to addiction itself. The rituals of preparation, the intensity of the craving, the brief moments of oblivion – these can take on a dark, compelling allure. The addict, in their pursuit of escape, may unconsciously craft a life defined by this pursuit, a life where the substance or behavior becomes the central, all-consuming aesthetic.

The dream of non-being, as realized through addiction, is a seductive but ultimately destructive illusion. It offers a temporary sanctuary from pain, but at the cost of life itself. The individual seeking escape through addiction is like a mariner who, fleeing a storm, deliberately steers their ship towards the siren song of oblivion, mistaking the promise of silence for the tranquility of peace. The tragedy lies in the fact that the very mechanisms designed to shield the self from suffering ultimately lead to its annihilation. The escape is not from the pain of existence, but from the possibility of transcending that pain through engagement, through growth, and through the full, messy, and often beautiful realization of one's own being. The addiction becomes a perverse aestheticization of erasure, a darkly compelling performance of a life that is slowly, deliberately, fading into nothingness. The ultimate escape is not a liberation, but a surrender to the void, a quiet dissolution that mirrors the very state of non-being the addict craved.

The human psyche, in its relentless pursuit of equilibrium, often employs elaborate mechanisms to shield itself from the slings and arrows of outrageous fortune, or indeed, from the more quotidian abrasions of existence. While addiction, as previously explored, represents a starkly destructive engagement with this impulse, a subtler, perhaps more insidious, form of escape resides in the construction and inhabitation of elaborate fantasy worlds. These are not mere daydreams, fleeting and insubstantial, but fully realized internal landscapes, meticulously crafted and deeply resonant, serving as potent psychic retreats. Individuals may construct rich inner lives, populate them with idealized selves or captivating companions, and engage in complex imaginary scenarios that offer a profound departure from the often-mundane or painful realities of their lived experience. This immersion is not simply a pastime; it can become the primary mode of existence, a chosen sanctuary from the demands and discontents of the external world.

The genesis of such elaborate fantasy worlds often lies in a deep-seated, unconscious drive to circumvent psychic pain. When the burdens of reality—be they existential dread, trauma, profound loneliness, or a sense of fundamental inadequacy—become overwhelming, the mind may seek refuge in the creation of an alternative locus of being. This is a defense mechanism, a sophisticated strategy for preserving the integrity of the self by withdrawing the locus of experience from a perceived hostile or unbearable external environment. The unconscious fantasy at play is one of creation and control: the fantasy of being able to conjure a world that is responsive, nurturing, and free from the arbitrary cruelty or crushing indifference of the actual. Within these constructed realms, the individual can transcend limitations, achieve idealized states of being, and experience a form of liberation unavailable in their waking lives.

Consider the individual who, facing the bleakness of social isolation and the perceived failure of their interpersonal relationships, retreats into a world populated by characters they have meticulously designed. These characters might embody idealized traits—loyalty, admiration, unwavering affection—that are conspicuously absent in their real-world interactions. The individual might engage in prolonged internal dialogues, orchestrate elaborate scenarios of social triumph, or experience profound emotional connection with these imaginary figures. This is not a conscious act of delusion, but a deeply ingrained psychic habit, a way of meeting unmet needs within the safe confines of the mind. The internal world becomes a more desirable reality, a place where the self is not only accepted but celebrated, where every interaction is affirming, and where the sting of rejection or misunderstanding is unknown. The vibrancy and perceived authenticity of these internal dramas can eclipse the muted tones of external life, leading to a gradual disengagement from the latter.

This withdrawal into internal fantasy can be seen as a form of symbolic death, a quiet secession from the external world. The individual does not necessarily cease to function outwardly, but their psychic energy, their emotional investment, and their sense of self become increasingly tethered to the imaginary domain. The external world, with its demands for compromise, its inherent unpredictability, and its capacity for inflicting pain, loses its allure. It becomes merely a stage upon which the internal drama plays out, or worse, an unwelcome intrusion upon the more cherished reality within. The richness of the fantasy world can create a profound sense of saturation, leaving little room for engagement with the external. The individual may become less responsive to their environment, their attention perpetually drawn inward, their inner landscape far more vivid and compelling than the world around them.

The rise of virtual realities and immersive online gaming environments has provided an unprecedentedly fertile ground for such psychic retreats. These digital worlds offer not just narrative depth and complex social interactions, but a fully sensory engagement that can rival, and in some aspects, surpass, the perceived limitations of physical reality. Here, individuals can adopt avatars that represent their idealized selves, shedding the constraints of physical appearance, social status, or personal history. They can engage in heroic quests, build elaborate virtual empires, or forge deep connections with others who share their passion for this digital existence. The allure lies in the active participation, the tangible sense of achievement within the game's framework, and the creation of a shared reality with a community of like-minded individuals. For some, these virtual worlds become so compelling that the distinction between the digital and the 'real' begins to blur, leading to a profound prioritizing of the former.

This immersion in virtual spaces can be understood as a sophisticated form of psychic escape, a deliberate construction of an alternative habitat for the self. The unconscious drive is to find a place where one can exert agency, experience mastery, and find belonging, all without the inherent vulnerabilities and disappointments of the analogue world. The rules of engagement are often clearer, the feedback more immediate, and the consequences, while sometimes significant within the virtual context, are ultimately contained. This containment is crucial; it allows for a powerful experience of engagement without the existential risks that often accompany real-world endeavors. The fantasy here is not merely to escape, but to

thrive in a constructed reality, to fulfill potentials that feel stifled or unrealized in the quotidian.

The danger, of course, lies in the potential for these constructed worlds to become prisons, albeit gilded ones. When the fantasy becomes the sole source of meaning and satisfaction, the individual risks a profound detachment from the lived reality, a state where the external world becomes increasingly alien and unmanageable. This withdrawal can manifest in neglecting responsibilities, isolating oneself from loved ones, and ultimately, experiencing a diminishment of the self as a fully embodied, socially connected being. The very act of escape, intended to preserve the self, can inadvertently lead to its erosion. The individual may become so accustomed to the curated perfection of their fantasy world that they lose the resilience and coping mechanisms necessary to navigate the complexities and imperfections of actual life.

The aesthetic of escape, in this context, finds its expression in the meticulous crafting and unwavering devotion to these alternative realities. There is an artistry in the construction of these internal or digital worlds, a dedication to detail that can be as profound as any artistic endeavor. The unconscious aim is to create a space of ultimate aesthetic satisfaction, a reality that resonates with the deepest desires of the self. However, this aestheticization of escape comes at a cost.

It can lead to a impoverishment of experience in the external world, a loss of the capacity to find beauty and meaning in the imperfect, the spontaneous, and the authentically human. The richness of lived experience, with its inherent messiness and unpredictable unfolding, is traded for the curated, predictable comfort of the imagined.

Furthermore, the process of constructing and inhabiting these fantasy worlds can be deeply solitary, even when undertaken within a shared virtual space. While the individual may interact with avatars or other players, the core of their experience—the processing of emotions, the integration of fantasy with reality—remains an intensely personal journey. This can lead to a profound sense of alienation, a feeling of being fundamentally misunderstood by those who inhabit the 'real' world. The fantasy, meant to be a refuge, can thus become a barrier, reinforcing the very isolation it was designed to alleviate. The unconscious wish is for connection, but the mechanism employed—a retreat into the self—often exacerbates the underlying lack.

The philosophical underpinnings of this phenomenon are rooted in the enduring human fascination with the idea of creating one's own reality. From Plato's allegory of the cave, which suggests our perceived reality might be but a shadow of a truer form, to the existentialist emphasis on radical freedom and self-creation, the notion of shaping our world is a recurrent theme. However, the escape into fantasy represents a deviation from the existentialist call to confront and shape reality through action and engagement. Instead, it is a flight from the authentic burden of that freedom, a surrender to the seductive ease of a world that requires no difficult choices, no confronting of limitations, no grappling with the fundamental uncertainties of existence.

The unconscious desire driving this retreat is multifaceted. It can be a yearning for a lost Eden, a primal state of unalloyed pleasure and freedom from suffering, often rooted in early childhood experiences of omnipotence or idealized parental figures. It can also be a desperate attempt to outrun the shadow of mortality, to create a form of existence that is impervious to decay and dissolution. In a world that constantly reminds us of our finitude, the ability to conjure an eternal, unchanging realm offers a potent illusion of control and permanence. The individual becomes the architect of their own eternity, the sovereign of their own domain, where time may stretch or contract at will, and where the specter of death holds no sway.

This retreat into fantasy, when it becomes a dominant mode of existence, can be understood as a profound psychological amputation. The individual has, in essence, severed a vital connection to the external world, opting for a less demanding, albeit less vital, form of being. The 'aesthetics of escape' here is not about appreciating a departure, but about inhabiting a state of perpetual departure, a sustained disengagement that preserves the self from the pain of direct experience. The vibrant hues of the imagined world obscure the muted tones of reality, and the individual, having perfected the art of inward gaze, may find themselves increasingly estranged from the very world they sought, perhaps unconsciously, to enhance through their withdrawal. The ultimate tragedy lies in the fact that the exquisite beauty of the constructed world, so meticulously crafted to preserve the self, can ultimately lead to its profound diminishment, a slow fading into a private, perfect, and ultimately empty, existence. This is not a surrender to the void, as in addiction, but a self-imposed exile into a perpetually self-renewing, yet ultimately sterile, paradise.

The human psyche, in its relentless pursuit of equilibrium, often employs elaborate mechanisms to shield itself from the slings and arrows of outrageous fortune, or indeed, from the more quotidian abrasions of existence. While addiction, as previously explored, represents a starkly destructive engagement with this impulse, a subtler, perhaps more insidious, form of escape resides in the construction and inhabitation of elaborate fantasy worlds. These are not mere daydreams, fleeting and insubstantial, but fully realized internal landscapes, meticulously crafted and deeply resonant, serving as potent psychic retreats. Individuals may construct rich inner lives, populate them with idealized selves or captivating companions, and engage in complex imaginary scenarios that offer a profound departure from the often-mundane or painful realities of their lived experience. This immersion is not simply a pastime; it can become the primary mode of existence, a chosen sanctuary from the demands and discontents of the external world.

The genesis of such elaborate fantasy worlds often lies in a deep-seated, unconscious drive to circumvent psychic pain. When the burdens of reality—be they existential dread, trauma, profound loneliness, or a sense of fundamental inadequacy—become overwhelming, the mind may seek refuge in the creation of an alternative locus of being. This is a defense mechanism, a sophisticated strategy for preserving the integrity of the self by withdrawing the locus of experience from a perceived hostile or unbearable external environment. The unconscious fantasy at play is one of creation and control: the fantasy of being able to conjure a world that is responsive, nurturing, and free from the arbitrary cruelty or crushing indifference of the actual. Within these constructed realms, the individual can transcend limitations, achieve idealized states of being, and experience a form of liberation unavailable in their waking lives.

Consider the individual who, facing the bleakness of social isolation and the perceived failure of their interpersonal relationships, retreats into a world populated by characters they have meticulously designed. These characters might embody idealized traits—loyalty, admiration, unwavering affection—that are conspicuously absent in their real-world interactions. The individual might engage in prolonged internal dialogues, orchestrate elaborate scenarios of social triumph, or experience profound emotional connection with these imaginary figures. This is not a conscious act of delusion, but a deeply ingrained psychic habit, a way of meeting unmet needs within the safe confines of the mind. The internal world becomes a more desirable reality, a place where the self is not only accepted but celebrated, where every interaction is affirming, and where the sting of rejection or misunderstanding is unknown. The vibrancy and perceived authenticity of these internal dramas can eclipse the muted tones of external life, leading to a gradual disengagement from the latter.

This withdrawal into internal fantasy can be seen as a form of symbolic death, a quiet secession from the external world. The individual does not necessarily cease to function outwardly, but their psychic energy, their emotional investment, and their sense of self become increasingly tethered to the imaginary domain. The external world, with its demands for compromise, its inherent unpredictability, and its capacity for inflicting pain, loses its allure. It becomes merely a stage upon which the internal drama plays out, or worse, an unwelcome intrusion upon the more cherished reality within. The richness of the fantasy world can create a profound sense of saturation, leaving little room for engagement with the external. The individual may become less responsive to their environment, their attention perpetually drawn inward, their inner landscape far more vivid and compelling than the world around them.

The rise of virtual realities and immersive online gaming environments has provided an unprecedentedly fertile ground for such psychic retreats. These digital worlds offer not just narrative depth and complex social interactions, but a fully sensory engagement that can rival, and in some aspects, surpass, the perceived limitations of physical reality. Here, individuals can adopt avatars that represent their idealized selves, shedding the constraints of physical appearance, social status, or personal history. They can engage in heroic quests, build elaborate virtual empires, or forge deep connections with others who share their passion for this digital existence. The allure lies in the active participation, the tangible sense of achievement within the game's framework, and the creation of a shared reality with a community of like-minded individuals. For some, these virtual worlds become so compelling that the distinction between the digital and the 'real' begins to blur, leading to a profound prioritizing of the former.

This immersion in virtual spaces can be understood as a sophisticated form of psychic escape, a deliberate construction of an alternative habitat for the self. The unconscious drive is to find a place where one can exert agency, experience mastery, and find belonging, all without the inherent vulnerabilities and disappointments of the analogue world. The rules of engagement are often clearer, the feedback more immediate, and the consequences, while sometimes significant within the virtual context, are ultimately contained. This containment is crucial; it allows for a powerful experience of engagement without the existential risks that often accompany real-world endeavors. The fantasy here is not merely to escape, but to

thrive in a constructed reality, to fulfill potentials that feel stifled or unrealized in the quotidian.

The danger, of course, lies in the potential for these constructed worlds to become prisons, albeit gilded ones. When the fantasy becomes the sole source of meaning and satisfaction, the individual risks a profound detachment from the lived reality, a state where the external world becomes increasingly alien and unmanageable. This withdrawal can manifest in neglecting responsibilities, isolating oneself from loved ones, and ultimately, experiencing a diminishment of the self as a fully embodied, socially connected being. The very act of escape, intended to preserve the self, can inadvertently lead to its erosion. The individual may become so accustomed to the curated perfection of their fantasy world that they lose the resilience and coping mechanisms necessary to navigate the complexities and imperfections of actual life.

The aesthetic of escape, in this context, finds its expression in the meticulous crafting and unwavering devotion to these alternative realities. There is an artistry in the construction of these internal or digital worlds, a dedication to detail that can be as profound as any artistic endeavor. The unconscious aim is to create a space of ultimate aesthetic satisfaction, a reality that resonates with the deepest desires of the self. However, this aestheticization of escape comes at a cost. It can lead to a impoverishment of experience in the external world, a loss of the capacity to find beauty and meaning in the imperfect, the spontaneous, and the authentically human. The richness of lived experience, with its inherent messiness and unpredictable unfolding, is traded for the curated, predictable comfort of the imagined.

Furthermore, the process of constructing and inhabiting these fantasy worlds can be deeply solitary, even when undertaken within a shared virtual space. While the individual may interact with avatars or other players, the core of their experience—the processing of emotions, the integration of fantasy with reality—remains an intensely personal journey. This can lead to a profound sense of alienation, a feeling of being fundamentally misunderstood by those who inhabit the 'real' world. The fantasy, meant to be a refuge, can thus become a barrier, reinforcing the very isolation it was designed to alleviate. The unconscious wish is for connection, but the mechanism employed—a retreat into the self—often exacerbates the underlying lack.

The philosophical underpinnings of this phenomenon are rooted in the enduring human fascination with the idea of creating one's own reality. From Plato's allegory of the cave, which suggests our perceived reality might be but a shadow of a truer form, to the existentialist emphasis on radical freedom and self-creation, the notion of shaping our world is a recurrent theme. However, the escape into fantasy represents a deviation from the existentialist call to confront and shape reality through action and engagement. Instead, it is a flight from the authentic burden of that freedom, a surrender to the seductive ease of a world that requires no difficult choices, no confronting of limitations, no grappling with the fundamental uncertainties of existence.

The unconscious desire driving this retreat is multifaceted. It can be a yearning for a lost Eden, a primal state of unalloyed pleasure and freedom from suffering, often rooted in early childhood experiences of omnipotence or idealized parental figures. It can also be a desperate attempt to outrun the shadow of mortality, to create a form of existence that is impervious to decay and dissolution. In a world that constantly reminds us of our finitude, the ability to conjure an eternal, unchanging realm offers a potent illusion of control and permanence. The individual becomes the architect of their own eternity, the sovereign of their own domain, where time may stretch or contract at will, and where the specter of death holds no sway.

This retreat into fantasy, when it becomes a dominant mode of existence, can be understood as a profound psychological amputation. The individual has, in essence, severed a vital connection to the external world, opting for a less demanding, albeit less vital, form of being. The 'aesthetics of escape' here is not about appreciating a departure, but about inhabiting a state of perpetual departure, a sustained disengagement that preserves the self from the pain of direct experience. The vibrant hues of the imagined world obscure the muted tones of reality, and the individual, having perfected the art of inward gaze, may find themselves increasingly estranged from the very world they sought, perhaps unconsciously, to enhance through their withdrawal. The ultimate tragedy lies in the fact that the exquisite beauty of the constructed world, so meticulously crafted to preserve the self, can ultimately lead to its profound diminishment, a slow fading into a private, perfect, and ultimately empty, existence. This is not a surrender to the void, as in addiction, but a self-imposed exile into a perpetually self-renewing, yet ultimately sterile, paradise.

Beyond the construction of elaborate internal or digital paradises, a more profound and perilous form of escape can manifest through dissociation. This is not merely a temporary disconnection, a mental stepping aside from an overwhelming moment, but a fundamental fracturing of psychic continuity. Dissociation, in its more extreme forms, is a deliberate, though often unconscious, mechanism by which the mind shields itself from unbearable psychic pain by fragmenting experience, memory, or identity. It is a defense against a reality so traumatic, so emotionally devastating, that direct engagement with it threatens to shatter the very core of the self. The allure of dissociation lies in its immediate, if temporary, cessation of suffering. When the weight of grief, terror, or shame becomes too immense to bear, the psyche may instinctively sever its connections, creating a gulf between the self and the unbearable experience.

This psychic cleavage can manifest in various ways. Individuals may find themselves unable to recall significant periods of their lives, particularly those marked by trauma. They might experience derealization, a sense of the external world being unreal or dreamlike, or depersonalization, a feeling of being detached from one's own body or thoughts, as if observing oneself from a distance. In its most severe presentations, dissociation can lead to the emergence of distinct personality states, a profound disruption of identity where different aspects of the self appear to operate independently. This is the mind's desperate attempt to compartmentalize the intolerable, to quarantine the wound so that the rest of the self can continue to function, however precariously.

The danger here lies in the very effectiveness of this defense. Dissociation, by its nature, creates a void. While it may offer immediate respite from acute pain, it simultaneously erodes the individual's capacity to integrate their experiences and to form a coherent sense of self. The memories, emotions, and aspects of identity that have been disavowed do not simply vanish; they remain, often festering in the psychic unconscious, exerting a subtle but persistent influence on the individual's life. This can lead to a pervasive sense of unease, fragmented emotional responses, and inexplicable behavioral patterns that baffle both the individual and those around them. The escape from pain is thus a flight into a state of psychic disarray, a fragmentation that leaves the individual less whole, less connected, and less able to navigate the complexities of life.

This is where the "aesthetic of escape" takes on a particularly chilling dimension. When dissociation becomes the primary mode of engaging with reality, the individual's trajectory can indeed be characterized by a profound severance from lived experience, a quiet fading or dissolution rather than a direct confrontation with the specter of mortality. It is an escape

from being, rather than an escape *to* something. The self, fragmented and disconnected, begins to unravel. The external world, stripped of its emotional resonance and subjective meaning, becomes a blurry, indifferent backdrop. The individual might continue to perform the motions of life, but the vital spark, the authentic engagement with existence, has been extinguished. This is not a dramatic self-destruction, but a slow, insidious diminishment, a gradual secession from the vibrant, messy, and ultimately meaningful tapestry of human life.

Consider the individual who, after enduring profound trauma, develops dissociative amnesia. They may wake up in a new location with no memory of how they got there, no recollection of their past identity, or even the names of their loved ones. This immediate escape from the memory of the trauma is absolute, but it comes at the cost of their personal history, their relationships, and their very sense of who they are. Their world becomes a series of disconnected moments, devoid of continuity or personal narrative. The "aesthetic" here is one of blankness, of erasure, a deliberate and devastating simplification of the complex human experience. The individual is effectively rendered a ghost in their own life, their existence a series of disconnected scenes performed without a script or a cohesive protagonist.

The long-term consequences of such profound dissociation are dire. Without the capacity to integrate traumatic memories and emotions, the individual remains perpetually at risk of re-traumatization. The fragmented aspects of the self, unable to communicate or find resolution, can lead to intense internal conflict, anxiety, and depression. The ability to form meaningful relationships is severely compromised, as genuine intimacy requires a stable and coherent sense of self to offer and to receive. The individual may find themselves caught in cycles of behavior that are self-defeating or destructive, driven by impulses and memories that they cannot consciously access or understand.

Furthermore, when dissociation becomes a deeply ingrained pattern, it can impede the natural process of grieving and healing. Instead of confronting loss and integrating it into one's life narrative, the disavowed emotions remain in a psychic limbo, preventing the individual from moving forward. The escape from pain becomes a perpetual stasis, a holding pattern that denies the possibility of growth and transformation. The aesthetic of escape, in this context, is the aesthetic of the perpetually unfinished, the eternally suspended, the life that never quite begins because the necessary foundational elements of identity and integrated experience have been shattered.

The ultimate endpoint of such a profound disengagement from reality, driven by dissociation, is a form of psychic dissolution. It is not a violent end, but a quiet fading into oblivion. The individual, so disconnected from their own internal world and the external reality, can become increasingly insubstantial. Their existence may dwindle to a mere shadow, their presence barely registered by themselves or others. This is the quiet end, the escape that becomes a final erasure. The self, in its desperate attempt to flee from unbearable pain, ultimately dissolves, leaving behind a void where a life once was. It is a tragic testament to the power of the human psyche to protect itself, but also a somber reminder of the profound interconnectedness of our thoughts, emotions, memories, and identity, and the devastating consequences when these fundamental threads are systematically severed. The allure of an immediate end to suffering can lead to an eternity of disembodiment, a fading into an existence that is neither alive nor dead, but a hauntingly empty space between the two. This is the ultimate, and most profound, aesthetic of escape – the escape from existence itself, orchestrated by the fractured, dissociative mind.

Chapter 6: Suicide Without Suicide

The landscape of self-destruction is far more variegated and insidious than the stark, unambiguous act of suicide. While the latter represents a direct confrontation with mortality, a conscious (or at least intentional) termination, there exists a vast and often overlooked terrain of *indirect* self-destructiveness. These are behaviors, often cloaked in the guise of impulsivity, carelessness, or even misguided self-care, that inexorably lead toward an end, yet lack the explicit intention of self-annihilation. This phenomenon, which we might term "suicide without suicide," operates through subtle, unconscious mechanisms, weaving a tapestry of self-sabotage that culminates in a fatal outcome. It is the quiet erosion, the gradual surrender, the prolonged dance with danger that, when the music finally stops, finds the individual no longer standing.

Understanding these patterns requires a shift in perspective, moving beyond the binary of "will to live" versus "will to die" to acknowledge a more complex psychic economy. Here, the death drive, that Freudian concept representing an instinctual urge toward dissolution and a return to an inorganic state, finds its expression not in an overt act, but in a pervasive inclination towards compromising one's own survival. This is not a rational calculation of risk and reward, but an unconscious mandate, a deeply ingrained imperative to punish, escape, or simply cease to be, without the burden of conscious acknowledgment. The unconscious mind, in its enigmatic wisdom, may orchestrate its own demise through a series of seemingly disparate and even contradictory actions, all serving the ultimate, hidden purpose.

The spectrum of indirect self-destructiveness is remarkably broad. At one end lie behaviors that involve a blatant disregard for personal safety, a flirtation with peril that borders on the suicidal, yet is often rationalized as an assertion of freedom, a pursuit of thrills, or a testament to one's resilience. This can include extreme risk-taking in physical activities – mountaineering without adequate preparation, engaging in high-speed pursuits, or participating in dangerous stunts. While the individual might articulate a love for adrenaline or a desire to push boundaries, the unconscious subtext is often a testing of fate, a dare to the universe, or an unconscious belief that survival is ultimately not worth the effort. The thrill derived from such activities can be seen as a temporary anesthetic, a potent distraction from deeper existential anxieties or unbearable emotional burdens. When the inevitable accident occurs, it is framed as a tragic miscalculation, a cruel twist of fate, rather than the culmination of a deeply ingrained self-destructive pattern.

Consider the life of an individual who habitually engages in a series of near-fatal car accidents. Each incident is explained away by external factors: poor road conditions, other drivers' negligence, a moment of inattention. Yet, upon closer inspection, a pattern emerges: a history of reckless driving, a disregard for safety regulations, and a seemingly insatiable appetite for putting oneself in harm's way. The unconscious motivation here is not necessarily to end one's life, but perhaps to feel intensely alive, to punish oneself for perceived transgressions, or to elicit a dramatic, attention-grabbing reaction from the external world that acknowledges their suffering or their existence in a way that passive living cannot. The ultimate fatal accident, then, is not an unforeseen event but the logical conclusion of a life lived on the precipice, a surrender to the very risks that were courted with such fervor.

Further along this spectrum, we find chronic neglect of one's physical and mental health. This is not a direct embrace of death, but a slow, deliberate disengagement from the processes that sustain life. It encompasses everything from persistent unhealthy eating habits, refusal to seek medical attention for serious ailments, to the chronic abuse of substances in ways that are not overtly about immediate oblivion but about a gradual poisoning. The unconscious drive here is often rooted in a deep-seated belief of worthlessness, a conviction that one does not deserve to live or to be well. The individual may passively accept illness, refuse treatment, or engage in behaviors that systematically undermine their physical integrity, all while professing a desire to live. The death that ensues is often attributed to natural causes, the "inevitability of disease," but the underlying reality is a self-imposed abdication of the responsibility for one's own well-being.

This chronic neglect can be seen as a form of passive suicide, a quiet withholding of the essential elements required for survival. The body, denied adequate nourishment, rest, and medical care, begins to fail. The mind, starved of stimulation and positive engagement, can also deteriorate. The individual may feel a pervasive sense of lethargy, depression, and hopelessness, which further reinforces their passive stance. They become spectators in their own decline, observing their body's deterioration with a detached resignation. The unconscious message is clear: "I am not worth the effort of keeping alive." This is not a sudden, dramatic gesture, but a slow, agonizing process of self-annihilation, a prolonged farewell that leaves no room for intervention because the desire to be saved, at an unconscious level, is absent.

Consider the individual with a chronic, untreated illness who actively sabotages any attempts at medical intervention. They may miss appointments, fail to take prescribed medication, or even dismiss dire prognoses with a shrug. Their conscious narrative might revolve around a fear of doctors, a distrust of Western medicine, or a belief in natural remedies that are demonstrably ineffective. However, the unconscious reality is often a desire to punish themselves for past perceived failings, or a deep-seated belief that suffering is their rightful due. The illness, rather than being a source of fear, becomes a perverse form of validation, a tangible representation of their internal suffering. When the illness finally claims their life, it is mourned as a tragedy, but the groundwork for that tragedy was laid years prior through a consistent pattern of self-neglect.

Another facet of indirect self-destructiveness lies in the realm of self-sabotage in relationships and careers. This is not a direct impulse toward death, but a pattern of behavior that systematically undermines one's ability to thrive, to connect, and to find meaning. It involves creating chaos, picking fights, alienating loved ones, and making poor professional choices that lead to professional ruin. While the individual may express confusion and frustration at their repeated failures, the unconscious motivation often stems from a fear of success, a deep-seated belief that they do not deserve happiness or stability, or an unconscious attempt to recreate familiar patterns of abandonment or conflict learned in childhood. The ultimate outcome of such patterns can be profound isolation, despair, and a loss of purpose, which can then pave the way for more direct forms of self-destructive behavior, or a general decline that leads to premature death.

The individual who, on the cusp of a significant career promotion or a deeply fulfilling relationship, inexplicably torpedoes it through their own actions—perhaps by revealing a hidden insecurity, picking a fight, or engaging in reckless behavior—is a prime example. Their conscious lamentations of bad luck or unfair circumstances often mask an unconscious fear of intimacy, success, or change. The known misery of self-sabotage becomes preferable to the unknown territory of happiness and fulfillment. This constant oscillation between potential success and inevitable failure can lead to a pervasive sense of hopelessness and existential despair, which can, in turn, diminish one's will to live and make one more vulnerable to accidents or illnesses. The unraveling of one's life, piece by piece, can be just as lethal as a single, decisive act.

The seductive nature of indirect self-destructiveness lies in its plausible deniability. Unlike overt suicide, which leaves little room for interpretation, these behaviors can be attributed to a myriad of external factors, personal failings, or unfortunate circumstances. This allows the unconscious death drive to operate with a degree of stealth, shielded from conscious awareness and external intervention. The individual can continue to deny any death wish, maintaining a facade of normalcy or even resilience, while their actions systematically dismantle their life. This makes identification and intervention incredibly challenging, as the individual may not recognize their own trajectory towards destruction and may resist any attempts to alter their course, perceiving them as external impositions rather than necessary salvations.

The "aesthetic" of suicide without suicide is not one of dramatic finality, but of gradual decay, of a slow unraveling. It is the aesthetic of the worn-out shoe, the neglected garden, the decaying building. There is a morbid beauty in the slow surrender, a quiet resignation that can be profoundly disturbing. It speaks to a deep-seated weariness with existence, a longing for peace that is achieved not through struggle and triumph, but through a relinquishing of the fight. The unconscious mind, in its infinite capacity for self-deception and self-punishment, finds a way to orchestrate an end that is both complete and, to the outside observer, seemingly accidental. It is the ultimate act of self-negation, a whispered farewell rather than a shouted declaration.

The philosopher Albert Camus, in his exploration of the absurd, touches upon this pervasive human tendency towards a kind of passive surrender. While he argues against suicide as a response to the meaninglessness of existence, he acknowledges the allure of simply ceasing to engage. This echoes the unconscious drive behind indirect self-destructiveness—a profound weariness with the demands of life, a desire to opt out of the struggle without the burden of conscious intent. The unconscious seeks an end, but it finds a more palatable, less confrontational route than the direct, active pursuit of death. It opts for a slow fading, a gradual withdrawal, a systematic dismantling of the self that ultimately achieves the same result.

Furthermore, the role of addiction, while a distinct category of self-destruction, often overlaps with indirect self-destructiveness. The chronic substance abuser, particularly one whose usage is not aimed at immediate oblivion but at numbing pain or escaping reality, engages in behaviors that steadily erode their health, relationships, and opportunities. While the individual may express a desire to quit, their continued use, often accompanied by a host of self-defeating behaviors, demonstrates an unconscious resistance to recovery. The addiction becomes a self-perpetuating cycle of destruction, a slow-motion train wreck that, even when the individual consciously wishes for a different outcome, continues its inexorable march towards a fatal conclusion. The substance becomes a proxy for death, a constant companion in the slow process of self-undoing.

The unconscious self-punishment that often underpins these patterns is particularly potent. For individuals who carry deep-seated guilt or shame, their own destruction can feel like a just consequence. They may unconsciously believe that they are unworthy of happiness, love, or a long life, and thus engineer situations that lead to their downfall. This self-punishment can manifest in a myriad of ways, from reckless endangerment to the chronic neglect of basic self-care. The external world, in these instances, becomes a stage for the enactment of an internal drama of guilt and retribution. The death that results is not merely an accident, but the fulfillment of an unconscious sentencing.

The exploration of "suicide without suicide" compels us to look beyond the overt act and to scrutinize the subtle currents of self-destruction that run beneath the surface of everyday life. It calls for a deeper understanding of the unconscious motivations that drive individuals to compromise their own well-being, to flirt with danger, and to passively surrender to forces that lead to their demise. It is a recognition that the death drive, that fundamental impulse toward dissolution, can find expression in a thousand quiet ways, ultimately leading to an end that is as absolute as any overt act, yet far more shrouded in ambiguity and denial. This understanding is crucial, not only for theoretical insight but for the development of more nuanced and effective therapeutic approaches to individuals who are, in essence, slowly and unconsciously killing themselves.

The siren song of the precipice, the exhilaration that blooms on the edge of oblivion—these are not merely expressions of a thirst for adventure. When risk-taking morphs into a chronic, pervasive pattern, it can betray a more profound, unconscious negotiation with the very forces of dissolution. Here, the individual does not consciously seek an end, but rather engages in a seductive dance with the possibility of it, a ritualistic testing of the boundaries of existence that, in its intensity, carries the implicit promise of annihilation. This is not about a rational assessment of odds; it is about a psychic imperative that finds expression through the extreme.

Consider the allure of extreme sports—the free climber scaling sheer rock faces with nary a rope, the wingsuit flyer plummeting through mountain canyons, the surfer challenging colossal waves. The conscious narrative is often one of mastery, of pushing human limits, of experiencing life in its most unadulterated, visceral form. Yet, beneath this veneer of intrepid spirit, a potent unconscious fantasy can be at play. It is the fantasy of confronting the ultimate arbiter, of engaging in a direct dialogue with fate. Each successful ascent, each daring dive, is not just an affirmation of skill but a temporary reprieve, a testament to the individual's perceived invincibility. But the precariousness, the ever-present specter of a fatal error, is precisely the point. It is in the stark confrontation with potential death that a perverse sense of vitality is often unearthed, a fleeting but potent antidote to a perceived emptiness or meaninglessness in everyday life. The body, pushed to its absolute physical and psychological limits, becomes a vessel for an amplified consciousness, a momentary triumph over the ennui that may otherwise gnaw at the soul.

This is not the same as simply enjoying a thrill. The chronic risk-taker exhibits a compulsive quality, a need to escalate, to constantly seek out situations that offer a higher degree of peril. Each successful feat, rather than satisfying, often serves only to fuel the desire for more extreme challenges. This escalation can be understood as a form of unconscious suicide, not in the sense of a deliberate desire to die, but as a self-engineered trajectory towards a statistically probable end. The individual is, in essence, constructing a life where the probability of accidental death is significantly amplified. They are not actively choosing the moment of cessation, but are setting the stage for it with an almost methodical precision, albeit an unconscious one. The near-misses become proof of their prowess, reinforcing the belief that they can indeed cheat death, further emboldening them to flirt with it again. When the inevitable accident occurs, it is often framed as a tragic misfortune, a consequence of an unforgiving environment or a split-second miscalculation, rather than the culmination of a life lived on the razor's edge, a life where such an outcome was not just possible, but probable.

The unconscious fantasy here can be multifaceted. For some, it might be a desperate attempt to feel alive in a world that feels muted or unreal. The sheer intensity of facing death provides a powerful, albeit temporary, jolt of existence. For others, it may be a form of rebellion against perceived limitations, whether imposed by society, biology, or their own internal constraints. By courting danger, they assert a radical freedom, a defiance of the natural order of things. Yet, this defiance is often tinged with a self-destructive hue. The pursuit of this heightened state of being necessitates proximity to its antithesis, and the unconscious mind, perhaps weary of the struggle for meaningful existence or burdened by unbearable guilt or shame, may find in this proximity a perverse form of peace.

Consider the individual who pursues a career in inherently dangerous professions, such as a firefighter, a deep-sea diver, or a soldier in a combat zone. While the conscious motivations are often altruistic or driven by a sense of duty, the constant immersion in life-threatening situations can, over time, exert a profound psychological toll. If the individual fails to adequately process the trauma and stress associated with their work, or if they possess an underlying predisposition towards self-neglect, these occupations can become vehicles for unconscious self-destruction. The routine exposure to danger can desensitize them, leading to a gradual erosion of caution. What was once a source of immense anxiety can become normalized, and the individual may find themselves unconsciously seeking out or accepting situations with an elevated risk, not out of recklessness, but as a consequence of a desensitized relationship with peril. The constant proximity to death, without adequate psychological containment, can subtly shift the individual's relationship with their own mortality, making them more susceptible to unconscious fatalism. They may not consciously wish for death, but their lived experience, the constant immersion in dangerous scenarios, can render them less vigilant about their own preservation. The line between heroism and self-annihilation becomes blurred, and the unconscious mind may find a peculiar solace in the familiar, albeit deadly, embrace of peril.

Reckless driving is another potent manifestation of this phenomenon. The driver who habitually exceeds speed limits, weaves through traffic, and engages in dangerous maneuvers is not necessarily aiming for a suicidal outcome. However, their actions demonstrably increase the probability of a fatal accident. The conscious rationale might be a desire for control, a need to feel powerful, or a simple impatience. But the unconscious undercurrent can be a potent cocktail of impulsivity, a disregard for consequences, and a testing of fate. Each journey becomes a gamble, a series of close calls that, for the unconscious mind, might serve to reinforce a sense of invincibility or, conversely, to punish oneself for perceived transgressions through the ever-present threat of annihilation. The thrill derived from narrowly avoiding a collision is a potent, albeit dangerous, form of emotional regulation. The car becomes an extension of the self, and its reckless operation a symbolic enactment of the driver's internal turmoil. When the inevitable crash occurs, it is often attributed to a momentary lapse in judgment, a mechanical failure, or the actions of another driver, obscuring the chronic pattern of self-endangerment that paved the way for the tragedy. The "accident" becomes the ultimate expression of a life lived on the brink, where the unconscious drive towards dissolution finds its physical manifestation.

The unconscious fantasy of "testing fate" is particularly compelling in this context. It is as if the individual is challenging the universe, daring it to deliver the ultimate blow. Each successful evasion of disaster is interpreted as a victory, a testament to their strength or their destiny. This can create a dangerous feedback loop, where the individual becomes increasingly convinced of their own immunity, leading them to take ever greater risks. The thrill is not just in the danger itself, but in the perceived triumph over it. This can be seen as a form of unconscious grandiosity, a narcissistic defense against feelings of helplessness or inadequacy. By confronting death and surviving, the individual seeks to affirm their own significance and power. However, this game of cosmic roulette cannot continue indefinitely. The universe, in its indifferent way, eventually collects its due, and the individual who has spent their life flirting with oblivion finds themselves finally unable to evade its grasp. The risk-taker, in their relentless pursuit of extreme sensation, may be unconsciously seeking not just to feel alive, but to find a dramatic, albeit fatal, resolution to their existential anxieties.

The concept of "vitality through peril" also plays a crucial role. For individuals who feel a profound sense of ennui, a pervasive lack of aliveness, the extreme risk can be a potent, albeit temporary, elixir. It injects a surge of adrenaline, a heightened awareness, a raw connection to the primal forces of life and death that is absent in their everyday existence. This is not a conscious choice to die, but a desperate, unconscious strategy to

feel alive by skirting the edge of not-being. The danger itself becomes a source of stimulation, a way to escape the perceived grayness of life. The closer they come to death, the more intensely they feel their own existence. This creates a dependency, where increasingly extreme situations are needed to achieve the same level of heightened sensation. The unconscious mind, in its relentless pursuit of this artificial vitality, can lead the individual down a path where the risks become unsustainable, and the ultimate price is paid not out of a desire for death, but out of a desperate, unconscious yearning for intense life.

This phenomenon is not limited to overt acts of physical danger. It can also manifest in more subtle ways, such as engaging in deeply toxic relationships, pursuing self-destructive career paths despite clear evidence of failure, or habitually putting oneself in emotionally compromising situations. While these may not carry the immediate threat of physical demise, they represent a consistent pattern of self-sabotage that can lead to profound despair, isolation, and a significant erosion of one's overall well-being, ultimately contributing to a premature end. The individual might unconsciously believe that they do not deserve happiness or stability, and thus gravitate towards situations that confirm these deeply held negative beliefs. The unconscious risk is not to life itself, but to the possibility of a fulfilling and meaningful existence. When this possibility is systematically dismantled, the individual is left with a life devoid of purpose and connection, a state that can be equally inimical to their long-term survival.

The psychological mechanism at play is often rooted in a complex interplay of defense mechanisms and unconscious beliefs. The individual might be using risk-taking as a way to avoid confronting deeper emotional pain, to distract themselves from unresolved trauma, or to punish themselves for perceived failings. The thrill and danger serve as a potent anesthetic, numbing the raw edges of their emotional reality. However, this anesthetic effect is fleeting, and the underlying pain and guilt remain, often driving the individual to seek even more extreme forms of stimulation. The unconscious mind, in its often paradoxical logic, can find a perverse comfort in the familiar cycle of danger and near-disaster, even as it leads towards an ultimate, irreversible conclusion. The individual is caught in a self-perpetuating loop, where the means of feeling alive become the very things that are slowly, systematically leading them towards their end.

The language of "testing fate" is symbolic of a deeper unconscious narrative. It speaks to a desire to confront the ultimate power, to gauge one's own strength against the forces that govern existence.

This can stem from a profound sense of powerlessness in other areas of life. By deliberately placing oneself in situations where life and death hang in the balance, the individual gains a sense of agency, however illusory. They are not passively subject to the whims of fate; they are actively engaging with it, attempting to control the uncontrollable. This can be a desperate attempt to reclaim a sense of self in the face of overwhelming external or internal pressures. However, this control is ultimately an illusion. The forces of chance and physics are indifferent to the individual's intentions, and the gamble with fate is a one-sided affair. The "victory" of surviving a dangerous situation is temporary, a brief reprieve before the next, perhaps final, encounter.

The concept of "suicide without suicide" provides a crucial lens through which to understand these behaviors. It moves beyond the simplistic dichotomy of wanting to live versus wanting to die, acknowledging a more nuanced and complex psychic landscape. Here, the death drive, that Freudian impulse towards dissolution, is not expressed through a direct, intentional act. Instead, it manifests indirectly, through a series of choices and behaviors that, while not overtly aimed at self-annihilation, inexorably lead towards it. Risk-taking, in its extreme and chronic forms, becomes a potent conduit for this unconscious imperative. It is a slow, deliberate, and often exhilarating march towards an end that is not consciously willed, but unconsciously orchestrated, a testament to the intricate and often perilous ways in which the human psyche navigates its own demise. The individual is not seeking an end, but is so consumed by the process of

not-ending—by the sheer effort of feeling intensely alive through peril—that they paradoxically engineer their own cessation. The act of survival becomes so consuming, so demanding of extreme circumstances, that it ultimately consumes the individual.

The body, often perceived as a mere vessel for the conscious mind, can instead become the ultimate theatre for psychic drama, a silent and devastating stage upon which unconscious conflicts play out their destructive denouement. When the direct, overt act of suicide is eschewed, the body itself can be enlisted in a slow, insidious campaign of self-annihilation. This is the realm of psychosomatic collapse, where the edifice of physical health is systematically undermined by the unseen forces of the psyche. Unresolved psychic pain, the gnawing burden of unexpressed grief, profound stress that has found no outlet, and a pervasive, often unconscious, form of self-neglect can coalesce, manifesting not as an acute crisis, but as a chronic, debilitating illness. The body, in this scenario, is not merely a passive recipient of psychic distress; it becomes an active participant, a battleground where the individual's own destructive impulses are enacted, leading to incapacitation and, ultimately, to a gradual and often tragic cessation of life. This is a profound testament to the intimate, unbreakable connection between our mental and physical states, a stark illustration of how psychic suffering can carve a deadly physical toll, an indirect, yet equally potent, pathway to an end.

Consider the chronic patient, their existence defined by a constellation of ailments that defy easy diagnosis or definitive cure. While the conscious mind may articulate a desire for health, for a return to vitality, the underlying psychic landscape may harbor a deeply buried, unconscious narrative of deserving illness, of being inherently flawed, or even of being fundamentally undeserving of a long and flourishing life. This narrative can be born from a myriad of sources: early childhood trauma that imprinted a sense of worthlessness, profound guilt over perceived transgressions, or the internalized voices of critical or neglectful caregivers. When these deeply entrenched beliefs remain unexamined and unaddressed, they can exert a relentless pressure on the organism. The body, in its earnest attempt to signal distress, begins to manifest these internal wounds. This is not a conscious choice to become ill; rather, it is a tragic consequence of the psyche's desperate, albeit misguided, attempt to make the invisible suffering visible, to give form to the formless despair. The symptoms themselves – chronic pain, debilitating fatigue, autoimmune disorders, intractable digestive issues – become the language of this hidden agony, the body's protest against an unbearable psychic reality.

The concept of "bodily betrayal" takes on a particular poignancy here. It is as if the body, the very instrument of our survival and experience in the world, turns against its inhabitant. Yet, from a psychoanalytic perspective, this betrayal is not arbitrary. It is a consequence, an echo of a deeper, more fundamental betrayal that has occurred within the psychic realm. This could be a betrayal of one's own needs and desires, a renunciation of joy and fulfillment due to internalized prohibitions, or a feeling of being fundamentally betrayed by life itself, by circumstances or by other individuals. When these feelings are too overwhelming to be consciously processed, they are often displaced, projected onto the physical self. The illness becomes, in a sense, an externalization of the internal damage, a way of separating the self from the unbearable pain by lodging it within the physical form. The individual may feel that their body has failed them, but in truth, it is acting out the script written by the unconscious mind, a script of disintegration and collapse.

The cumulative effect of chronic stress, often a precursor to psychosomatic illness, cannot be overstated. When the stress response system, designed for acute, short-term threats, is perpetually activated, it begins to wreak havoc on the body. Hormones like cortisol flood the system, suppressing immune function, increasing inflammation, and disrupting a multitude of physiological processes. While the external stressors might be tangible – a demanding job, financial hardship, difficult relationships – the internal amplification of these stressors, often fueled by anxiety, rumination, and a pervasive sense of helplessness, can be the most damaging. In the absence of effective coping mechanisms or the ability to disengage from the stressor, the body enters a state of chronic overdrive, depleting its resources and becoming increasingly vulnerable. This physiological erosion, driven by psychic strain, becomes a potent pathway towards collapse.

Consider the case of individuals who live with persistent, unexpressed rage or resentment. This emotional energy, denied conscious expression, does not simply dissipate. It can fester, becoming a corrosive force within the psyche and, by extension, within the body. The constant internal battle to suppress these powerful emotions can lead to muscular tension, headaches, digestive disturbances, and a heightened susceptibility to illness. The immune system may be compromised, making the individual more vulnerable to infections. Over time, this ongoing internal conflict can contribute to the development of more serious chronic conditions, such as cardiovascular disease, inflammatory bowel disease, or even certain types of cancer. The body, in its desperate attempt to manage the unmanageable emotional burden, begins to break down under the strain. This is not a conscious desire to become ill, but a tragic manifestation of suppressed emotional energy finding a destructive outlet.

The role of unconscious self-neglect is central to understanding psychosomatic collapse. This is not necessarily about overt acts of self-harm, but a more subtle, pervasive pattern of disregard for one's own well-being. It can manifest as a consistent pattern of poor diet, lack of sleep, avoidance of medical care, or an inability to set boundaries and protect oneself from harmful situations. These behaviors are often rooted in deeply ingrained beliefs about one's own worthlessness or a feeling that one does not deserve to be well or cared for. The individual may unconsciously feel that tending to their own needs is selfish or inappropriate, leading them to prioritize the needs of others or to simply neglect themselves entirely. This self-neglect creates fertile ground for illness to take root and flourish, as the body lacks the necessary resources and support to maintain its health and resilience.

Furthermore, the body can become a repository for collective or intergenerational trauma. When individuals carry the weight of unprocessed suffering from previous generations, or when they are exposed to pervasive societal stressors such as discrimination or poverty, their bodies can bear the brunt of this burden. Chronic stress, epigenetic changes, and a heightened sense of vulnerability can be passed down or acquired, predisposing individuals to illness. In such cases, the psychosomatic collapse is not solely an individual phenomenon but is deeply interwoven with broader social and historical contexts. The body's illness becomes a testament to a history of suffering, a silent scream against injustice, and a tragic, albeit indirect, culmination of a life lived under immense pressure.

The trajectory towards psychosomatic collapse is often characterized by a gradual erosion of vitality, a slow dimming of the life force. Unlike the acute crisis of a deliberate suicide attempt, here the process is more insidious. The individual might experience a series of minor ailments that gradually worsen, or a persistent, low-grade malaise that slowly saps their energy and will. Each illness, each flare-up of chronic pain, takes a further toll, both physically and psychologically. The individual may become increasingly isolated, their capacity for engagement with the world diminished by their physical suffering. This isolation, in turn, can exacerbate their psychic pain, creating a vicious cycle where illness breeds further distress, and distress fuels further illness.

The insidious nature of this process makes it particularly challenging to address. Because there is no overt act of intentional self-destruction, the underlying self-destructive dynamic can remain hidden, even from the individual themselves. Medical professionals may focus on treating the symptoms, without fully addressing the underlying psychic roots of the illness. Friends and family may offer support for the physical ailments, but may be unaware of the profound psychological suffering that is driving the disease. This lack of awareness can leave the individual trapped in a cycle of illness, with their unconscious drive towards dissolution going unrecognized and unaddressed.

The body, in its remarkable capacity to manifest our deepest psychological states, can become the ultimate canvas for a life lived in silent desperation. When the impulse towards an end cannot find direct expression, it can seep into the very fabric of our being, manifesting as chronic illness, debilitating pain, and a gradual loss of physical capacity. This psychosomatic collapse is a profound form of "suicide without suicide," a testament to the complex and often tragic ways in which the human psyche navigates its darkest impulses. It is a reminder that our minds and bodies are not separate entities, but are inextricably linked, and that psychic suffering, when left unaddressed, can indeed carve a deadly path towards oblivion. The body, in its silence, speaks volumes, revealing the hidden narratives of pain, despair, and the unconscious yearning for release that lie beneath the surface of our conscious lives. This journey, marked by bodily betrayal, is not one of aggression, but of an agonizing, slow surrender, a quiet capitulation to the weight of an unbearable inner world.

The following is the content of the subsection:

The shadow of self-destruction, when it veils the explicit act of suicide, can manifest in a life trajectory that, from an external vantage point, appears merely unfortunate, a series of poor decisions, or a confluence of bad luck. Yet, within the depths of the psyche, these unfolding events are often orchestrated by an unconscious imperative, a slow, deliberate dismantling of the self. This is the territory of what we might term "suicide without suicide," a process where the individual, driven by subterranean forces, effectively engineers their own demise without ever consciously contemplating or intending it. To illustrate this phenomenon, we turn to a clinical vignette, a composite sketch drawn from observed patterns, depicting a life unconsciously oriented towards its own premature conclusion. For the purposes of this discussion, we will refer to this individual as "Elias."

Elias's life, from his earliest recollections, was marked by a peculiar dissonance between outward potential and inward fulfillment. He possessed a keen intellect, a creative spark, and a capacity for deep empathy, qualities that should have served as fertile ground for a rich and rewarding existence. However, Elias was perpetually drawn to situations and relationships that, while initially appearing promising, ultimately led to his diminishment. It was as if an invisible hand guided him, time and again, towards the precipice, not with a violent push, but with a series of subtle nudges that gradually led him off course.

His early academic career, for instance, was a testament to this pattern. He excelled in his initial years, earning accolades and the admiration of his professors. Yet, as significant opportunities for advancement arose – prestigious internships, scholarship applications, thesis proposals that promised groundbreaking research – Elias would invariably falter. Not through a lack of capability, but through a seemingly inexplicable inertia. Deadlines would loom, and instead of diligently working, he would find himself engrossed in tangential, unproductive pursuits, or simply paralyzed by an overwhelming sense of anxiety that he could not articulate. The outcome was always the same: missed opportunities, a sense of profound disappointment, and a lingering feeling of inadequacy that he internalized as definitive proof of his own inherent flaws.

This pattern extended with striking regularity into his personal relationships. Elias possessed a deep yearning for connection, for love and intimacy. Yet, he seemed incapable of sustaining healthy, reciprocal bonds. He would often gravitate towards individuals who were emotionally unavailable, critical, or even overtly damaging. Initially, these relationships might have offered a semblance of validation, perhaps by Elias's attempts to "fix" or "save" his partner, a dynamic that unconsciously mirrored a deeper need to expiate some unarticulated guilt. However, these relationships inevitably became sources of immense emotional strain, leaving Elias depleted, heartbroken, and further convinced of his inability to attract or maintain genuine affection. The pattern was not one of actively seeking out abuse, but rather of an unconscious susceptibility to dynamics that, in their destructive arc, ultimately served to reinforce his negative self-perception. He would often describe these relationships with a bewildered detachment, as if a force beyond his control had steered him into these tumultuous waters.

A crucial element in Elias's self-sabotaging trajectory was his relationship with his own well-being. He frequently engaged in behaviors that were detrimental to his physical and mental health, not out of ignorance, but as if by some internal dictate. He would neglect crucial medical advice, undereating when stressed, overindulging in substances that offered temporary solace but long-term harm, and consistently deprioritizing rest and self-care. These were not acts of overt self-harm, but a chronic, low-grade erosion of his vitality. It was as if his body, the very instrument of his being in the world, was being systematically neglected, left vulnerable to the ravages of stress and poor health, not through an active assault, but through a profound and persistent omission of care.

The unconscious drivers behind Elias's life trajectory are complex and deeply rooted. One can hypothesize a powerful undercurrent of guilt, perhaps stemming from early life experiences or internalized prohibitions. This guilt might manifest as a deeply held, albeit unconscious, belief that he did not deserve happiness, success, or even a long life. Consequently, every opportunity for advancement, every potential for joy, would be unconsciously perceived as a threat to this deeply ingrained sense of deserved punishment. By unconsciously engineering his own failures and suffering, Elias was, in essence, fulfilling an unconscious sentence, a form of self-imposed penance.

Another possible contributing factor could be a profound sense of unworthiness. If, from an early age, an individual internalizes the message that they are fundamentally flawed, inadequate, or unlovable, they may unconsciously seek to validate these beliefs through their life experiences. Elias's repeated failures, his tumultuous relationships, and his neglect of his own well-being served as constant, albeit agonizing, affirmations of his perceived inadequacy. Each setback reinforced the internal narrative: "See? I told you you weren't good enough." This self-reinforcing cycle creates a powerful inertia, making it exceedingly difficult to break free from destructive patterns, as the very act of seeking a different outcome would challenge the foundational beliefs upon which the individual's sense of self is precariously built.

There is also the possibility of a pervasive, unconscious fear of success or of authentic connection. Success can be terrifying for those who feel they do not deserve it, as it brings with it increased visibility, heightened expectations, and the potential for greater loss. Similarly, genuine intimacy can be frightening for individuals who have learned to associate vulnerability with pain or betrayal. In such cases, self-sabotage becomes a defense mechanism, a way of preemptively dismantling any potential for deep connection or significant achievement before it can be fully realized and thus, potentially, be lost. By keeping himself at a safe distance from genuine fulfillment, Elias might have been unconsciously protecting himself from a deeper, more unbearable pain.

The cumulative effect of Elias's life trajectory was a gradual but inexorable decline. His physical health deteriorated, his social network dwindled, and his spirit became increasingly despondent. He would often express a vague sense of dissatisfaction, a feeling that life had dealt him a poor hand, without ever recognizing the extent to which he had unconsciously been the architect of his own misfortunes. The ultimate outcome, when it arrived, was not a dramatic suicide, but a fatal illness exacerbated by years of neglect and stress, or perhaps a fatal accident that occurred during a period of profound emotional distress and impaired judgment. The end was not a sharp, decisive break, but a slow, drawn-out unraveling, a life that had been unconsciously unspooled thread by thread.

This case of Elias vividly illustrates the concept of "suicide without suicide." It is a testament to the profound power of unconscious forces to shape our lives, guiding us towards destruction even in the absence of conscious intent. His story underscores the idea that the drive towards dissolution can manifest not only in a single, overt act, but in a lifelong pattern of self-defeat, a gradual surrender to the forces that undermine our well-being. It is a tragic reminder that the most formidable enemy can reside not in the external world, but within the unexplored depths of our own psyche. The body, in this context, becomes not the target of an explicit act of violence, but a neglected garden, left untended and vulnerable, slowly succumbing to the weeds of despair and the harshness of the elements, its eventual collapse an inevitable consequence of prolonged, unconscious neglect. The story of Elias is a somber elegy for a life unconsciously surrendered, a life where the silence of the unconscious held a louder, more destructive voice than any spoken plea for help. His was a slow, deliberate drift away from the shores of life, a journey undertaken without the compass of conscious intent, yet with an undeniable, albeit tragic, destination.

The insidious nature of such self-sabotaging life trajectories lies in their capacity to disguise their destructive core behind a facade of misfortune or poor judgment. To the outside observer, Elias's life might appear as a series of unfortunate events, a symphony of missed chances and bad luck. This external perception is often mirrored internally, with the individual themselves struggling to identify the root cause of their persistent unhappiness and their inability to achieve their potential. They may feel like a victim of circumstance, lamenting the unfairness of life, while remaining oblivious to the unconscious scripts that are being enacted through their choices and behaviors. This lack of self-awareness is not a sign of intellectual deficiency, but rather a testament to the sheer power of unconscious dynamics to operate beneath the surface of conscious awareness, shaping our reality in profound and often devastating ways.

Consider the concept of "learned helplessness," a psychological state where an individual, after experiencing repeated uncontrollable aversive events, ceases to attempt to escape or improve their situation, even when opportunities to do so become available. In Elias's case, his repeated failures in academics and relationships could have fostered such a learned helplessness. Each time he attempted to forge a path towards success or meaningful connection and was met with disappointment or destruction, his internal locus of control would diminish. He might have begun to believe, at an unconscious level, that his efforts were futile, that external forces were perpetually arrayed against him, or that he was simply incapable of influencing the trajectory of his own life. This belief system, once entrenched, becomes a powerful self-fulfilling prophecy, leading to a cessation of genuine effort and an embrace of passivity, which, in turn, further perpetuates the cycle of failure and despair.

The relational aspect of this self-sabotage is particularly poignant. When individuals like Elias are drawn to unhealthy relationships, they may not consciously recognize the patterns at play. They might be attracted to the intensity of drama, the perceived challenge of "saving" someone, or the familiar echoes of early relational wounds. Unconsciously, these relationships might serve to keep them occupied, to drain their emotional and psychic energy, thereby preventing them from focusing on their own development, their own potential for happiness, or their own need for self-care. The drama of a tumultuous relationship can act as a powerful distraction from the deeper, more painful work of self-exploration and healing. It provides a readily available, albeit destructive, outlet for their emotional turmoil, preventing that energy from being channeled into more constructive pursuits.

Furthermore, the very act of repeatedly choosing suboptimal paths can subtly erode an individual's sense of agency and self-efficacy. If one consistently finds themselves in situations where their efforts are thwarted or their choices lead to negative outcomes, their belief in their ability to make effective decisions is undermined. This can lead to a pervasive sense of doubt and indecisiveness, making it even more challenging to break free from the established patterns. The unconscious drive for self-destruction, in this regard, can be seen as a cruel irony: by attempting to avoid perceived threats or fulfill unconscious needs, the individual inadvertently paralyzes their capacity to make choices that would lead to genuine well-being and fulfillment.

The concept of the "shadow" in Jungian psychology is also highly relevant here. The shadow represents the repressed, unconscious aspects of the personality, the parts we deem unacceptable and deny. In cases of self-sabotage, the shadow can become particularly potent. Unacknowledged aspects of aggression, dependency, or a profound sense of worthlessness can be projected onto external circumstances or relationships, creating a distorted perception of reality. Elias might have been unconsciously acting out his own unacknowledged destructive impulses, projecting them onto the situations and people he encountered. His external world, in this sense, becomes a mirror reflecting the disowned parts of his psyche, a stage upon which his internal dramas are played out with devastating consequences.

The physical manifestations of this unconscious self-destruction, as alluded to in the previous context, are not mere coincidences. The chronic stress that accompanies a life of perpetual struggle and disappointment takes a significant toll on the body. The immune system is compromised, making individuals more susceptible to illness. Inflammation, a key factor in many chronic diseases, can become pervasive. Digestive issues, chronic pain, fatigue, and sleep disturbances are common companions to chronic psychological distress. Elias's physical ailments, when viewed through this lens, are not simply the result of poor lifestyle choices, but are the somatic expressions of a deeper, unaddressed psychic pain. His body, in its own way, is screaming for help, signaling the immense burden that his unconscious conflicts are imposing upon his physical being.

The notion of "punishment" as an unconscious motivator is a recurring theme in understanding such trajectories. If an individual harbors deep-seated guilt or a belief that they are inherently bad or deserving of suffering, then any success or happiness they experience might feel alien, undeserving, and ultimately anxiety-provoking. The unconscious mind, in its effort to restore a sense of psychic equilibrium – albeit a distorted one – may then engineer situations that lead to failure or suffering, thereby reaffirming the individual's core beliefs about themselves. This is a tragic paradox: the very experiences that would lead a healthy individual to seek joy and fulfillment become, for the self-sabotager, triggers for seeking out the familiar pain of their perceived deserved retribution.

The journey of Elias, as a representative figure, highlights the profound ethical and therapeutic challenges posed by "suicide without suicide." How does one intervene when the very mechanisms of self-destruction are cloaked in unconscious intent and disguised as misfortune? Traditional approaches to suicide prevention, focused on identifying overt suicidal ideation and intent, may be insufficient here. The task requires a deeper dive into the unconscious, an exploration of the hidden narratives that guide an individual's life choices, and a patient, compassionate process of helping the individual to excavate and reframe those deeply held beliefs that are leading them towards their own demise. It necessitates an understanding that the most insidious forms of self-destruction are often not acts of sudden violence, but the slow, relentless erosion of a life, guided by unseen forces from within. The body, in its silent suffering, becomes the ultimate witness to this internal war, its gradual decline a poignant testament to a life unconsciously dedicated to its own undoing. The individual, in their bewilderment, may lament their fate, unaware that the script has been written, and is being enacted, by the hidden architects of their own destiny.

The concept of "suicide without suicide," as illuminated by the case of Elias, leads us to a deeper contemplation of its underlying mechanisms. Beyond the immediate manifestations of self-sabotage, we encounter a more profound psychological phenomenon: an unconscious negotiation with death itself. This is not a conscious contemplation of mortality, but rather a complex, often unspoken pact, a subterranean dialogue with annihilation that shapes a life's trajectory towards its own premature conclusion. It is as if the individual, driven by forces beyond their awareness, engages in a subtle, protracted bargaining with the ultimate cessation of being, seeking a form of control over an experience that is inherently uncontrollable.

This negotiation can take myriad forms, each reflecting a distinct facet of the individual's relationship with their own mortality. For some, it manifests as a series of calculated risks, a deliberate courting of danger that, while not overtly suicidal, pushes the boundaries of survival. Think of individuals who repeatedly engage in high-risk behaviors without adequate precautions, perhaps driving recklessly, participating in extreme sports with insufficient training, or even venturing into dangerous environments without proper preparation. From an external perspective, these actions might be dismissed as thrill-seeking, recklessness, or simply poor judgment. However, from a psychoanalytic viewpoint, they can be interpreted as an unconscious attempt to wrest agency from a life that feels otherwise powerless. By choosing the circumstances of potential peril, the individual is, in a peculiar way, dictating terms to death, attempting to impose a sense of order and control on the chaotic and terrifying unknown. It is a defiant posture, a whispered challenge: "If I am to face oblivion, I will do so on my own terms, by my own choosing."

Conversely, this unconscious negotiation can also manifest as a profound surrender, a slow, voluntary drift towards a state of passive succumbing. This is less about actively seeking danger and more about passively allowing oneself to be overtaken by it. It is the relinquishing of the will to live, not through an act of violent self-termination, but through a gradual abdication of responsibility for one's own well-being. This resonates deeply with the neglect observed in Elias's life. His consistent disregard for his physical health, his failure to seek medical attention, his poor dietary habits, and his chronic sleep deprivation are not merely passive lifestyle choices; they can be seen as a subtle yet persistent yielding to the forces of decay. It is an unconscious agreement that the effort of maintaining life is too burdensome, too fraught with the potential for disappointment and pain. In this scenario, death is not a vanquished foe, but a welcome release, an inevitable end to a struggle that the individual has, at an unconscious level, already conceded. This is a form of resignation, an unspoken dialogue that whispers, "I am tired. Let it be."

The internal landscape of this negotiation is often populated by complex fantasies. These are not conscious daydreams but unconscious imaginings that fuel the individual's trajectory. One such fantasy might be that of a heroic or tragic, albeit silent, martyrdom. The individual, unconsciously believing themselves to be fundamentally flawed or undeserving of a conventional life, may harbor a hidden desire to make a profound, albeit self-destructive, statement. This statement could be directed towards perceived betrayers, negligent figures from their past, or even an indifferent universe. The "suicide without suicide" becomes a grand, tragic gesture, a posthumous vindication of their suffering, a way of saying, "See what you have done?" The prolonged suffering and eventual demise are, in this unconscious narrative, the ultimate testament to their victimhood. The death, when it comes, is not just an end, but a climactic event that validates a lifetime of unspoken pain and perceived injustice.

Another potent fantasy can be one of reunion or merging with a lost object or a desired state of being. For individuals who have experienced profound loss or who feel deeply disconnected, the idea of oblivion might unconsciously represent a return to a primal state of oneness, a dissolution back into the undifferentiated whole. This can be particularly compelling for those who feel alienated from the world, for whom existence is a constant experience of separation and loneliness. Death, in this context, is not an annihilation but a homecoming, a dissolution of the lonely ego into a larger, more comforting entity. The self-neglect and risk-taking behaviors can be seen as unconscious attempts to accelerate this perceived reunion, to shed the burdensome shell of the individual self and merge with something more profound and all-encompassing. It is a desire to cease to be a separate, suffering entity and to become one with the universe, or with a beloved, lost figure.

The paradox of this unconscious negotiation lies in its attempt to exert control over an inherently uncontrollable event. By engaging in self-destructive behaviors, the individual is, in a twisted way, trying to manage their encounter with mortality. They are not passively awaiting death; they are actively, albeit unconsciously, participating in its approach. This participation can be a source of a perverse sense of power in lives that otherwise feel devoid of agency. The individual may feel a sense of heightened aliveness in moments of extreme risk, a fleeting but intense sensation of being fully present and in control, even as they are on a path towards self-annihilation. This is the intoxicating allure of the precipice – the illusion of mastery over the ultimate unknown.

Furthermore, this unconscious negotiation often involves a complex dance with annihilation itself. It is not necessarily a wish for oblivion, but a deep, often unacknowledged, fascination with the void. The "suicide without suicide" can be a way of skirting the edges of non-being, of drawing near to the abyss without fully succumbing. This proximity can be both terrifying and strangely exhilarating, a testament to the human psyche's complex relationship with its own limits. It is as if the individual is testing the boundaries of existence, pushing themselves closer and closer to the edge, not necessarily to jump, but to feel the sensation of being on the brink, to experience the thrill of proximity to the ultimate release from the burdens of life.

This negotiation is also intimately tied to the individual's capacity for hope and their belief in the possibility of a different future. When hope has been systematically eroded, when the belief in a better tomorrow has been extinguished, the unconscious mind may begin to explore alternatives to continued existence. The "suicide without suicide" becomes a way of enacting this loss of hope, of demonstrating, through life choices, the absence of a future worth striving for. The consistent pattern of failure, the inability to sustain positive relationships, and the neglect of one's own well-being are all, in essence, a living testament to the absence of hope. The individual, in their unconscious dealings with death, is signaling the cessation of their engagement with life's possibilities.

The challenge for therapeutic intervention in these cases is immense. How does one approach an individual who is engaged in a silent, unconscious negotiation with death? The overt suicidal patient presents with a clear and present danger that demands immediate attention. However, the individual who is slowly, imperceptibly dismantling their own life requires a different approach, one that is sensitive to the subtle language of the unconscious. It necessitates helping the individual to become aware of the unconscious pact they have made, to understand the underlying fantasies and fears that drive their self-destructive trajectory. It involves illuminating the subtle ways in which they have been bargaining with mortality, and gently encouraging them to renegotiate the terms of their existence, to find a new dialogue with life rather than with death.

This process requires patience and a deep understanding of the symbolic language of the psyche. The seemingly irrational choices, the repeated misfortunes, and the profound neglect are not simply random occurrences. They are often the outward manifestations of an internal, unconscious drama, a complex negotiation with the profound mystery of mortality. By bringing these unconscious processes into the light of awareness, it becomes possible to disrupt the self-destructive cycle and to foster a renewed engagement with the possibilities of life. The ultimate aim is not to banish the contemplation of death, but to transform the unconscious negotiation with it into a conscious dialogue, one that allows for a more integrated and life-affirming experience of one's own finitude. The body, in this context, is not merely a vessel to be neglected or a stage for risk-taking, but a living testament to the ongoing, often silent, internal negotiations that define our relationship with existence and its inevitable end. The individual, in their complex dance with mortality, is attempting to script their own ending, even if that script is written in the invisible ink of unconscious desires and fears. This negotiation, though often veiled, reveals the profound human drive to assert some measure of control over that which seems most uncontrollable, to find meaning, or at least agency, in the face of ultimate cessation.

Chapter 7: Childhood Narratives and the Death Script

The specter of our ultimate end, the cessation of being that we call death, is not a concept that arrives fully formed in the adult psyche. Rather, it is a shadow that lengthens gradually, cast from the earliest moments of our existence. The psychic architecture that will eventually house our understanding, or more accurately, our unconscious negotiation with mortality, begins to take shape in the crucible of infancy and early childhood. Here, amidst the nascent stirrings of consciousness, the foundational templates for our relationship with loss and separation are etched, laying the groundwork for what might be termed the 'fantasmatic signature' of death. These initial encounters, often fraught with primal terror and profound vulnerability, become the unconscious blueprints that will, in subtle and far-reaching ways, inform how we ultimately perceive and, in a deeply symbolic sense, 'play out' our own endings.

Central to this early psychic formation are the experiences of separation and loss. For the infant, the primary caregiver – typically the mother – represents the entire universe, the source of sustenance, comfort, and safety. The temporary absence of this figure, even for a short duration, can be experienced as an existential threat, a terrifying glimpse into a world devoid of connection and meaning. This primal fear of abandonment, the terror of being left alone in a vast and indifferent cosmos, becomes an indelible part of the infant's emotional landscape. When this separation is prolonged, or when the primary caregiver is lost permanently, the impact is magnified exponentially. Such profound losses, whether through death, divorce, or emotional unavailability, create fissures in the developing psyche, imprinting a deep-seated anxiety about finality and irrecoverable separation. These early wounds do not simply fade with time; they lodge themselves within the unconscious, becoming potent sources of dread and shaping the individual's unconscious narratives about death. The fear of death, in this context, is often inextricably linked to the fear of absolute, irreversible separation, a return to that terrifying state of primal aloneness.

Consider the child who experiences the death of a parent or sibling during their formative years. This is not merely a biographical event; it is a seismic shift in their psychic universe. The fabric of their reality is torn, and the concept of permanence is shattered. The unconscious mind, struggling to comprehend such an absolute absence, begins to construct narratives that attempt to make sense of this irretrievable loss. Death, in this nascent understanding, becomes synonymous with ultimate abandonment, with the irreversible severing of bonds that were perceived as eternal. The child may internalize the belief that love itself is fragile and transient, that those who are loved are destined to vanish, leaving behind an unfillable void. This can foster a deep-seated pessimism about the nature of existence and relationships, a gnawing suspicion that all connections are ultimately doomed to end. The 'fantasmatic signature' of death, in such cases, becomes indelibly marked by the terror of final separation, a visceral dread of being left utterly alone.

Beyond the direct experience of loss, anxieties surrounding the parents' own mortality can also profoundly influence a child's developing understanding of death. Children are acutely attuned to the emotional climate of their families, and they absorb their parents' unspoken fears and anxieties. If a parent harbors a deep, unexpressed fear of death, this anxiety can permeate the child's environment, creating a pervasive sense of unease. The child may interpret the parent's hushed conversations, their worried glances, or their avoidance of certain topics as evidence of an impending, ever-present danger. In an attempt to understand and perhaps manage this ambient dread, the child may develop their own unconscious theories about death, often colored by their limited cognitive and emotional capacities. These early, often distorted, interpretations can become internalized narratives that shape their future perceptions. For instance, a child might unconsciously believe that death is a punishment, a consequence of misbehavior, or a terrifying entity that lurks just beyond the periphery of awareness, waiting to claim those deemed worthy.

Furthermore, the way parents themselves grapple with the concept of death – or their attempts to shield children from it entirely – can inadvertently shape the child's fantasmatic signature. Overly protective parents, who attempt to sanitize the reality of death and present it as something that simply 'doesn't happen' or is merely a temporary 'sleep,' can leave a child unprepared for its inevitable presence. This can lead to a profound disconnect between the child's internal narrative and the external reality, fostering a sense of confusion and even denial when confronted with loss. Conversely, parents who communicate about death in a fearful, agitated manner can instill a primal terror in the child, associating the concept with overwhelming dread and helplessness. The ideal scenario, of course, involves age-appropriate and honest conversations that acknowledge the reality of death while also offering comfort and reassurance, framing it within a larger context of life and continuity. However, the reality of family dynamics often falls short of this ideal, leaving children to construct their own often-frightening interpretations.

These early imprints, formed in the crucible of primal separation, loss, and parental anxieties, do not remain static. They evolve, coalesce, and become woven into the complex tapestry of the unconscious, forming the bedrock upon which the individual's later relationship with mortality will be built. The 'fantasmatic signature' of death is, therefore, not a singular, monolithic entity, but a constellation of deeply embedded fears, desires, and defenses, forged in the fires of early experience. These primal scripts become the unconscious templates that guide our perceptions, influencing our choices, our relationships, and ultimately, our symbolic engagement with our own finitude. The anxiety of final separation, the terror of absolute aloneness, the conviction that loss is an inevitable fate – these are the whispers of our earliest encounters with the unthinkable, the echoes that will resonate throughout our lives, shaping the narrative of our eventual return to the silence from which we emerged. They represent the foundational psychic material that establishes our unique, unconscious relationship with the ultimate separation, the final act of an existence that began with profound dependence and vulnerability.

The unconscious mind, in its relentless effort to make sense of overwhelming experiences, employs symbolic representation. For a child grappling with the profound absence of a loved one, death may not be understood as a biological event, but as a form of profound, irreversible departure. This 'departure' fantasy can take many forms, often reflecting the child's developmental stage and their emotional resources. It might manifest as the belief that the lost person has simply gone on a very long journey, from which they will never return. This seemingly simple narrative, however, carries within it the heavy weight of permanent absence. The child's psyche, in its attempt to contain the unbearable reality of death, transforms it into a story of irretrievable leaving. This narrative, once established, can become a powerful unconscious driver, influencing how the individual later perceives their own potential endings. The idea of 'leaving' or 'departing' can become a deeply ingrained metaphor for death, a psychic placeholder for the unnameable terror of non-being.

In cases where the loss is not of a person but of a fundamental sense of security or belonging, the early fantasies of separation can be equally potent. Imagine a child whose parents are emotionally distant or preoccupied, creating an environment of chronic neglect. The child's experience is one of profound abandonment, not necessarily in the form of a dramatic disappearance, but in a constant, gnawing lack of attunement. This can foster an unconscious belief that they are fundamentally unlovable, unworthy of sustained connection. The fantasy here is not necessarily of a single, cataclysmic loss, but of a pervasive, ongoing state of being 'left behind' by life. Death, in this context, might be unconsciously perceived as a final, ultimate validation of this belief – the ultimate confirmation of their inherent separateness and lack of worth. It becomes a perverse form of resolution, an ending that aligns with their deeply ingrained, albeit painful, self-perception. The 'fantasmatic signature' is one of inherent unworthiness, leading to an unconscious acceptance, perhaps even a seeking, of an end that confirms this profound sense of disconnection.

The anxiety surrounding parental mortality can also contribute to these foundational fantasies. A child who witnesses a parent's brush with death, or hears of such an event, may develop an unconscious fear that their own existence is precarious, contingent on the survival of others. The fantasy here might be one of being orphaned, of being thrust into a world without the protective figures who safeguard them. This can foster a deep-seated vulnerability and a heightened sense of the fragility of life. Death, in this instance, is not merely a personal end but a disruption of the very order of their universe, a potential collapse of the structures that hold their world together. The child may unconsciously absorb the parents' fear and translate it into a personal narrative of impending doom, a sense that their own life is perpetually at risk, tethered to the survival of those they depend upon. This can create a psychic environment ripe for the development of a death script that is characterized by a pervasive sense of dread and a constant anticipation of catastrophe.

These early fantasies are not static. They are dynamic, evolving entities that are continuously shaped by subsequent experiences. However, the foundational patterns established in childhood often persist, exerting a powerful, unconscious influence. The way a person approaches intimacy, their tolerance for risk, their capacity for self-care, and their overall outlook on life can all be subtly informed by these early imprints. For example, an individual who experienced profound parental abandonment may develop an unconscious fear of true intimacy, pushing away potential partners before they can be 'left,' thereby unconsciously enacting their early separation fantasy. Similarly, someone who grew up with anxious parents preoccupied with their own mortality might develop a tendency towards hypochondria or a heightened sense of personal vulnerability, constantly anticipating their own demise.

The concept of the 'death script' emerges from this interplay of early experience and unconscious fantasy. It is not a conscious plan, but an internalized narrative, a set of unconscious expectations and beliefs about how one's life will end. This script is written in the language of primal emotions and symbolic representations, born from the earliest encounters with separation, loss, and the mysteries of mortality. The 'fantasmatic signature' of death, therefore, is the unique imprint left by these formative experiences, a deeply personal emblem that guides an individual's unconscious journey towards their final cessation. It is the emotional and symbolic resonance of our earliest fears of being alone, of being irrevocably separated, and of the terrifying unknown that lies beyond the bounds of familiar connection. This foundational material is crucial for understanding the subsequent manifestations of self-neglect and risk-taking behaviors discussed earlier, as these actions often serve as unconscious enactments of these deeply embedded, early scripts. The individual is, in essence, unconsciously playing out a drama that was scripted in the dawn of their consciousness, a drama centered around the ultimate separation.

The persistence of these early fantasies underscores the deeply ingrained nature of our relationship with mortality. They are not simply childhood anxieties that are outgrown; rather, they become woven into the fabric of the unconscious, shaping our perceptions and influencing our behaviors throughout life. When an individual engages in behaviors that seem to court danger or neglect their well-being, it is often not a conscious desire for self-destruction, but a complex, unconscious enactment of these early-formed 'death scripts.' The fear of final separation, for instance, may lead to an unconscious sabotage of relationships, a preemptive strike against the possibility of being abandoned. The fantasy of the lost caregiver can be replayed in a cycle of seeking out unavailable partners, unconsciously hoping to finally achieve the reunion that was denied in childhood. In this sense, the individual is not consciously choosing death, but rather enacting a deeply ingrained, unconscious narrative that equates their ultimate end with a primal, albeit distorted, resolution of early separation trauma.

Consider the impact of parental loss on the development of the 'fantasmatic signature' of death. When a child loses a primary caregiver, the experience is not just one of grief; it is a profound disruption of their sense of self and their understanding of permanence. The world, once perceived as stable and predictable, is suddenly revealed as fragile and ephemeral. The unconscious mind grapples with this shattering reality by constructing narratives that attempt to contain the incomprehensible. Death becomes, in this context, a terrifying embodiment of absolute abandonment. The child may internalize the belief that love itself is fleeting, that those closest to them are destined to vanish, leaving an irremovable void. This can foster a pervasive sense of existential dread, a feeling that life itself is inherently precarious and that loss is an inevitable, perhaps even deserved, fate. The unconscious script that emerges from such experiences is often one of profound isolation, where death is perceived not merely as an end, but as the ultimate confirmation of a life lived in the shadow of irretrievable separation. The yearning for connection, so fundamental to human existence, becomes perverted into a silent anticipation of the final, ultimate disconnection.

This early imprinting of separation anxiety also influences how individuals perceive their own bodies and their physical well-being. For a child who has experienced neglect or emotional abandonment, the body can become a symbol of vulnerability, a site where their deep-seated fears of being uncared for are played out. Self-neglect, therefore, is not simply a passive act of failing to care for oneself; it can be an unconscious re-enactment of earlier experiences of being uncared for. The body, in this scenario, becomes a stage for the unconscious drama of abandonment, its deterioration a silent testament to the profound ache of being alone and uncared for. The 'fantasmatic signature' of death, in such cases, is imbued with a deep-seated belief that their physical existence is inherently fragile and destined for decay, mirroring the emotional decay they experienced in childhood. Death, in this light, can become an unconscious surrender to this perceived fate, a final confirmation of their body's inherent worthlessness and their ultimate isolation.

Moreover, the anxieties surrounding a parent's own mortality can further shape these early fantasies. Children are incredibly perceptive of the emotional undercurrents within their families. If a parent harbors a deep, unarticulated fear of death, this anxiety can permeate the child's environment, creating a pervasive sense of unease. The child may unconsciously absorb this fear, translating it into their own narrative about the nature of existence. Death, in this context, might be unconsciously perceived as a menacing force, an ever-present threat that looms over their loved ones and, by extension, over themselves. This can foster a heightened sense of vulnerability and a predisposition towards what might be termed a 'vigilant' approach to life, where the individual is constantly on guard against potential disaster. The 'fantasmatic signature' of death, therefore, becomes one of impending doom, a pervasive dread that their world, and their own existence within it, is perpetually at risk of being extinguished. This unconscious anticipation of catastrophe can lead to a life lived under a shadow, where the possibility of one's own end is never far from conscious or unconscious awareness.

The interplay between these early experiences – primal separation, profound loss, and parental anxieties about mortality – creates a unique 'fantasmatic signature' for each individual. This signature is the unconscious imprint that shapes their relationship with death, a deeply personal template that influences how they perceive their own finitude. It is not a conscious choice, but an internalized narrative, a constellation of fears, desires, and defenses forged in the crucible of early life. This signature dictates the symbolic language through which death is understood and, in a crucial sense, enacted. The individual, unaware of the script being played out, moves through life guided by these deeply ingrained unconscious expectations, their actions and choices subtly orchestrated by the echoes of their earliest encounters with loss and the terrifying prospect of ultimate separation. The profound impact of these foundational experiences cannot be overstated; they lay the psychic groundwork for the complex and often self-destructive relationship with mortality that characterizes so many lives. The unconscious, in its relentless pursuit of meaning and resolution, draws upon these early imprints to construct a symbolic narrative of death that resonates with the individual's deepest fears and most primal wounds.

The Oedipal drama, a foundational tempest in the psychic development of every individual, does not simply recede into the mists of childhood once we have navigated its turbulent waters. Instead, its potent currents continue to shape the contours of our unconscious, casting long shadows that can profoundly influence our most ultimate engagement with life's final act: death. The unresolved desires, the fierce rivalries, the gnawing guilt that characterize this primal period do not vanish; they are internalized, transformed, and woven into the very fabric of our being, becoming silent architects of our personal 'death script.' Death, in its absolute finality, can emerge as a symbolic stage upon which these deeply ingrained dramas are replayed, offering a perverse kind of resolution or a stark re-enactment of our earliest existential conflicts.

The Oedipal complex, as theorized by Freud, centers on the child's intense, often unconscious, attachment to the parent of the opposite sex and their simultaneous feelings of rivalry and hostility towards the parent of the same sex. This triangular dynamic, replete with forbidden desires, jealousies, and fears of retaliation (particularly castration anxiety in boys, and its psychic equivalents in girls), creates a profound internal conflict. The resolution of this complex typically involves the internalization of parental prohibitions, the formation of the superego, and the sublimation of these primal drives into more socially acceptable pursuits. However, the resolution is rarely absolute. Vestiges of these early desires and rivalries, particularly the guilt associated with them, can remain deeply embedded in the unconscious, shaping our internal landscape for decades. When we consider the unconscious script of death, we must therefore account for the enduring echoes of this Oedipal struggle.

The finality of death offers a unique and potent arena for the unconscious reprisal of Oedipal themes. For an individual who has grappled with intense, unresolved Oedipal desires, the concept of death can become unconsciously associated with the ultimate fulfillment or, more often, the ultimate denial of those desires. The overwhelming power of the parental figure, once a source of both love and terror, can be re-envied or re-projected onto figures of authority in adulthood, and ultimately, onto the very concept of annihilation. If, for instance, the unconscious guilt surrounding forbidden desires towards the parent of the opposite sex remains potent, death can be unconsciously experienced as a profound punishment, a terrifying consequence for these primal transgressions. This guilt, never fully expiated, finds its ultimate reckoning in the inescapable finality of non-being. The superego, born from the internalization of Oedipal prohibitions, exerts its relentless judgment, and death becomes the ultimate surrender to this internal tribunal.

Conversely, the rivalry aspect of the Oedipal complex can also color an individual's death script. The unconscious struggle for dominance and recognition with the same-sex parent can translate into a lifelong pattern of seeking to 'outdo' or 'surpass' perceived authorities or rivals. In the context of death, this might manifest as an unconscious defiance or a desire to confront mortality on one's own terms, a final act of rebellion against the ultimate authority figure – be it fate, God, or simply the inexorable march of time. This can manifest in risk-taking behaviors that appear to court danger, a subconscious desire to prove one's strength and resilience in the face of the inevitable. It is a symbolic wrestling match with the primal rival, projected onto the grandest possible stage of existence. The fear of being 'overpowered' or 'castrated' by the primal rival can morph into a deeper fear of simply ceasing to exist, of being utterly vanquished by a force beyond one's control.

Furthermore, the Oedipal complex instills in us a deep-seated understanding of power dynamics and authority. The relationship with the parents, particularly the punitive or idealized aspects of the parental figures, shapes our internal model for dealing with authority throughout our lives. When we face the ultimate authority of death, these internalized dynamics come to the fore. An individual who felt oppressed or controlled by a powerful parental figure might unconsciously view death as the ultimate act of subjugation, a final surrender to an oppressive force. This can fuel a sense of despair or a desperate, often unconscious, struggle against the inevitable. The death script, in such a case, is one of tragic inevitability, a narrative of being crushed by an overwhelming power that mirrors the perceived omnipotence of the early parental figures.

The guilt generated by the Oedipal complex is perhaps one of its most enduring legacies, and it plays a crucial role in shaping the death script. The child's aggressive wishes towards the rival parent and their possessive desires towards the other parent are invariably accompanied by overwhelming guilt and the fear of severe punishment. This guilt does not dissipate; it becomes a pervasive undercurrent in the psyche. When confronted with the concept of death, this internalized guilt can lead to an unconscious belief that one is fundamentally deserving of punishment, that one's very existence is a transgression that warrants cessation. The finality of death can then be unconsciously perceived as a just deserts, a logical and inevitable consequence of one's inherent flaws and past transgressions. This self-punishing tendency can manifest in various ways, from subconscious self-sabotage in life to an unconscious welcoming of death as a release from the burden of unbearable guilt. The death script, in this instance, becomes a narrative of expiation, where the ultimate act of dying serves as the final payment for an unpayable debt.

The resolution of the Oedipal complex also involves the repression of primal sexual and aggressive drives. If this repression is incomplete, these drives can resurface in symbolic forms throughout life, and death can become a powerful symbolic container for them. For instance, the primal energy associated with incestuous desires or aggressive impulses can become unconsciously linked to the ultimate taboo – death. The fascination with death, for some, can be an unconscious channeling of these repressed, powerful energies. The 'forbidden' nature of Oedipal desires finds a potent echo in the forbidden nature of dwelling too deeply on death. The intensity of these early drives, when unmet or unresolved, can create a psychic pressure that seeks an outlet, and death, as the ultimate mystery and ultimate cessation, can become a focal point for this displaced energy. The death script, here, is less about guilt and more about the powerful, unresolved forces of primal desire seeking their ultimate expression or annihilation.

Consider the impact of unresolved Oedipal rivalries on one's relationship with authority figures in later life. These patterns are often unconsciously replicated. When such individuals face the ultimate authority of death, their established patterns of defiance, submission, or appeasement come into play. The death script can be shaped by whether they unconsciously perceive death as a benevolent, albeit stern, parental figure, a tyrannical oppressor, or a rival to be overcome. The anxiety surrounding castration, a core element for boys in the Oedipal drama, can translate into a fear of annihilation, a fear of losing one's potency, one's very essence, which death promises. This fear of 'losing everything' can become a driving force behind the unconscious death narrative, painting it as a tragedy of ultimate diminishment and loss.

The concept of 'completion' or 'resolution' is deeply tied to the Oedipal complex. Successful navigation of this stage allows for a sense of psychic integration and forward movement. When the Oedipal complex remains largely unresolved, there can be a pervasive sense of being stuck, of being unable to move beyond certain primal conflicts. Death, in this context, can be unconsciously viewed as the only possible 'completion,' a final end to an internal struggle that has been raging since childhood. The individual might unconsciously feel that life itself is a continuation of this unresolved drama, and death offers the only escape, the only true end to the internal torment. The death script, therefore, becomes a narrative of longed-for release, a final punctuation mark on a life defined by an internal stalemate.

The legacy of the Oedipal complex extends to our understanding of love and loss. The intensity of the early love for the parent of the opposite sex, coupled with the rivalry towards the same-sex parent, creates a complex matrix of attachment and potential betrayal. If the unconscious fear of losing the primary love object (stemming from the Oedipal period) is particularly strong, death can become unconsciously associated with the ultimate abandonment, a confirmation of the deepest, primal fear of being left alone. The death script, in this scenario, is imbued with profound grief and a sense of irretrievable loss, mirroring the imagined or real loss of the parental love object in childhood. The final separation of death becomes the ultimate enactment of this primal separation anxiety.

In essence, the unconscious death script is not merely a premonition of physical demise; it is a deeply symbolic narrative forged in the crucible of our earliest relational dramas. The Oedipal complex, with its potent mix of desire, rivalry, guilt, and fear, provides a rich and enduring source for this script. The finality of death offers an ultimate stage for the unconscious to enact these primal conflicts, to seek a resolution – however distorted or tragic – for the battles waged in the nursery. Whether it manifests as a sense of deserved punishment, a defiant struggle against authority, a profound mourning for lost love, or a longed-for escape from internal torment, the echoes of the Oedipal drama are undeniable, casting a long and often unconscious shadow over our eventual return to silence. These unresolved familial dynamics continue to whisper to us, shaping our perception of our ultimate fate, guiding our unconscious towards an end that symbolically reflects the beginning of our psychic lives. The very act of dying, in this psychoanalytic view, can become a final, albeit unconscious, reenactment of the most formative dramas of our youth, a testament to the enduring power of early experiences in shaping the narrative of our entire existence, right up to its very conclusion.

The echoes of our earliest experiences do not fade into the background noise of adult life; instead, they often orchestrate a recurring performance, a deeply ingrained choreography of the unconscious that compels us to revisit and re-enact patterns established in the fertile soil of childhood. This phenomenon, vividly described by Sigmund Freud as the "compulsion to repeat," offers a profound lens through which to understand the seemingly inexplicable ways individuals navigate their lives, often finding themselves ensnared in cyclical dramas that appear beyond their conscious control. This compulsive tendency is not limited to the mundane routines of daily existence; it extends its tendrils into the most profound and ultimate act of life – death. The way we approach, experience, and even symbolically enact our demise can be profoundly shaped by these unconscious repetitions, transforming death itself into a final, climactic performance of an age-old internal play.

The compulsion to repeat is a fundamental psychic mechanism, a kind of internal imperative that drives individuals to unconsciously recreate past situations, particularly those that were emotionally charged, traumatic, or unresolved. This is not born of a conscious desire for self-destruction, but rather from an unconscious attempt to master, or at least to find a form of resolution for, experiences that overwhelmed the psyche in its nascent stages. It is as if the unconscious mind, unable to fully process and integrate certain events or emotional states, insists on replaying them, seeking a different outcome, a more favorable resolution, or simply a sense of familiarity in the face of overwhelming newness. This repetition can manifest in a myriad of ways: choosing similar relationship dynamics, gravitating towards familiar professional environments that echo past conflicts, or even manifesting physical symptoms that mirror past illnesses or traumas. The unconscious mind, in its relentless pursuit of integration, orchestrates these repetitions as a form of therapy, albeit a painful and often counterproductive one, hoping to achieve mastery through re-enactment.

When we turn this understanding towards the finality of death, the implications become particularly poignant. The death script, the unique narrative that unfolds around an individual's end, can be seen as the ultimate stage for these repetitive patterns. Individuals may unconsciously steer their lives towards scenarios that mirror the unresolved conflicts or traumas of their past. This is not to suggest a conscious, deliberate drive towards a specific end, but rather a subtle, pervasive influence that guides choices, perceptions, and even the very conditions under which one faces mortality. For instance, someone who experienced early childhood neglect might, in their adult life, unconsciously recreate scenarios of abandonment, perhaps through strained relationships or a tendency to isolate themselves, and this pattern might culminate in a death that is experienced in profound loneliness, mirroring the primal fear of being left behind. The aesthetic of their ending, the particular hues of their dying, are thus painted with the brushstrokes of these deeply ingrained, repetitive gestures.

Consider the individual whose childhood was marked by overwhelming control and criticism from a parental figure. This experience can instill a deep-seated sense of inadequacy and a desperate yearning for autonomy. In adulthood, such an individual might unconsciously repeat this dynamic by engaging in self-sabotaging behaviors that limit their potential or by entering into relationships that replicate the controlling atmosphere of their youth. The compulsion to repeat can lead them to inadvertently create situations that reinforce their core beliefs about their own worthlessness or their inability to escape external judgment. When it comes to their death, this pattern might manifest as a surrender to an illness that feels imposed upon them, a sense of being utterly powerless against an invading force, or even a preoccupation with final judgments and criticisms, as if the ultimate authority figure from their past has returned to deliver a final verdict. The narrative of their passing becomes a somber echo of the constant critique and control they experienced in their formative years, a performance of the very powerlessness they struggled against throughout their lives.

Similarly, a childhood marked by intense, unresolved sibling rivalry can shape an adult's propensity to engage in competitive struggles, constantly seeking to prove themselves superior or to outmaneuver perceived rivals. This drive for dominance, rooted in early familial dynamics, can extend into professional life, social circles, and even into how one confronts existential challenges. In the context of death, this repetitive pattern might manifest as a defiant stance against mortality, a refusal to "go down without a fight," even when the fight is medically or realistically unwinnable. It can manifest as a desire to be remembered as a victor, to have their passing be a testament to their strength and resilience, even in the face of inevitable defeat. The death script, in this instance, becomes a grand, final competition, a last stand against the ultimate rival – oblivion itself. The aesthetic of their end is one of struggle, of defiance, of a final, desperate attempt to assert control and superiority against an opponent that cannot be outmaneuvered.

The repetitive nature of these unconscious patterns is not merely about the content of the experience but also about the emotional tone and the underlying dynamics. Even seemingly positive repetitions can be driven by this compulsion. For example, an individual who experienced profound love and security in early childhood might unconsciously seek out relationships that provide a similar sense of comfort and safety, replaying the warmth of their early attachments. However, when this compulsion extends to more difficult or traumatic experiences, it becomes a source of distress. The unconscious mind does not discriminate between helpful and harmful repetitions; it simply seeks to re-engage with what is familiar, what is known, in an attempt to integrate and master it.

The concept of "working through" in psychoanalysis directly addresses this compulsion to repeat. It is through the painstaking process of analysis, by bringing these unconscious patterns into conscious awareness, that individuals can begin to break free from their cyclical grip. However, in the absence of such therapeutic intervention, these patterns often continue their relentless performance throughout life, and death becomes the ultimate, often tragic, stage upon which they are re-enacted. The individual might unconsciously recreate the very circumstances that led to past trauma or suffering, not out of a desire to relive the pain, but from an unconscious belief that this time, perhaps, the outcome will be different, or that by re-enacting it, they can finally gain a measure of control.

This brings us to a crucial point: death itself can become the ultimate repetition, a symbolic fulfillment of these deeply ingrained psychic patterns. It is the final act in a play that has been rehearsed throughout a lifetime, an end that mirrors the beginning in its unconscious dynamics. For the individual who experienced profound feelings of guilt in childhood, perhaps stemming from imagined transgressions or forbidden desires, death can be unconsciously perceived as the ultimate expiation, the final punishment that absolves them of their perceived sins. The fear of death might be intertwined with the fear of judgment, of facing the consequences of their lifelong internal struggles. Their death script is one of grim inevitability, a narrative of paying a final, deserved price for a lifetime of unconscious transgression. The aesthetic of their ending might be one of somber resignation, of a release from the burden of guilt, or even a sense of dark satisfaction at finally meeting the fate they unconsciously believed they deserved.

Furthermore, the compulsion to repeat can explain why individuals might be drawn to certain types of narratives or imagery surrounding death. A person whose life has been characterized by a constant struggle against overwhelming odds might be drawn to heroic narratives of death, where they are the protagonist fighting a noble battle. Conversely, someone who has felt victimized throughout their life might unconsciously gravitate towards a death that is perceived as tragic and unjust, thereby repeating the narrative of their lived experience. The aesthetic of their end is thus not simply a biological event but a deeply psychological and symbolic reconstruction of their life's central dramas.

The aesthetic of an individual's ending, therefore, is intimately tied to the repetitive patterns that have shaped their unconscious landscape. It is the unique stylistic signature of their final act, a reflection of the internal logic that has governed their life's narrative. This aesthetic can be perceived in the manner of dying – whether it is peaceful or turbulent, solitary or surrounded, defiant or resigned. It can also be seen in the surrounding circumstances, the relationships, the final words spoken, or the unspoken emotions that fill the space. These elements are not arbitrary; they are often the unconscious elaborations of the repetitive motifs that have played out throughout the individual's life.

The unconscious mind, in its attempt to resolve or master past experiences, can also lead individuals to seek out symbolic forms of repetition that are not directly life-threatening but carry a significant psychic weight. For example, an individual who experienced a profound loss in childhood might unconsciously seek out careers or hobbies that involve themes of preservation, remembrance, or even the reconstruction of damaged objects. This is a way of symbolically engaging with and attempting to repair the original wound. When these patterns are left unexamined, they can continue to influence the individual's relationship with mortality. The fear of loss, the desire for repair, can become woven into the fabric of their death script, perhaps manifesting as a deep concern for the legacy they leave behind, or a profound fear of being forgotten, of experiencing a final, irretrievable loss.

The compulsive element is what makes these repetitions so potent and, at times, so destructive. It is not a matter of choice in the conscious sense, but a driven, almost instinctual, compulsion to return to the familiar, even when that familiarity is fraught with pain. This is where the therapeutic challenge lies: to help the individual recognize these patterns, understand their origins, and consciously choose a different path, thereby disrupting the repetitive cycle. Without this conscious intervention, the unconscious script plays out, and death becomes its ultimate, often poignant, conclusion. The individual's final moments, therefore, are not merely a physical cessation but a profound symbolic event, a testament to the enduring power of early experiences and the unconscious drives that shape our journey from birth to death. The aesthetic of their ending is the signature of this journey, the unique style with which they perform the final act of their life's deeply ingrained drama. The compulsion to repeat ensures that this drama, with all its unresolved tensions and familiar gestures, finds its ultimate expression, shaping the contours and character of our final farewell.

The unconscious mind, a vast and intricate theater of the self, often stages elaborate productions that draw heavily from the scripts of our earliest experiences. These deeply etched narratives, particularly those born of trauma, do not merely reside in memory; they pulsate with a life of their own, dictating the rhythm of our days and, more profoundly, choreographing the very unfolding of our end. This section delves into such a phenomenon, presenting a clinical vignette that illuminates how a specific childhood trauma narrative can unconsciously shape the "fantasmatic signature" of death. It is a story of how the past, unacknowledged and unintegrated, can cast a long shadow, ultimately dictating the symbolic contours of one's final exit.

Consider the case of "Elias" (a pseudonym), a man whose life trajectory was marked by an almost palpable sense of being pursued, an underlying current of dread that seemed to color every significant decision and interpersonal dynamic. Elias presented in his late fifties with a constellation of anxieties and a pervasive feeling of impending doom, though the specific nature of this threat remained nebulous. His life was a series of near misses, of opportunities that slipped through his grasp, and relationships that inevitably dissolved into mutual misunderstanding and, for him, a profound sense of abandonment. He described a persistent, almost physical sensation of being watched, of an unseen force lurking just beyond his periphery, ready to pounce. This pervasive sense of being under siege, of an external threat that was both omnipresent and indefinable, was the very air he seemed to breathe.

As the psychoanalytic work progressed, the fragmented narratives of Elias's childhood began to coalesce, revealing a deeply traumatic event that occurred when he was approximately four years old. This event, which had been largely suppressed and fragmented in his conscious recall, involved a terrifying encounter with a figure of authority during a period of familial upheaval. His parents, engaged in a bitter and volatile divorce, had left him briefly in the care of a stern and emotionally distant relative. During this unsupervised interval, Elias, driven by childish curiosity and a desperate need for reassurance, had wandered into a restricted area of the relative's imposing house. He had been discovered by this figure, not with the gentle correction he might have unconsciously hoped for, but with an explosive outburst of rage and accusation. The relative, a man known for his severe disposition, had cornered the terrified child, his face contorted with anger, his voice booming with condemnations that Elias, even at his young age, understood as a dire threat. The specific accusations were lost in the fog of Elias's memory, but the overwhelming emotional residue – the sheer terror, the sense of being utterly helpless and condemned, the palpable menace emanating from the adult – remained indelibly imprinted on his psyche. He remembered the feeling of being trapped, the desperate urge to escape, and the chilling certainty that he was facing a profound and irreversible danger, a judgment from which there could be no appeal.

This primal scene, with its potent cocktail of fear, helplessness, and condemnation, became the unconscious template for Elias's later life. The relative's imposing presence, his booming voice, and the overwhelming sense of being trapped and judged were not just memories; they were internalized psychic structures that shaped Elias's perception of the world and his place within it. The dynamic of being discovered in a forbidden space, of having his actions met with disproportionate wrath, and of facing an authority figure who instilled an existential terror, began to play itself out in various forms throughout his adult life.

Elias repeatedly found himself in situations where he felt exposed and vulnerable, as if he had stumbled into a forbidden territory of adult life. He would unconsciously gravitate towards professions where he felt constantly scrutinized and judged, areas where a single mistake could lead to devastating consequences. His career choices were often characterized by a restless pursuit of excellence, driven not by intrinsic motivation but by a desperate, almost neurotic, need to avoid the critical gaze he had experienced in childhood. He would oscillate between periods of intense overwork and subsequent burnout, a pattern that mimicked the initial transgression followed by the overwhelming consequence. The fear of discovery, of being caught doing something "wrong," became a pervasive anxiety that fueled his actions, pushing him to constantly prove his worth and to preempt any potential accusation.

His relationships were similarly colored by this dynamic. He was drawn to partners who, consciously or unconsciously, mirrored the critical authority figure of his past. These relationships were often characterized by a power imbalance, where Elias would feel infantilized, criticized, and ultimately controlled. He would attempt to appease these figures, to anticipate their every need and desire, in a desperate attempt to avoid the explosive condemnation he so deeply feared. When inevitably, these relationships would falter, Elias would interpret their dissolution not as a consequence of the unhealthy dynamic but as confirmation of his own inherent inadequacy and his inability to meet the standards of others. He would feel, once again, like the small child caught in a forbidden space, utterly exposed and condemned.

The "fantasmatic signature" of Elias's death, as it began to emerge through the therapeutic process, was intimately tied to this primal scene. While he did not suffer from a terminal illness in the conventional sense, his life was slowly being consumed by the chronic stress and anxiety generated by his internal dramas. He developed a series of stress-related ailments, each one seemingly a physical manifestation of his psychological torment. There was a recurring pattern of his symptoms intensifying during periods of perceived professional or interpersonal threat, mirroring the childhood incident where his trespass was met with a swift and terrifying response.

As Elias approached the end of his life, his narrative around mortality began to crystallize around themes of exposure and final judgment. He became increasingly preoccupied with his legacy, not in terms of achievements, but in terms of how he would be perceived after his death. He expressed a profound fear of being "found out," of his perceived flaws and failures being laid bare for all to see. This was a direct echo of the childhood terror of being discovered in a forbidden space and facing the wrath of an authority figure. His death, in his unconscious projection, was to be the ultimate act of exposure, the final moment where all his carefully constructed defenses would crumble, leaving him vulnerable to an unappealable verdict.

He would often speak of a "reckoning," a sense that his life's accounting would be tallied, and that he would have to face the consequences of his perceived transgressions. This "reckoning" was not necessarily a religious concept for Elias, but a deeply internalized psychological one, a fear of facing the ultimate authority – whether it be societal judgment, the judgment of loved ones, or perhaps even an internal, self-imposed judgment – and being found wanting. The imposing figure of his childhood relative, with his booming voice and accusatory stance, re-emerged in Elias's dreams and waking thoughts as a spectral judge, overseeing the final audit of his life.

The circumstances of Elias's dying mirrored this internal drama. He spent his final weeks in a state of heightened anxiety, often isolating himself, believing that his suffering was a private matter that would only burden others. He refused to allow many visitors, fearing that they would witness his decline and confirm his deepest fears of inadequacy. His room, once a place of comfort, became a stage where he felt perpetually observed, though by whom, he could not articulate. He became fixated on small details, obsessively tidying his belongings, as if preparing for an inspection, an anxious attempt to present a facade of order and control in the face of overwhelming internal chaos.

His final moments were not marked by a sudden cessation of breath but by a slow, agonizing surrender to what he perceived as an inevitable judgment. He reportedly whispered fragmented phrases about being "found out" and "it's not fair," utterances that spoke to the enduring power of the original trauma. The "fantasmatic signature" of his death was, therefore, the symbolic re-enactment of being discovered in a forbidden place and facing an overwhelming, condemnatory authority. While the literal circumstances of his childhood encounter were vastly different from the process of dying, the psychic mechanism, the core emotional dynamics of terror, helplessness, and the dread of judgment, remained eerily consistent.

This case vividly illustrates how an early, unresolved traumatic experience can cast a long and pervasive shadow, dictating not only the trajectory of one's life but also the symbolic language of one's death. Elias did not consciously choose to re-enact his childhood trauma; rather, the unconscious imperative to revisit and somehow master this deeply wounding experience propelled him towards a final act that bore its indelible mark. The defenses he erected throughout his life – the constant striving, the people-pleasing, the avoidance of exposure – ultimately proved insufficient to contain the primitive terror of that early encounter. Death, in this context, became the ultimate symbolic fulfillment of that unresolved trauma, the final scene in a lifelong play rehearsed in the depths of the unconscious.

The therapeutic work with Elias had begun to bring these unconscious dynamics into conscious awareness. He had started to recognize the repetitive patterns in his relationships and career choices, and to understand their roots in that terrifying childhood encounter. He had begun to question the accusatory voice in his head, to challenge its authority. However, the work was ongoing, and the deeply ingrained patterns had taken such hold that their ultimate expression seemed almost inevitable. The analysis provided a space to understand, to witness, and to begin the arduous process of disentanglement, but the momentum of the unconscious script was powerful.

The question that arises from such a case is not whether individuals *can* escape these patterns, but rather how the process of facing one's mortality can, paradoxically, become the very arena where these deeply embedded scripts are most dramatically played out. Elias's death was not a mere biological event; it was a deeply symbolic act, a final, albeit tragic, testament to the enduring power of early life experiences and the unconscious drives that shape our journey. The "fantasmatic signature" of his end was the unique style, the psychological imprint, of this lifelong drama, a drama that found its ultimate, poignant conclusion on the stage of his dying. It is in these moments, as consciousness recedes and the unconscious comes to the fore, that the most deeply buried narratives often find their final, potent expression, shaping the aesthetic of our farewells in ways that are both profound and, at times, deeply unsettling. The compulsion to repeat, in its most absolute form, ensures that the familiar gestures of our inner world are performed one last time, even as the final curtain falls.

The human psyche, in its ceaseless endeavor to make meaning, has for millennia turned to narrative. Long before the advent of individual psychotherapy or the clinical dissection of personal trauma, humanity wrestled with the profound mystery of death through the telling of stories. These tales, passed down through generations, function as a collective unconscious repository of wisdom, fear, and hope regarding the ultimate human experience. They are not mere entertainment; they are distillations of shared psychological landscapes, archetypal dramas that resonate across cultures and epochs. Within the rich tapestry of fairy tales and myths, we find potent symbolic frameworks that can, often unconsciously, inform and shape an individual's personal death script. These ancient narratives offer a shared language, a cultural scaffolding upon which we build our understanding of endings, influencing the very aesthetic and symbolic contours of our final moments.

Fairy tales, often dismissed as simple children's stories, possess a remarkable depth and complexity. They frequently feature protagonists who embark on perilous journeys, face insurmountable obstacles, and confront profound loss. Within these narratives, death often appears not as a sterile biological event, but as a transformative passage, a natural, albeit often tragic, conclusion to a particular phase of life or a quest. Consider the pervasive motif of sacrifice. In countless tales, a hero or heroine must give up something precious – their life, their love, their innocence – for the greater good, for the salvation of their community, or for the fulfillment of a prophecy. This archetypal sacrifice speaks to a deep-seated human understanding that endings can be imbued with profound meaning, that the cessation of individual existence can serve a larger purpose. Such narratives, when internalized, can shape an individual's unconscious perception of their own end, leading them to imbue their dying with a sense of purpose or redemptive significance, even if this meaning is only symbolically enacted. The fairy tale of "The Little Mermaid," for instance, is a poignant exploration of sacrifice for love, where the protagonist willingly surrenders her voice and endures immense pain for the chance to win the prince's heart. Her eventual dissolution into sea foam, rather than a terrifying annihilation, becomes a poetic transformation, a testament to the depth of her love and the ultimate sublimation of her individual desires into the elemental forces of nature. This narrative can, for an individual unconsciously drawn to such themes, inform a death that is experienced as a quiet fading, a dissolving into a greater whole, a sacrifice of self for the idealized image of love or belonging.

Similarly, the archetypal journey, so central to myth and legend, often involves a confrontation with mortality. The hero's descent into the underworld, a common trope found in Greek myths like that of Orpheus and Eurydice, or in the epic of Gilgamesh, represents a symbolic journey into death. These narratives are not simply about overcoming obstacles; they are about confronting the fear of oblivion, about grappling with the finitude of human existence. Orpheus's tragic failure to retrieve Eurydice, his glance back sealing her fate, speaks to the profound difficulty, perhaps even the impossibility, of truly conquering death or fully retrieving what has been lost to its embrace. This motif can resonate with individuals who, in their own dying process, find themselves wrestling with the finality of loss, perhaps reliving moments of missed opportunity or irreparable separation. The "death script" might, in such cases, be characterized by a pervasive sense of regret or a desperate, albeit unconscious, attempt to recapture what has irrevocably passed. The aesthetic of such a death might be one of poignant melancholy, a lingering gaze into the shadows of what was, rather than a resolute stride into the unknown.

The archetype of the tragic lover, immortalized in stories like "Romeo and Juliet," also offers a powerful framework for understanding the death script. Here, death is not merely an end but a final, dramatic affirmation of love, a union forged in the face of insurmountable societal or familial opposition. The lovers' double suicide, a desperate act of defiance and devotion, becomes their ultimate, albeit tragic, triumph. This narrative archetype can unconsciously influence individuals who have experienced intense, perhaps unfulfilled or forbidden, loves. Their death might be unconsciously staged as a final, passionate act of devotion, a symbolic reunion with the lost beloved in the realm beyond life. The "fantasmatic signature" of such a death would likely be charged with an intense emotionality, a theatricality that mirrors the grand passions of the story. It might involve a profound sense of longing, a final embrace of imagined arms, or a quiet fading away with the name of the beloved on their lips, a final whisper into the void that echoes the intensity of their earthly affections.

Beyond individual journeys and romantic entanglements, myths and fairy tales also explore the cyclical nature of destruction and renewal. Many creation myths begin with a primordial chaos, a formless void from which the world emerges through a process of separation and ordering. Conversely, apocalyptic narratives often depict the end of an era, a cataclysmic event that purges the old to make way for the new. This understanding of death as a necessary precursor to rebirth, or as a part of a larger cosmic cycle, can deeply inform an individual's acceptance or resistance to their own mortality. For some, their death script might reflect a belief in reincarnation or a spiritual continuation, an unconscious identification with the archetypal promise of renewal. The death is not an absolute end but a transition, a shedding of the old form to allow for a new manifestation. Such a death might be experienced with a sense of peace and inevitability, a quiet relinquishing of the physical form, much like the falling leaves that herald the dormant period before spring's awakening. The aesthetic here is one of quiet dignity and acceptance, a harmonious participation in the grand rhythm of existence.

The power of these archetypal narratives lies in their ability to tap into the collective unconscious, a reservoir of shared human experiences and predispositions, as Carl Jung described it. They provide a pre-existing symbolic language for navigating the most profound aspects of human existence, including death. When an individual's personal history intersects with these archetypal patterns, the ancient stories can provide a ready-made script, an unconscious blueprint for the manner and meaning of their dying. This is not to suggest that these narratives dictate a predetermined fate, but rather that they offer readily available symbolic frameworks that can unconsciously shape the subjective experience of death. The specific details of a person's life – their traumas, their loves, their regrets, their triumphs – are woven into these archetypal patterns, creating a unique yet recognizably resonant death script.

For instance, the archetype of the wise elder or the sage, often depicted in myths as possessing profound knowledge and facing death with equanimity, can influence those who have lived long lives and have accumulated a wealth of experience. Their dying process might be characterized by a quiet wisdom, a sense of acceptance, and a desire to impart final lessons to those around them. Their death is not a defeat but a culmination, a final act of teaching and guidance. The aesthetic is one of serene authority, a peaceful surrender of the reins of life to the next generation. Conversely, the archetype of the fool or the trickster, often living a life of chaotic energy and unpredictability, might manifest in a death that is sudden, unexpected, and perhaps even absurd. The trickster's ultimate trick might be on death itself, a final evasion or a subversion of the expected solemnity of the end.

The very language we use to describe death is often steeped in these archetypal narratives. We speak of "passing away," "crossing over," "making one's final journey," or "succumbing to fate." These phrases are not merely euphemisms; they carry the weight of ancient stories, invoking images of movement, transition, and an encounter with forces beyond our immediate control. The "death script" is not just about the physical process of dying; it is about the narrative surrounding it, the symbolic drama that unfolds in the hearts and minds of the dying and those who witness their end. The fairy tale's enduring appeal lies in its distillation of complex human emotions and experiences into potent, easily digestible symbols. When these symbols resonate with our deepest, often unconscious, anxieties and desires surrounding death, they can become powerful drivers of our personal narratives of ending.

Consider the pervasive fear of abandonment that can fuel a death script. Many fairy tales feature orphans or protagonists who are cast out, forced to fend for themselves in a hostile world. Their journey is often one of arduous survival, marked by loneliness and the yearning for belonging. If such a narrative has deeply imprinted itself on an individual's psyche, their dying might be characterized by a profound sense of isolation, a feeling of being utterly alone in their final moments, even if surrounded by loved ones. The unconscious fear is not just of death itself, but of the ultimate abandonment, the final separation from all that is known and cherished. The aesthetic of such a death might be one of quiet sorrow, a withdrawal into oneself, a fading light that mirrors the perceived dimming of connection and belonging.

The archetype of the innocent victim, destined for sacrifice or suffering, is also a powerful force in shaping death narratives. Tales of innocent maidens betrayed, or noble figures unjustly persecuted, tap into our collective sense of vulnerability and the often arbitrary nature of suffering. For individuals who have experienced significant injustice or trauma, their dying might unconsciously reenact this narrative of victimhood. There might be a sense of profound unfairness, a feeling of being punished for unknown transgressions, or a quiet resignation to a fate that feels predetermined and unjust. The "fantasmatic signature" here is one of poignant tragedy, a life ending under a cloud of sorrow and perceived injustice, leaving behind a lingering sense of what might have been if fate had been kinder.

However, it is not solely tales of woe and tragedy that inform our death scripts. The archetype of the hero, the one who faces death with courage and defiance, also holds significant sway. Stories of valiant warriors, determined explorers, or individuals who fight valiantly against overwhelming odds can imbue a death with a sense of triumph, even in defeat. The dying process, in this context, might be characterized by a fierce determination, a refusal to yield, a final surge of energy and will. The "death script" becomes one of valiant struggle, where the cessation of life is seen not as a surrender but as the ultimate act of bravery. The aesthetic is one of powerful resilience, a final stand against the inevitable, leaving behind an impression of strength and unwavering spirit.

The presence of magic and the supernatural in fairy tales and myths also provides a rich symbolic language for understanding the transition of death. The idea of a magical cure, a transformation, or a journey to an enchanted realm offers comfort and meaning in the face of mortality. For individuals who hold strong spiritual or metaphysical beliefs, their death script might be heavily influenced by these archetypal themes. The dying process could be experienced as a passage into a spiritual realm, a reunion with a divine presence, or a miraculous transformation. The "fantasmatic signature" would be one of transcendence, of a movement beyond the physical constraints of the body into a realm of light, peace, or spiritual fulfillment. The aesthetic is one of luminous wonder, a final, awe-inspiring journey into the heart of the sacred.

Ultimately, fairy tales and myths provide a shared cultural grammar for discussing and understanding death. They offer a canvas upon which individuals can unconsciously project their deepest fears, their most cherished hopes, and their most profound understandings of what it means to cease to be. These archetypal narratives equip us with symbols and scenarios that can help to structure the ineffable experience of dying, imbuing it with meaning, purpose, or at least a sense of order. They remind us that the human confrontation with mortality is not a solitary, unprecedented event, but a part of a vast, ancient tapestry of human experience. The "fantasmatic signature" of our death, therefore, is rarely a purely personal invention; it is a complex interplay between our individual life history and the timeless echoes of the stories that have shaped our collective consciousness, stories that continue to guide us, consciously or unconsciously, through the twilight of existence. They are the whispered lore of our ancestors, offering solace, warning, and a profound sense of connection as we navigate the final, inevitable chapter of our lives. The very act of storytelling, in its most ancient forms, can be seen as an attempt to wrestle with the silence of death, to fill it with meaning and form, and in doing so, to make it a little less terrifying, a little more understandable, and perhaps, even beautiful in its own profound and mysterious way.

Chapter 8: The Unconscious Desire for the Real

The unconscious, a realm of shadow and potent, untamed desire, is often perceived as seeking resolution, a movement towards coherence and meaning. Yet, within its deepest currents lies a paradoxical pull, an undeniable allure towards that which resists all sense, all order: Lacan's concept of 'The Real'. This is not the tangible world of everyday experience, nor the realm of fantasy, but rather the unvarnished, brute fact of existence itself, that which lies beyond the grasp of language, beyond the comforting structures of symbolization. It is the traumatic kernel, the irreducible core of being, which language can only skirt around, describe in oblique terms, or represent through its devastating absence. The unconscious, in its most radical explorations, can harbor a fascination with this abyss, a morbid curiosity that draws it towards the very edge of annihilation, the point where meaning dissolves and sheer presence, unmediated and raw, asserts itself with terrifying force.

The terror of 'The Real' is precisely this unassimilable quality. It is the encounter with an alterity so profound that it shatters our meticulously constructed symbolic universes. Imagine staring into the void, not the romantic, starlit void of poets, but a void that stares back, devoid of all reflection, all intelligibility. This is the terror that Lacan locates at the heart of existence, the irreducible gap that our symbolic apparatus attempts, and ultimately fails, to bridge. This terror is not merely an abstract philosophical concept; it is a visceral, felt experience that can manifest in the most profound anxieties and desires. The unconscious, in its yearning for what it cannot articulate, can oscillate between a desperate flight from this overwhelming presence and a perilous, almost suicidal, yearning for its full immersion. It is a complex dance on the precipice, where the desire for dissolution and the instinct for self-preservation engage in a perpetual, often agonizing, struggle.

This oscillation can be observed in the symbolic architecture of death. The death drive, as conceptualized in psychoanalysis, is not simply a death wish in the common parlance, but a fundamental tendency within the psyche to return to an inorganic state, to undo the complexities of being, to return to a primal stillness. When this drive intersects with the profound terror of 'The Real', it can manifest as a desire not merely for an end, but for an end that obliterates all trace of symbolic meaning, an end that plunges the individual into the unmediated reality of their own dissolution. This is not the peaceful fading of a narrative arc, or the noble sacrifice, but a terrifying confrontation with sheer nothingness, a regression to a state prior to differentiation, prior to language, prior to consciousness itself. The unconscious might, in its more extreme manifestations, harbor a desire for this ultimate encounter, a yearning to shed the burden of symbolization and to merge with the raw, untamed essence of existence, even at the cost of annihilation.

The terror is amplified by the fact that 'The Real' is fundamentally unspeakable. We can only point to its effects, the gaps it leaves in our discourse, the moments of breakdown in our symbolic systems. When individuals confront their own mortality, they are, in a profound sense, confronting the limits of what can be known and articulated. The sheer fact of finitude, the absolute cessation of being, resists all attempts at narrative containment. It is here that the unconscious might manifest a paradoxical desire: to both flee from the unbearable intensity of this confrontation and to rush headlong into it. This creates a complex internal dynamic, a push and pull between the instinctual drive towards self-preservation, which urges us to maintain our symbolic coherence, and the more radical, perhaps even masochistic, pull towards the unmediated experience of dissolution.

Consider the experiences of those who, in the face of terminal illness, describe a profound disorientation, a sense of their own identity dissolving not into a transcendent realm or a comforting narrative, but into a terrifying formlessness. They may articulate a feeling of "going nowhere," a sense of being untethered from all meaning and purpose. This is not the acceptance of a cyclical transition, nor the heroic struggle against fate; it is the encounter with a sheer void, an utter lack of symbolic grounding. The terror here stems from the realization that all the narratives that have structured their existence – their relationships, their achievements, their very sense of self – offer no solace, no bridge to this ultimate reality. 'The Real' asserts itself as the unyielding bedrock of non-being, against which all symbolic constructions crumble.

The unconscious desire for 'The Real', in this context, is not a conscious wish for death, but a subterranean current that seeks to unravel the symbolic tapestry of life. It is a powerful counter-movement to the life drive, a regression towards a state of undifferentiation. This can manifest as an attraction to the chaotic, the destructive, the utterly alien. In literature, for example, characters who are drawn to madness or self-destruction often embody this unconscious pull towards the unassimilable. They are not seeking a romanticized end, but a complete obliteration of the self as a constructed entity, a plunge into the primal soup of existence, stripped of all pretense and form. Their undoing becomes a perverse form of seeking truth, an attempt to touch the unvarnished, horrifying core of being.

This encounter with 'The Real' can also be understood through the lens of trauma. Traumatic experiences, by their very nature, exceed our capacity to symbolize them. They leave us with a wound in our psychic fabric, a point where the symbolic order breaks down. The unconscious, in its attempt to process or, paradoxically, to fully succumb to this trauma, might oscillate between repression and a relentless re-exposure to the unbearable. In the context of one's approaching death, this trauma can be the fundamental existential trauma of finitude itself. The unconscious might then be drawn to a death that mirrors the overwhelming, unmediated quality of the original trauma, a death that offers no narrative resolution, no symbolic meaning, but a pure, raw confrontation with the abyss.

The terror of 'The Real' is intrinsically linked to the experience of the sublime, as it was understood by philosophers like Edmund Burke. The sublime arises from an encounter with something vast, powerful, and potentially dangerous, something that overwhelms our senses and our capacity for comprehension. It inspires a mixture of awe and terror, a recognition of our own fragility in the face of overwhelming forces. In Lacanian terms, the sublime is an intimation of 'The Real' that pushes the boundaries of our symbolic containment. When we are faced with our own mortality, we are confronted with the ultimate sublime, the ultimate overwhelming force that threatens to dissolve our very being. The unconscious desire, in this state, can be a complex yearning for this dissolution, a desire to finally be overwhelmed, to cease the struggle against the inevitable, and to merge with the vastness that lies beyond all representation.

This desire is not necessarily a wish for annihilation in the sense of self-destruction. Rather, it is a desire for a state beyond the confines of the ego, beyond the limitations of our symbolic identities. It is a yearning for a return to a primordial unity, a state before the sundering of self and other, before the imposition of language and meaning. This primal unity, however, is not a comforting embrace, but a terrifying indifference. 'The Real' is not a benevolent mother figure, but a blind, impersonal force. The unconscious desire, therefore, is a dangerous one, a flirtation with the very forces that threaten to unmake us. It is the desire to touch the ungraspable, to confront the unthinkable, and to experience the raw, unmediated truth of existence, even if that truth is a terrifying void.

The process of dying, when viewed through this lens, becomes a potential site for the manifestation of this unconscious oscillation. For some, the terror of 'The Real' might prompt an overwhelming desire to cling to every last vestige of symbolic order, to frantically construct narratives of meaning, purpose, and transcendence. This is a flight from the abyss, a desperate attempt to shore up the collapsing walls of meaning. For others, however, the terror can paradoxically fuel a yearning for the very dissolution that is feared. This is the perilous allure of 'The Real', the unconscious desire to finally let go of the struggle, to cease the futile attempt to symbolize the unsymbolizable, and to surrender to the raw, unmediated truth of non-being. The death that such a desire might unconsciously script would be one devoid of redemption, of transcendence, of comforting narratives—a stark, unadorned encounter with the ultimate fact of existence and its inevitable cessation. It is a terrifying prospect, yet one that the deepest currents of the unconscious may, in its relentless pursuit of ultimate confrontation, find itself inexorably drawn towards. The human psyche, in its enigmatic depths, harbors a profound fascination with the limits of being, and in the face of death, this fascination can manifest as a terrifying, yet irresistible, draw towards the unassimilable core of existence—'The Real'.

The finality of death, stripped bare of all comforting platitudes and metaphysical assurances, presents itself as the ultimate bastion of the unsymbolizable. It is the absolute cessation, the irreducible fact of non-being, that eludes the grasp of language and the scaffolding of symbolic systems that have hitherto structured our reality. The unconscious, in its enigmatic depths, may not merely fear this ultimate encounter but, in a profound and often disturbing oscillation, may even gravitate towards it. This is not a conscious yearning for oblivion, but a subterranean current that seeks the absolute undoing of the symbolic order, a return to a primal state prior to differentiation, to meaning, to the very structures that define our existence as conscious beings. The unconscious, in its most radical exploration, can find itself drawn to the very edge of intelligibility, where sheer, unmediated presence – or in this case, its absolute absence – asserts itself with a force that language can only ever gesture towards.

Consider the nature of certain deaths, those that erupt from the fabric of life with a ferocity that obliterates all narrative coherence. Extreme violence, the sudden obliteration of self through catastrophic accident, or even the prolonged, agonizing disintegration of the body in certain terminal illnesses, can be viewed not merely as tragic ends but as potent, albeit terrifying, approximations of the encounter with the unsymbolizable. In such instances, the meticulously constructed symbolic edifice of a life – its relationships, achievements, its very narrative arc – is not gently folded but violently shattered. The survivor, and indeed the dying individual themselves, is left confronting a raw, brutal fact that resists all attempts at integration into a meaningful story. The language of grief, of remembrance, of legacy, falters in the face of such utter dissolution. What can be said about a life that ends not in a crescendo or a diminuendo, but in a sudden, deafening silence, or a chaotic shriek that echoes into nothingness? This is where the unconscious may find a chilling resonance, a confirmation of its more primal impulses towards deconstruction, towards the unmaking of the symbolic.

The unconscious, in its ceaseless dynamic, can project onto death a desire for the erasure of the signifier, the ultimate release from the burden of representation. This is not a desire for peace, but a desire for a radical nullification, a return to a state so utterly devoid of symbolic form that it verges on the pre-natal, the undifferentiated matrix of existence before the ego's formation and the subsequent imposition of language. Certain deaths, by their sheer gratuitousness, can seem to embody this unconscious fantasy. Think of the soldier obliterated by an unseen mine, leaving no trace but a shattered landscape. Or the child lost to a sudden, inexplicable illness, whose potential narratives are extinguished before they could even begin to unfold. These are not deaths that lend themselves to dignified eulogies or consoling narratives of a life well-lived. They are abrupt ruptures, instances where the symbolic order is not merely challenged but utterly annihilated, leaving behind a void that screams its unsymbolizable reality. The unconscious, in its most extreme expressions, might perceive such an ending not as a tragedy to be overcome by meaning-making, but as a pure, unadulterated expression of the Real, a death that truly

is nothing more than a cessation of being, unadorned by any symbolic vestige.

This gravitational pull towards the unsymbolizable can also be discerned in the morbid fascination that certain forms of death exert on the human psyche, particularly when these deaths are characterized by extremity, by an apparent lack of meaning or purpose that paradoxically draws our attention. The horrific accidents meticulously detailed in news reports, the unexplained disappearances, the suicides that defy psychological explanation – these events, while deeply disturbing, often hold a strange, compelling power. They represent a rupture in the predictable flow of our symbolic universe, a glimpse into an abyss of pure contingency that the unconscious may, in its more radical flights, find itself drawn to. This fascination is not necessarily a conscious desire for such an end, but rather an unconscious recognition of a death that mirrors the unassimilable kernel of existence itself. It is a death that refuses to be contained within the comforting narratives of fate, karma, or divine plan. It is, in essence, a death that is

just death, pure and unadulterated, and the unconscious may, in its complex interplay with the desire for dissolution, find this terrifying purity deeply alluring.

The very nature of the 'Real' – that which resists symbolization – is intrinsically linked to the traumatic. Trauma, by definition, is an event that exceeds our capacity to process it symbolically. It leaves an indelible mark on the psychic apparatus, a wound in the symbolic fabric that can never be fully healed or integrated into a coherent narrative. Death, in its ultimate dimension, can be seen as the archetypal trauma, the fundamental existential wound of finitude. For the unconscious, then, the confrontation with death is a confrontation with the ultimate source of trauma, with that which fundamentally breaks down our symbolic systems. In this context, the desire for the unsymbolizable death becomes a desire to confront the primal trauma in its purest form, to experience a dissolution that mirrors the initial shattering of the symbolic order, that trauma inevitably brings. Certain deaths, by their sheer uncontainability, their inherent senselessness, can feel like a re-enactment of this primal traumatic encounter, offering a terrifying validation of the unconscious's more destructive impulses.

Consider the philosophical attempts to grapple with the boundary of language and experience. Wittgenstein, in his later work, famously suggested that philosophical problems arise when language "goes on holiday," detaching itself from its "ordinary language" grounding. This "going on holiday" can be seen as a metaphor for the breakdown of symbolization, a state where words lose their anchoring and begin to drift into a realm of pure abstraction or, conversely, into a brute, unmediated presence that resists linguistic formulation. Death, as the absolute limit of our experience and our symbolization, represents the ultimate "holiday" of language. It is the point where our words fail us, where even the most eloquent pronouncements become hollow echoes against the silence of non-being. The unconscious, in its quest for the Real, might be drawn to this ultimate linguistic desert, this realm where the signs of life are extinguished, and only the stark, unvarnished fact of absence remains. A death that is brutally abrupt, devoid of any lingering presence or symbolic trace, can thus serve as a stark, albeit terrifying, manifestation of this unconscious pull towards the unsymbolizable.

The language of the sublime, as explored by thinkers like Burke and Kant, offers another avenue for understanding this paradoxical attraction. The sublime arises from an encounter with something vast, overwhelming, and terrifyingly powerful that lies beyond our capacity to fully comprehend or contain. It evokes a mixture of awe and dread, a recognition of our own finitude in the face of immense forces. Death, in its ultimate and absolute nature, is the most profound source of the sublime. When this sublime encounter is stripped of any mitigating narratives of transcendence, redemption, or spiritual continuity, it becomes a pure confrontation with the Real. The unconscious, in its more radical and perhaps masochistic tendencies, might be drawn to such an unmediated sublime, to the terrifying grandeur of absolute annihilation, a death that is not softened by meaning but presented in its raw, unassimilable horror. This is not the romanticized death of the poet, but a stark, existential encounter with the void.

Furthermore, the concept of the "jouissance" in Lacanian theory, that excessive, non-prohibitable enjoyment that lies beyond the pleasure principle, can be relevant here. Jouissance is often associated with the Real, with a transgression of the symbolic order that brings a certain ecstatic intensity, even if it is painful or destructive. Certain deaths, particularly those that are violent or shocking, can evoke a morbid fascination that borders on jouissance for the observer. For the individual experiencing such a death, it can represent a terrifying plunge into an experience that shatters all ordinary modes of being and pleasure, a form of ultimate, albeit annihilating, jouissance. The unconscious, in its pursuit of this radical, transgressive experience, might unconsciously seek out a death that embodies this principle, a death that is utterly excessive and beyond the bounds of normal symbolic experience. This is a desire not for simple oblivion, but for an absolute dissolution that is, in its very extremity, a form of ultimate, forbidden pleasure.

The unsymbolizable aspect of death is also deeply intertwined with the ineffable nature of suffering. Extreme physical or psychological pain can often transcend language, leaving the sufferer in a state of raw, unmediated experience that defies articulation. When such suffering culminates in death, the death itself can be perceived as an extension or culmination of this ineffable agony. The unconscious, in its desire to confront the Real, might be drawn to a death that is a direct continuation of such unresolvable suffering, a death that offers no release into meaning or understanding, but simply an absolute cessation of an experience that was already beyond words. This can manifest as a morbid fascination with deaths that are prolonged, agonizing, and seemingly without reason, where the sheer intensity of the suffering becomes the dominant, unsymbolizable element that culminates in an equally unsymbolizable end.

In essence, the unconscious desire for the unsymbolizable death is a profound testament to the human psyche's complex and often paradoxical relationship with its own finitude. It is a desire that operates beneath the surface of conscious thought, a subterranean current that seeks the ultimate confrontation with that which lies beyond the grasp of language and meaning. Certain deaths, by their very nature – their extremity, their senselessness, their utter finality – serve as potent symbols, or rather, as stark manifestations, of this ultimate unsymbolizable reality. They are the points where the carefully constructed edifice of our symbolic universe crumbles, revealing the raw, terrifying core of existence and its inevitable, unutterable end. This is not a desire to be understood, but a desire to be utterly undone, to merge with the primal silence from which all symbolization ultimately emerges and into which it must inevitably recede. The allure of such deaths lies not in their narrative potential, but in their absolute resistance to narrative, their pure, unadulterated presence as the ultimate, unspeakable truth of being.

This inherent pull towards the unsymbolizable, a theme woven through our exploration of death's ultimate resistance to meaning, finds its most potent and disturbing expression when we move beyond Freud's foundational concept of the death drive and consider a more profound, indeed, a more absolute unconscious orientation: the drive towards annihilation. While Freud's formulation of the *Todestrieb* articulated a fundamental psychic impetus towards a return to the inorganic, a release from the tension of life, the drive to annihilation ventures into a territory of absolute dissolution, a yearning not merely for stasis or an undoing of tension, but for a complete erasure of being itself. This is not the simple cessation of biological function, nor is it solely the repetition compulsion that Freud identified as a sign of the death drive's relentless operation. Instead, it is a more radical, a more totalizing desire, a psychic signature etched into the deepest strata of the unconscious, that seeks the utter obliteration of the self and its entire existential landscape.

This drive towards annihilation finds its conceptual anchor in what might be termed the 'fantasmatic signature' of death. It is the unconscious fantasy that animates not just the

how of dying, but the *what* of the end itself. This is not about a conscious wish for oblivion, nor is it a straightforward suicidal ideation, which often carries its own complex symbolic and psychological burdens. Rather, it is a more fundamental psychic orientation that gravitates towards endings characterized by a complete dissolution of selfhood and existence. Imagine, for a moment, a death that offers no lingering trace, no narrative redemption, no symbolic afterlife. Consider the sheer, unadorned concept of absolute void, of being utterly unmade. This is where the drive to annihilation finds its purest, albeit terrifying, expression. It is a psychic trajectory that seeks not simply rest, but a complete and irreversible unravelling, a return to a state prior to any form of differentiation, prior to any mark left upon the fabric of reality.

This is a drive that transcends the biological imperative for stasis, which Freud alluded to as a fundamental property of matter. It is not merely about a reduction of tension or a return to an inorganic equilibrium. The drive to annihilation is a distinctly psychic phenomenon, a yearning for an existential

ex nihilo, a complete vanishing that leaves no residue. It is a radical embrace of the void, not as an absence to be filled or mourned, but as an ultimate aesthetic. In this view, the void becomes the final, perfect canvas upon which existence has been painted, and the annihilation drive is the impulse to wipe it clean, to return it to its pristine, unblemished state of non-being. This confrontation with the Real, in its most unmediated and absolute form, becomes a perverse form of ultimate encounter, a catastrophic aesthetic of escape from the burdens of consciousness, representation, and the very fact of existence.

The unconscious, in its relentless pursuit of the Real, may therefore find itself drawn to this absolute erasure. It is a recognition that the most potent confrontation with the unsymbolizable is not simply the cessation of breath, but the utter disintegration of the symbolic edifice that constitutes the self. This can manifest in a myriad of subtle, and often disturbing, ways. It is in the fascination with extreme, almost incomprehensible forms of death, those that defy rationalization and leave behind only a stark, unnerving absence. Think of the narratives that surround individuals who seemingly vanish without a trace, leaving behind no explanation, no final message, no discernible reason for their departure. The unconscious may perceive in such disappearances a potent, albeit terrifying, enactment of its own desire for absolute dissolution. It is a death that, in its very lack of trace, embodies the drive towards utter non-being.

This is not to say that such deaths are consciously sought or desired. The unconscious operates through complex mechanisms of repression, sublimation, and projection. However, the psychic energy directed towards annihilation can shape our phantasies, our anxieties, and even our understanding of life's ultimate purpose. It is a subterranean current that can subtly influence the narratives we construct around mortality, pushing them towards extremes of dissolution. Consider the appeal of certain nihilistic philosophies or artistic expressions that emphasize entropy, decay, and the ultimate futility of human endeavour. While these may be intellectual or aesthetic pursuits on a conscious level, they can resonate with a deeper, unconscious drive towards erasure, finding validation in their stark pronouncements of ultimate meaninglessness.

The drive to annihilation can also be understood through the lens of a profound fatigue with existence itself. Life, with its constant demands, its relentless negotiations with reality, its perpetual striving and suffering, can become an unbearable burden. While the pleasure principle seeks to minimize pain, and the reality principle moderates our desires, the drive to annihilation offers a more radical form of escape: the complete abdication of the struggle. It is an imagined peace found not in the cessation of conflict, but in the utter vanishing of the combatant. This is a tempting proposition for the unconscious, a siren call towards an ultimate silence where the demands of being no longer intrude. The aesthetics of this silence are not necessarily serene; they can be terrifyingly absolute, the silence of non-existence, which, for a psyche exhausted by the noise of life, might hold an irresistible allure.

This pursuit of annihilation can also be seen as a hyper-sophisticated response to the terror of existence. Faced with the overwhelming complexity of consciousness, the burden of self-awareness, and the inherent contingency of life, the unconscious may recoil towards the simplest, most absolute resolution: non-being. It is a form of ultimate surrender, a recognition that the attempt to symbolize, to create meaning, to simply

be within the symbolic order, is a Sisyphean task. The drive to annihilation then becomes a psychic shortcut, an embrace of the void as the only true escape from the exhausting and often painful labor of existence. The Real, in its terrifying finality, is not just the absence of meaning, but the absence of the very burden of consciousness.

Furthermore, the concept of "negative theology," which attempts to describe the divine by what it is

not, offers a curious parallel. While theological, it touches upon the limits of symbolization. The drive to annihilation can be seen as a psychological echo of this negative approach applied to existence itself. It seeks to define the ultimate state by its absolute negation of all positive attributes of being. It is a state of absolute *un-being*, an ultimate "not-there" that stands as the antithesis to all that is. For the unconscious, this negation can become a potent object of phantasy, a realm of ultimate freedom from the constraints of positive being. The aesthetic of this absolute negativity is one of pure erasure, a canvas wiped clean of all representation, all presence, all existence.

The concept of the "limit-experience" in existential psychology and philosophy also provides a framework for understanding this drive. These are experiences that push individuals to the very edge of their being, forcing a confrontation with their finitude, their freedom, and the fundamental groundlessness of existence. Death, in its absolute sense, is the ultimate limit-experience. However, the drive to annihilation suggests a psychic orientation that actively seeks to

resolve this limit-experience through complete dissolution. It is not about enduring the terror of the limit, but about surrendering to it, about allowing the limit to swallow the self entirely. This is a radical form of confronting the Real, where the boundary between being and non-being is not merely tested, but utterly collapsed.

Consider also the phenomenon of what might be termed "existential ennui," a profound sense of boredom and meaninglessness that can afflict individuals who have seemingly achieved all their conscious goals. While often treated as a psychological malaise requiring therapeutic intervention, it can, in its extreme forms, hint at a deeper psychic yearning. This ennui can arise when the symbolic narratives that have structured a life no longer hold sway, leaving a void that is not filled by pleasure or engagement. For the unconscious oriented towards annihilation, this void is not a problem to be solved but an opening, a precursor to the ultimate erasure it craves. The lack of meaning becomes an invitation to complete non-being.

The drive to annihilation, then, is not merely a morbid curiosity or a destructive impulse; it is a fundamental psychic orientation towards the ultimate Real, a yearning for an absolute undoing that transcends the biological and even the aggressively destructive. It is the unconscious's most radical attempt to escape the burden of existence, to find in the absolute void the ultimate aesthetic of non-being. This drive shapes our phantasies of death, not as an end to be feared or understood, but as a potential for utter dissolution, a final, annihilating embrace of the Real. It is a testament to the unfathomable depths of the unconscious, where the desire for being can, in its most extreme manifestations, transform into a powerful, subterranean current pulling towards absolute non-being. This is not simply an end; it is an unmaking, a return to a primal silence that predates all form, all meaning, all existence.

The shadow of the absolute, the phantom limb of existence that aches for its own absence, finds its most arresting and unsettling manifestation not in abstract philosophical pronouncements or poetic metaphor alone, but in the stark, irreducible reality of human experience. Within the sanctum of the consulting room, where the carefully constructed edifices of the self are laid bare, we sometimes encounter individuals whose psychic trajectory seems inexorably drawn towards an abyss, a descent into a realm where the symbolic order crumbles and the raw, unmediated terror of being – or non-being – takes center stage. This is not a surrender to conventional despair, nor a simple embrace of nihilism. It is, rather, a profound, unconscious orientation towards *The Real*, a desire to touch, to merge with, or perhaps to be utterly consumed by that which resists symbolization, that which lies beyond the grasp of language and meaning.

Consider, for instance, the case of a patient I shall refer to as "Elias." Elias presented with a life that was, from its inception, a tapestry woven with threads of extremity. Not necessarily in the overt, dramatic sense of sensational headlines, but in the subtle, pervasive way in which certain lives seem to skirt the edges of the normative, brushing against the unspeakable with an unnerving frequency. His early childhood was marked by a profound sense of displacement, a feeling of being fundamentally out of sync with his environment, as if he were a foreign entity deposited into a world he could not fully comprehend or inhabit. This was not simply shyness or social anxiety; it was a deeper estrangement, a sense that the very air he breathed, the language spoken around him, held an alien resonance. His parents, though not overtly abusive, operated within a sphere of unspoken tensions and pervasive melancholia, a psychic atmosphere thick with unresolved loss that Elias absorbed not as a conscious understanding, but as a felt, somatic reality. He learned, early on, to navigate a world where direct emotional expression was rare, replaced by a language of omission, of glances that held more than they revealed, of silences that screamed.

As Elias matured, this sense of existential dislocation intensified. He found himself drawn to experiences that pushed the boundaries of ordinary perception and social convention. His adolescence was not a period of typical rebellion, but a quiet, almost obsessive exploration of what lay beyond the ordinary. He would spend hours in abandoned buildings, not for thrill-seeking, but for the palpable sense of decay, of a world that had surrendered its symbolic order and was slowly returning to a primal state. He sought out the periphery, the liminal spaces where the edges of reality seemed to blur. This included a fascination with extreme sports, not for the adrenaline rush in itself, but for the moments of near-death, where the self was stripped down to its barest existence, a precarious flicker against an overwhelming backdrop of potential annihilation. In these moments, he reported a peculiar clarity, a sense of being intensely alive precisely because he was so close to the edge of non-being. It was as if, in the face of absolute cessation, the stark reality of *is* was momentarily, luminously present.

His relationships, when they formed, were marked by a similar pattern. He was drawn to individuals who themselves seemed to exist on the fringes, those who carried within them an aura of profound sadness, of lives lived in the shadow of trauma or loss. He would often become the confidante, the silent witness to their deepest pain, absorbing their narratives of suffering with an almost unnerving equanimity. It was as if he were collecting fragments of the unspeakable, piecing together a mosaic of human agony that mirrored his own internal landscape. Yet, despite this profound empathy, he struggled with genuine emotional intimacy. His defenses, though not robust in the conventional sense of repression, were more akin to a profound detachment, a psychic habit of observing suffering from a distance, even when he was intimately involved in its telling. This detachment allowed him to engage with the abyss without being fully consumed by it, to observe the disintegration without losing his own precarious hold on existence.

The analytical work with Elias was arduous, characterized by long stretches of silence punctuated by cryptic, often disquieting, pronouncements. He spoke of dreams that were not narratives but sensory impressions – the feeling of falling endlessly, the sensation of melting into an undifferentiated mass, the sound of an immense, deafening silence. These were not symbolic representations of anxiety; they felt like direct transmissions from a pre-symbolic realm, echoes of a terrifying primal state. He described moments of derealization, where the solid world would momentarily lose its substance, becoming a flimsy façade, a deceptive construct. In these instances, he felt a fleeting glimpse of what lay beneath, a raw, unmediated reality that was both horrifying and, in a perverse way, exhilarating. He spoke of a "terrible beauty" in this void, an aesthetic that transcended conventional notions of good and bad, beautiful or ugly. It was the beauty of absolute truth, he explained, a truth that lay beyond human interpretation or comfort.

Elias's unconscious trajectory was not directed towards a conscious desire for suicide, though suicidal ideation had, at times, flickered at the edges of his consciousness. Instead, his drive seemed to be towards a more existential form of annihilation, a yearning for an absolute erasure of selfhood that would not necessarily be violent or self-willed, but more akin to a dissolution, a merging back into the undifferentiated source from which he felt he had so unnaturally emerged. He described this not as an end, but as a return, a shedding of the burdensome individuality that had always felt like an imposition.

This desire manifested in his professional life as well. He found himself unable to sustain any career that required consistent engagement with the symbolic demands of the world – building relationships, creating products, contributing to a collective narrative. Each attempt felt like a betrayal of his fundamental orientation. He would gravitate towards jobs that were temporary, detached, or involved a degree of isolation, allowing him to observe rather than to participate actively. He was a night watchman, a remote data entry clerk, a seasonal park ranger. These roles offered a certain degree of invisibility, a freedom to exist in the liminal spaces of the working world.

The crucial turning point in Elias's analysis, and indeed in his life, came with an incident that, though seemingly minor in its outward presentation, held profound symbolic weight. He had been living in a remote cabin for several months, seeking further isolation, when a severe storm hit. The cabin was small, battered, and the surrounding wilderness became a maelstrom of wind and rain. For three days, Elias was effectively cut off from any form of communication or rescue. During this period, his internal state mirrored the external chaos. He described a profound surrender, a letting go of the struggle to maintain his individual self. The boundaries between himself and the storm, between his consciousness and the roaring void of nature, began to dissolve. He reported moments where he felt he was no longer Elias, but the wind, the rain, the very earth groaning under the onslaught. He was not afraid; he was, in his words, "becoming one with the unmaking."

When the storm finally abated, Elias was found by a concerned neighbor, huddled in the remains of his cabin, which had partially collapsed. He was physically unharmed, though disoriented. However, the Elias who emerged from that experience was fundamentally different. The analytic sessions that followed were marked by a profound stillness, a quietude that had not been present before. He spoke of a completion, a finality that had been achieved. He no longer seemed to be struggling against the current; he had, in a sense, been swept away.

His narrative shifted. He no longer spoke of the allure of the void, but of its terrifying reality. The "terrible beauty" he had once described now seemed to him to be a profound and absolute emptiness, a chilling absence of anything that could be called being. He described the experience not as a merging, but as an encounter with an absolute nothingness that had, for a terrifying moment, almost succeeded in erasing him. The near-dissolution had not been a resolution, but a stark confrontation with the possibility of utter unmaking. The Real, in its most unadulterated form, had presented itself not as a liberating truth, but as a vast, indifferent abyss.

This confrontation, paradoxically, became the very thing that stabilized him, not by providing answers, but by offering a definitive experience of the limit. He had, in essence, come to the brink of that which he had unconsciously sought, and in the profound terror of that near-annihilation, a new, albeit fragile, sense of self began to emerge. It was a self that was acutely aware of its own tenuousness, its profound vulnerability to the forces of dissolution. But it was also a self that had, through direct encounter, finally understood the difference between symbol and the unsymbolizable, between the narrative of existence and the raw fact of non-existence.

The ending of Elias's story, in this context, is not a triumphant overcoming, nor a descent into madness. It is a testament to the profound psychic gravity of the unconscious drive towards the absolute, towards the Real that lies beyond our symbolic grasp. Elias's life became a living enactment of this drive, a journey towards an abyss that promised ultimate truth and found only an unbridgeable void. His experience highlights how, for some individuals, the unconscious quest for meaning can paradoxically lead to a fascination with meaninglessness, a desire to confront the ultimate void not as an end to be feared, but as a fundamental aspect of existence that demands acknowledgment. His life, and its near dissolution, served as a stark, unvarnished illustration of the terror and the perverse allure of the unassimilable, a poignant reminder of the abyssal depths that lie at the core of the human psyche, always yearning for a confrontation with that which lies beyond the comfort of symbol and the order of meaning. The void, in its absolute purity, had nearly claimed him, but in that near-annihilation, a new, fragile awareness was born – an awareness of the precipice itself, and the profound, unsettling reality of the groundless ground upon which all being precariously rests. His case underscores the profound human, or perhaps,

post-human, impulse to seek out the ultimate Real, even when that Real offers not solace, but the stark, unvarnished terror of utter non-being.

The inherent paradox of our endeavor, as analysts, philosophers, and indeed as sentient beings, lies in our persistent attempt to map the unmappable, to chart the contours of that which, by its very nature, defies cartography. We are creatures of symbol, weavers of meaning, our very consciousness a product of the linguistic and conceptual frameworks we inhabit. Yet, the unconscious, that vast and unruly territory of desire, trauma, and primal drives, often thrusts upon us glimpses of a reality that eludes our carefully constructed nets of signification. This is particularly acute when we approach the threshold of the "Real," that Lacanian abyss of pure jouissance and unmediated terror, the unassimilable kernel of existence that lies beyond the pale of symbolization. Our tools – language, theory, even the evocative power of art – are inherently symbolic. They are the very mechanisms by which we render the world intelligible, by which we suture the tears in the fabric of our subjective experience. To employ these tools in the service of apprehending that which fundamentally resists them is a task fraught with inherent limitation, a Sisyphean endeavor that nonetheless defines the very edge of our intellectual and psychic exploration.

Psychoanalysis, in its clinical practice, often finds itself in this precarious position. The consulting room, that enclosed space where the subject is invited to speak their truth, becomes a crucible for the negotiation between the symbolic and the unsymbolizable. When a patient recounts a dream, a fantasy, or a traumatic memory, they are, in essence, attempting to translate an internal, often visceral, experience into a communicable form. This act of translation is never neutral; it is always an interpretation, a shaping, a symbolic rendition. Even the most fragmented, nonsensical pronouncements, those that seem to shatter the expected coherence of discourse, are themselves symbolic gestures. They are fragments of a shattered mirror, reflecting a reality that refuses to be pieced back together into a coherent whole. The analyst's task, then, is not to simply decipher these fragments as if they were a code, but to bear witness to the

struggle of symbolization itself, to the very point where meaning falters and collapses. This involves a deep attunement to the affect, the rhythm, the silences that punctuate the narrative, for it is often in these gaps, these moments of linguistic failure, that the Real makes its most potent, albeit indirect, appearance. We learn to listen not just to what is said, but to what is *refused* by language, to the traumatic kernel that the symbolic order can only allude to, never fully encompass.

Philosophy, too, grapples with this fundamental limit. From the Eleatic paradoxes that question the very possibility of motion and change, to Kierkegaard's existential dread and Heidegger's meditations on Being and Nothingness, philosophical inquiry has consistently circled the unsymbolizable. Thinkers have employed paradox, metaphor, and a relentless questioning of categories to prod at the boundaries of human understanding. The concept of the "absolute," the "unconditioned," the "divine" – these are all terms that attempt to point beyond the finite, the conditioned, the mediated. Yet, any attempt to define or describe these ultimate realities inevitably traps them within the very symbolic structures they seek to transcend. We can speak of God, but the word "God" is a symbol, a placeholder for an experience or a reality that remains, for the human mind, fundamentally opaque. We can articulate the terrifying emptiness of absolute nothingness, but the very act of articulation, of naming it, imbues it with a certain conceptual existence, thereby distinguishing it from the pure absence it represents. This is the philosopher's bind: to illuminate the unknown by bringing it into the light of language, and in doing so, to inevitably alter its essential nature.

Art, in its myriad forms, offers a unique avenue for exploring this liminal space. A painting can evoke a profound sense of dread or awe that transcends words. A piece of music can tap into emotions for which we have no names. A poem, through its careful orchestration of rhythm, imagery, and metaphor, can create a resonance that hints at profound truths without explicitly stating them. These artistic expressions do not

explain the unsymbolizable; rather, they create an affective encounter with it. They create a space where the viewer, listener, or reader can, for a moment, touch upon that which lies beyond conceptual grasp. Think of the unsettling stillness in a Rothko painting, the dissonant harmonies in a Shostakovich symphony, or the stark, haunting imagery in a poem by T.S. Eliot. These are not straightforward narratives or logical propositions. They are invitations to an experience, to a feeling that bypasses the rational mind and speaks directly to the core of our being. Art, in this sense, is a powerful tool for creating symbolic inroads into the unsymbolizable. It gestures towards the abyss, not by describing its depth, but by creating a sense of vertigo, a palpable awareness of the sheer drop. It offers not an answer, but a profound, often disquieting, question that echoes in the soul.

When we consider the notion of "phantasmatic death" within this framework, the tension between the symbolic and the unsymbolizable becomes particularly acute. The unconscious, in its enigmatic workings, can manifest a "desire" for an end, for an annihilation, for a return to the primal state of undifferentiation. This desire, however, is almost always expressed through symbolic means. A dream of falling, a fantasy of dissolution, a repetitive reenactment of trauma – these are symbolic formations that represent the unconscious drive towards what is perceived as the Real of non-being. Yet, the actual experience of this "death," if it were to occur in its pure, unsymbolized form, would be an absolute cessation, an absence of any subject to witness it, to articulate it, to imbue it with meaning. The very idea of a "phantasmatic" death implies that it is a concept, a representation, a symbol that we can apprehend, even if it points to something beyond our full comprehension.

The horror, and indeed the perverse allure, of the Real lies in its resistance to such symbolic capture. It is not a narrative to be told, nor a concept to be understood. It is a brute fact, an encounter that can shatter our symbolic universe. When Elias, in his intense proximity to the storm, felt himself dissolving into the elements, he was, in a sense, touching upon this unsymbolizable Real. The experience was not fully communicable through language, not because he lacked the words, but because the very fabric of his being, the symbolic apparatus through which he apprehended reality, was being unraveled. His subsequent description of the "terrifying emptiness" was an attempt to translate this profound encounter back into the symbolic realm, a testament to the human need to make sense, even of that which defies sense.

This attempt to use symbolic means to explore the unsymbolizable is not merely an intellectual exercise; it is a deeply psychological and existential necessity. We are creatures who live by stories, by meanings, by the symbolic order that organizes our perception of the world and ourselves. To confront that which lies beyond this order is to risk dissolution, to face the abyss of meaninglessness. Yet, it is precisely in this confrontation that the boundaries of our symbolic universe are tested and, sometimes, expanded.

The analyst, therefore, must become adept at navigating this delicate terrain. They must be able to hold the patient's narrative, recognizing its symbolic weight, while simultaneously sensing the tremors of the Real that lie beneath. This requires a certain analytic discipline, a willingness to sit with ambiguity, to resist the urge to prematurely "fix" or "explain" that which is inherently resistant to such interventions. It means understanding that the patient's struggle with language, their silences, their moments of apparent regression, are not failures of communication, but rather the very sites where the unconscious grapples with its most profound encounters.

Consider the role of metaphor in this process. When a patient describes feeling "empty," they are using a spatial metaphor to convey a psychic state. This is a symbolic bridge, a way of articulating an internal experience. However, the "emptiness" they feel may be a resonance with the void, a primal lack that precedes language and conceptualization. The analyst does not simply accept the metaphor at face value, but uses it as a point of departure to explore the deeper affect and the underlying psychic reality. Similarly, the metaphor of "death" itself is a symbolic construct. The unconscious desire for annihilation may be a yearning for a state of pure being, or perhaps a release from the unbearable pressures of existence, a desire for a merging that obliterates the painful individuated self. But the absolute cessation of being, the ultimate Real of non-existence, is not something that can be symbolized or desired in any meaningful sense, for to desire is to exist.

This paradox is central to our understanding of the unconscious desire for the Real. It is a desire that, by its very nature, cannot be fully realized or articulated. It is a perpetual reaching towards a horizon that recedes as we approach it. The symbolic forms it takes – the dreams, the fantasies, the destructive impulses – are not mere representations; they are also the very means by which the unconscious attempts to both approach and distance itself from this terrifying limit. They are both expressions of the drive and defenses against its full impact.

The artistic response to this predicament is particularly illuminating. Artists often explore themes of death, void, and disintegration not to provide answers, but to evoke the feeling, the affective resonance of these states. They understand that the Real cannot be spoken, but it can be

felt. A sculptor might carve a form that suggests a body collapsing in on itself, not as a literal depiction of death, but as an evocation of the experience of disintegration. A writer might employ stream-of-consciousness to mimic the breakdown of symbolic order, creating a textual landscape that mirrors the internal chaos of confronting the unsymbolizable. These artistic endeavors are not failures of communication; they are sophisticated uses of the symbolic to gesture towards the ineffable. They acknowledge the limit of representation while simultaneously pushing against it, creating a liminal space where the viewer can have a fleeting, embodied experience of that which lies beyond symbolization.

In the consulting room, the analyst acts as a kind of interpreter of this symbolic gesturing. They are not translating a foreign language, but rather facilitating a dialogue between the patient's symbolic world and the unsymbolizable core of their experience. This might involve helping the patient to recognize the recurring patterns in their dreams or fantasies, not to explain them away, but to understand how these symbolic formations are attempts to grapple with an overwhelming affective reality. It might involve attuning to the subtle shifts in the patient's tone or affect, recognizing that these non-verbal cues can carry as much, if not more, symbolic weight than the spoken words.

The very act of analysis, of bringing the unconscious into the realm of the symbolic, is a way of attempting to contain and integrate that which threatens to overwhelm us. It is a process of weaving the threads of the Real into the larger tapestry of the self, not to master it, but to learn to live with its presence. When Elias, after his near-dissolution in the storm, reported a newfound stillness, it was not because he had conquered the void, but because he had, in a profound and terrifying way, encountered its absolute reality. This encounter, though deeply unsettling, had paradoxically provided a new foundation for his existence, one built not on solid ground, but on the stark awareness of the precipice. His subsequent narratives, though still tinged with a profound awareness of existential fragility, were no longer driven by an unconscious yearning for dissolution, but by a conscious wrestling with the meaning of having, for a moment, touched the unsymbolizable. This shift underscores the crucial insight that the symbolic attempt to grasp the Real, while always incomplete, is nonetheless a vital and necessary human endeavor, a testament to our indomitable drive to make meaning in the face of an existence that often offers only silence.

Chapter 9: The Unconscious and the Narrative of Life

The tapestry of a human life, as it unfolds, is rarely a straightforward chronicle. Beneath the surface of conscious decisions and perceived intentions lies a deeper, more intricate design, woven by the threads of the unconscious. This chapter delves into the profound connection between the narrative we consciously construct of our lives and the often-unacknowledged "fantasmatic signature" of death that operates at a deeper psychic level. It is our contention that the way we narrate our existence—the preoccupations that define us, the traumas that shape us, the desires that propel us—unconsciously prefigures the narrative of our ending. Our life's trajectory, therefore, is not merely a sequence of events, but a dynamic process imbued with an unconscious foreshadowing, a developing plot and character arc that inevitably leads to the symbolic resolution of death. The unconscious, in its subtle yet persistent manner, orchestrates the choices we make, the paths we tread, and the meanings we ascribe to our experiences, all of which contribute to weaving the fabric of our life's story and, by extension, setting the stage for its final, inevitable act.

Consider, for instance, the individual who, throughout their life, has been driven by an insatiable need for control. This might manifest in meticulous planning, a resistance to spontaneity, and a deep-seated anxiety surrounding any perceived loss of agency. Such a life narrative, rich with instances of careful management and strategic maneuvering, may, on an unconscious level, be preparing for an ending that mirrors this lifelong pursuit. The anxiety surrounding loss of control, when amplified and projected onto the ultimate loss of control that is death, can lead to a potent unconscious fantasy of dying in a manner that attempts, paradoxically, to exert some vestige of mastery over the inevitable dissolution. This might be a fantasy of dying "on one's own terms," a carefully orchestrated exit, or perhaps a more subtle, unconscious striving to preserve a sense of autonomy even in the face of biological surrender. The life narrative, in this case, becomes a prolonged rehearsal for a death that aligns with its core thematic preoccupations. The relentless pursuit of order, the avoidance of chaos, the meticulous charting of a course – these are not simply the habits of a personality, but the unconscious scripting of a final scene, where the ultimate loss of control becomes the central dramatic conflict.

Conversely, a life marked by a pervasive sense of helplessness, by experiences of profound victimization, or by an unconscious belief in one's own inherent fragility might weave a different prefiguration of death. The narrative here might be filled with accounts of being overwhelmed, of succumbing to external forces, of a passive acceptance of fate. The unconscious investment in this narrative of helplessness can imbue the fantasy of death with a sense of inevitability, a resigned surrender rather than a struggle. The ending, in this scenario, becomes less a confrontation and more a final, perhaps even welcome, release from the burden of a life lived under constant duress. The themes of powerlessness, of being buffeted by circumstances, of an inability to effect change, which have characterized the conscious and unconscious life story, find their ultimate expression in a death that is perceived as an unavoidable consequence, a final act of succumbing. The unconscious signature of death here is one of relinquishment, a quiet fading that mirrors the perceived lack of agency that has permeated the lived experience.

The role of trauma in this unconscious prefiguration is particularly significant. Traumatic experiences, by their very nature, shatter the existing narrative of self and world, leaving behind fragments and fissures. The unconscious response to trauma often involves complex mechanisms of defense, such as repression, dissociation, and denial. These mechanisms, while serving to protect the psyche in the immediate aftermath, can profoundly shape the subsequent life narrative. An individual who has experienced profound betrayal, for example, might unconsciously dedicate their life to seeking retribution or, conversely, to meticulously avoiding any situation that evokes a similar sense of vulnerability. Their life story becomes a testament to this ongoing, often unconscious, struggle. The fantasmatic signature of death, in such cases, might be deeply colored by the original trauma. It could manifest as a recurrent, symbolic reenactment in dreams of the traumatic event, or a persistent, underlying fear of a violent or sudden end that mirrors the original experience of terror and helplessness. The narrative of life, in its attempt to contain and process the unprocessable, becomes a protracted engagement with the ghost of a past event, a narrative that unconsciously directs the individual towards a resolution that echoes its initial rupture.

Consider the unconscious drive for repair or atonement that can shape a life. A person who carries a profound, perhaps unconscious, guilt from a past transgression may dedicate their life to acts of service, to alleviating the suffering of others, or to striving for a personal purity that seeks to erase the perceived stain of their past. Their life story is a conscious and unconscious effort to "make amends." The death narrative, in this context, might be imbued with a desire for forgiveness or absolution. It could be a hope for a peaceful passing, a sense of having achieved some form of spiritual redemption, or even a fantasy of sacrifice that offers a final, ultimate act of expiation. The unconscious logic at play is that by living a life dedicated to rectifying an imagined or real wrong, one can arrive at an ending that signifies a successful atonement, a return to a state of grace. The life narrative becomes a long, arduous journey towards a death that promises a symbolic cleansing.

The concept of the "death drive," as posited by Freud, offers a crucial lens through which to understand this unconscious prefiguration. While often understood as a destructive impulse towards annihilation, it can also be viewed as a fundamental striving towards a return to an inorganic state, a dissolution of psychic tension. This inherent tension between the life drive (Eros) and the death drive (Thanatos) is played out continuously throughout a life, shaping our choices, our relationships, and our very sense of self. The narrative of a life can be seen as the way in which these drives are woven together, with certain choices and experiences unconsciously reinforcing one drive over the other, or creating complex tensions between them. The unconscious "fantasmatic signature" of death, then, is the unique expression of this balance, or imbalance, of drives, as it is unconsciously projected onto the ultimate cessation of being. A life characterized by an overwhelming repression of instinctual desires and a constant striving for order might unconsciously harbor a powerful death drive, seeking release from the relentless pressure of inhibition. Its death narrative might therefore be one of explosive, sudden release, a violent eruption of repressed energy, or conversely, a slow, suffocating decline that symbolizes the crushing weight of lived repression.

Furthermore, the "object" of our unconscious desire plays a pivotal role in this prefiguration. What we unconsciously seek, what we yearn for at the deepest levels of our being, can powerfully shape the narrative arc of our lives and, consequently, the symbolic meaning of our death. If the unconscious object of desire is one of union and dissolution, a merging with something greater than the self, then the life narrative might be characterized by a constant seeking of engulfment, a blurring of boundaries in relationships, or an immersion in experiences that evoke a sense of ecstatic loss of self. The death narrative, in this instance, could be unconsciously fantasized as a complete dissolution, a final, ecstatic merger with the universe, a true return to the primordial unity. The life, in its conscious and unconscious manifestations, has been a journey towards this ultimate state of indistinguishable being.

Conversely, if the unconscious object of desire is one of autonomy, of absolute self-possession, then the life narrative might be a relentless pursuit of independence, a resistance to entanglement, and a deep-seated fear of annihilation of the self. The death narrative, for such an individual, might be unconsciously framed as a final act of defiance, a sovereign departure where the self remains intact and in control until the very last moment. The life has been a testament to the unyielding preservation of selfhood, and death becomes the ultimate, albeit tragic, affirmation of that solitude.

The very act of storytelling—how we choose to narrate our lives to ourselves and to others—is a crucial element in this dynamic. We select certain events, emphasize particular emotions, and weave them into a coherent (or perhaps deliberately fragmented) account. This conscious narration, however, is not entirely divorced from the unconscious. It is often shaped by, and in turn shapes, the unconscious phantasies that are at play. A person might consciously focus on their achievements, their triumphs, as the defining elements of their life story. This conscious emphasis, however, may serve as a defense against an unconscious fear of failure, or an unconscious sense of inadequacy. The unconscious "fantasmatic signature" of death, therefore, might be one that contrasts sharply with the conscious narrative – perhaps a sudden, ignominious end that belies the carefully constructed image of success. The unconscious narrative is often the more potent director of our ultimate symbolic fate.

The unconscious, in its relentless pursuit of psychic equilibrium, seeks a certain coherence, even in its most chaotic expressions. The narrative of a life, from birth to death, is one such attempt at imposing order and meaning. The unconscious "fantasmatic signature" of death acts as a powerful organizing principle for this life narrative. It is the unseen architect, guiding the placement of events, the development of character, and the eventual conclusion. It is the hidden resonance that gives the life story its underlying tonality, its particular emotional flavor. This signature is not a static blueprint, but a dynamic force, constantly shaping and reshaping the unfolding narrative. It is the murmur beneath the conscious discourse, the silent counterpoint to the spoken words, the ghost in the machine of our lived experience, subtly dictating the rhythm and cadence of our final exit. The life, in essence, becomes the intricate and often unconscious prelude to the death that its own internal logic has already begun to compose. It is a symphony played out in slow motion, where every note, every chord, is a deliberate, albeit often unconscious, step towards the grand finale. The conscious narrative is the melody we hear, but the unconscious signature is the harmonic structure that gives it its profound, and sometimes terrifying, meaning.

The unconscious, a vast and often inscrutable realm within the psyche, acts as an unseen editor of the memoir of our lives. It is a relentless curator, sifting through the immense archive of our experiences, selectively highlighting certain passages while discreetly, or sometimes brutally, downplaying or even erasing others. This editorial process is not a neutral act of cataloging; it is a deeply charged, emotionally resonant selection that shapes not only how we perceive ourselves and the meaning of our existence, but also, crucially, how we unconsciously script our death. The patterns and themes that this internal editor favors—the recurring motifs of struggle, the celebrated arcs of triumph, the poignant melodies of love, the stark landscapes of loss—these are not merely biographical data. They are the very substance of the narrative, and they invariably find their echo in the symbolic form of our final exit. This internal narrative construction, this shaping of our life's story by an unconscious hand, is foundational to understanding the intricate dance between life and death.

Consider the individual whose life, from a conscious perspective, appears to be a relentless pursuit of external validation. They might meticulously curate their achievements, dwelling on accolades, promotions, and public recognition. Every success is amplified, every setback minimized or rationalized away. This conscious narrative, however, may be a carefully constructed façade, masking a deeper, unconscious belief in their own inherent worthlessness. The unconscious editor, in this scenario, is working overtime to ensure that the "published" version of the memoir is one of perpetual triumph, a bulwark against the gnawing fear of inadequacy. But what does this selective editing portend for the unconscious script of death? It is possible that this relentless pursuit of validation, this constant striving to prove one's worth to the external world, unconsciously predisposes the individual towards an ending that mirrors this lifelong emphasis. The death, rather than being a peaceful cessation, might be experienced or fantasized as a final, desperate bid for recognition, a dramatic exit intended to elicit a powerful, perhaps even salvific, response from the world. The unconscious editor has ensured that the final chapter, no matter how painful or tragic, will still be about the pursuit of something external, a testament to the very mechanism that defined the life narrative. The focus remains resolutely outward, a desperate, final attempt to secure the validation that was never truly found within. The editor, in its zeal to present a heroic figure, may have inadvertently written a tragic finale, one where the last act is a desperate plea for applause in an empty theatre.

Conversely, imagine a life narrative that is saturated with the theme of sacrifice. The conscious story is filled with accounts of selflessness, of putting others' needs before one's own, of enduring hardship for the sake of loved ones. The unconscious editor, in this case, might be highlighting these acts of renunciation, celebrating the saintly aspects of the individual's character. This narrative can be a source of pride, a defining characteristic that brings a sense of purpose and virtue. Yet, beneath the surface, there may be a profound, unconscious narrative of self-negation, a belief that one's own desires and needs are inherently invalid or even dangerous. The editor's choice to emphasize sacrifice might be a way of managing this deeper unease, of presenting a palatable, virtuous version of a life lived in avoidance of the self. When this narrative is projected onto the unconscious script for death, it can manifest in a number of ways. The individual might unconsciously fantasize a death that is itself a supreme act of sacrifice, a final, ultimate offering that absolves them of any perceived selfishness or imperfection. This could be a death that directly saves others, or a death that is perceived as a noble, perhaps even heroic, martyrdom. The unconscious editor has ensured that the final pages continue the theme of giving oneself away, a culmination of a lifetime spent diminishing the self in favor of a perceived greater good. The narrative arc, however virtuous it appears, leads inexorably to an ending that perpetuates the erasure of the individual's own existence. The editor has, in essence, dictated that the final act must be the ultimate act of self-effacement.

The role of idealized relationships within a life narrative also offers a compelling example of the unconscious editor at work. A person might consciously focus on a singular, profound love affair, recounting it with an almost religious fervor. The unconscious editor may then elevate this relationship to the supreme significance, making it the central organizing principle of the entire life story. Other relationships, friendships, or familial bonds might be relegated to footnotes or even entirely omitted, deemed less important in the grand tapestry. This selective focus can be a way of warding off feelings of loneliness, or of maintaining an idealized image of oneself as capable of profound, all-consuming connection. However, this intensely focused narrative can unconsciously prefigure a death that is deeply intertwined with the fate of this idealized object. The unconscious script might involve a desire to die united with the beloved, or a fear of dying alone, separated from this central figure. The narrative might even unconsciously drive the individual towards a shared demise, or towards an ending where the absence of the beloved becomes the primary catalyst for dissolution. The editor, by fixating on this singular bond, has woven a narrative where life and death are inextricably linked to the presence or absence of another, a potent if potentially tragic thematic resolution.

The editor's preference for a singular, luminous star has cast a long shadow, dictating that the final fade to black must occur in its orbit.

Consider, too, the unconscious editor's treatment of conflict and resolution. Some individuals, consciously or unconsciously, have a life narrative that is characterized by continuous struggle. Every victory is hard-won, every peace temporary, and the underlying tone is one of perpetual engagement with adversity. The unconscious editor may meticulously document each battle, each moment of tension, presenting a life story as a continuous war of attrition. The narrative might be rich with accounts of overcoming obstacles, of resilience in the face of overwhelming odds. This emphasis on conflict can serve various unconscious purposes, perhaps a way of asserting one's strength, or a deeply ingrained belief that life itself is inherently fraught with peril. When this theme of struggle is projected onto the unconscious script for death, it can lead to a fantasy of dying in the midst of a battle, of going down fighting, or of experiencing death as the ultimate, unavoidable conflict. The ending, for such an individual, might be unconsciously framed as a final, epic showdown, a culmination of a lifetime spent in opposition. The unconscious editor, by consistently highlighting the drama of conflict, has written a final act that is a grand, perhaps violent, climax, a testament to a life lived in perpetual resistance. The editor, in its preference for the dramatic, has ensured that the final curtain falls not in quiet resignation, but in a thunderous crescendo.

Conversely, a life narrative that is consciously constructed around themes of avoidance and peace-seeking presents a different editorial hand. The conscious story might emphasize periods of tranquility, a deliberate steering clear of conflict, and a profound desire for harmony. The unconscious editor might then downplay or even erase moments of internal discord or external tension, presenting a smoother, more serene biography. This narrative construction can be a powerful defense against underlying anxieties or traumatic memories, a way of creating a safe, placid inner world. The unconscious editor, by smoothing over the rough edges, creates a narrative of gentle progression. When this thematic preference for peace is translated into the unconscious script for death, it can lead to a fantasy of a peaceful, uneventful passing. The death might be imagined as a gentle fading, a quiet slipping away into oblivion, a final surrender to the serenity that has been a hallmark of the life. The unconscious editor has ensured that the concluding chapter is a soft diminuendo, a peaceful lullaby sung to the dying embers of existence. The editor's preference for stillness has dictated that the final act must be one of profound quietude.

The unconscious editor's role is also evident in how it handles formative relationships. A childhood marked by profound neglect might be consciously remembered as "tough but character-building." The unconscious editor, however, might highlight the moments of abandonment, the gnawing emptiness, the deep-seated feelings of unworthiness that stem from that neglect. These experiences, though perhaps minimized in conscious recollection, become the bedrock of the individual's internal narrative, shaping their perception of love, trust, and self-worth. The editor might compulsively revisit these early wounds, weaving them into the fabric of subsequent relationships, always unconsciously seeking either to repeat the pattern or to desperately find a corrective experience. When this underlying narrative of neglect and unworthiness is projected onto the unconscious script for death, the ending can take on a particularly poignant or even tragic cast. The individual might unconsciously fantasize a death that mirrors the early experience of abandonment, a solitary passing, or an ending where their final moments are marked by a profound sense of being unseen or uncaringly left behind. The unconscious editor, by fixating on the primal wound, ensures that the final scene reflects the original trauma, a painful echo of a forgotten beginning. The editor has, in its relentless focus on the initial rupture, ensured that the concluding silence is a profound testament to that original emptiness.

The unconscious editor's influence extends to the very emotional texture of our life's memoir. Some lives are narrated, consciously and unconsciously, with a dominant hue of melancholy. Moments of joy are fleeting, tinged with an underlying sadness, and the overarching tone is one of gentle sorrow or a pervasive sense of loss. The unconscious editor amplifies these melancholic experiences, magnifying the sense of impermanence, the ephemeral nature of happiness, and the inevitability of suffering. This creates a life narrative that is rich in pathos, imbued with a profound understanding of the human condition's inherent suffering. When this dominant emotional tone is projected onto the unconscious script for death, it can lead to a fantasy of a sorrowful, perhaps even beautiful, demise. The death might be imagined as a poignant farewell, a moment of profound emotional resonance, imbued with the weight of all the sadness that has been experienced. The unconscious editor, by consistently emphasizing the melancholic, has written a final act that is a tear-jerking elegy, a somber masterpiece that resonates with the deepest chords of sorrow. The editor's preference for a somber palette has dictated that the final masterpiece be a dirge.

Conversely, a life narrative that is consciously, and unconsciously, imbued with a spirit of defiant optimism presents a different editorial choice. Even in the face of adversity, the narrative emphasizes resilience, the unwavering belief in a brighter future, and the capacity for joy even in the darkest of times. The unconscious editor will highlight these moments of hope, these acts of courage, and the persistent spark of life that refuses to be extinguished. This creates a narrative of indomitable spirit, a testament to the power of the human will. When this optimistic orientation is projected onto the unconscious script for death, it can lead to a fantasy of a triumphant end, a passing that is met with courage and a sense of peace, or even a final affirmation of life's inherent goodness. The unconscious editor, by consistently highlighting the light, has written a final act that is a hopeful anthem, a testament to the enduring power of the human spirit. The editor's commitment to the radiant has ensured that the final illumination is one of enduring brilliance.

The selective nature of this unconscious editing is what gives each individual's life memoir its unique character and, crucially, its particular foreshadowing of death. It is not merely the events themselves, but the

way in which they are remembered, emphasized, or suppressed by the unconscious editor that crafts the overarching narrative. This narrative is a living, breathing entity, constantly being revised and reinterpreted, but its core thematic preoccupations, dictated by the editor's preferences, remain remarkably stable. These preoccupations, these favored motifs and emotional resonances, are the threads that are woven into the very fabric of our being, and they invariably lead to a death that is, in its symbolic form, a fitting conclusion to the story that the unconscious has so diligently, and so powerfully, edited. The unconscious editor, in its ceaseless work, does not merely record life; it shapes it, guiding it towards an ending that is a mirror, however distorted or sublime, of the narrative it has so carefully constructed. The memoir, when read with an understanding of this editorial hand, reveals not just what happened, but what the unconscious *wished* had happened, and what it unconsciously decrees must be the final, resonant note.

The unconscious, a vast and often inscrutable realm within the psyche, acts as an unseen editor of the memoir of our lives. It is a relentless curator, sifting through the immense archive of our experiences, selectively highlighting certain passages while discreetly, or sometimes brutally, downplaying or even erasing others. This editorial process is not a neutral act of cataloging; it is a deeply charged, emotionally resonant selection that shapes not only how we perceive ourselves and the meaning of our existence, but also, crucially, how we unconsciously script our death. The patterns and themes that this internal editor favors—the recurring motifs of struggle, the celebrated arcs of triumph, the poignant melodies of love, the stark landscapes of loss—these are not merely biographical data. They are the very substance of the narrative, and they invariably find their echo in the symbolic form of our final exit. This internal narrative construction, this shaping of our life's story by an unconscious hand, is foundational to understanding the intricate dance between life and death.

Consider the individual whose life, from a conscious perspective, appears to be a relentless pursuit of external validation. They might meticulously curate their achievements, dwelling on accolades, promotions, and public recognition. Every success is amplified, every setback minimized or rationalized away. This conscious narrative, however, may be a carefully constructed façade, masking a deeper, unconscious belief in their own inherent worthlessness. The unconscious editor, in this scenario, is working overtime to ensure that the "published" version of the memoir is one of perpetual triumph, a bulwark against the gnawing fear of inadequacy. But what does this selective editing portend for the unconscious script of death? It is possible that this relentless pursuit of validation, this constant striving to prove one's worth to the external world, unconsciously predisposes the individual towards an ending that mirrors this lifelong emphasis. The death, rather than being a peaceful cessation, might be experienced or fantasized as a final, desperate bid for recognition, a dramatic exit intended to elicit a powerful, perhaps even salvific, response from the world. The unconscious editor has ensured that the final chapter, no matter how painful or tragic, will still be about the pursuit of something external, a testament to the very mechanism that defined the life narrative. The focus remains resolutely outward, a desperate, final attempt to secure the validation that was never truly found within. The editor, in its zeal to present a heroic figure, may have inadvertently written a tragic finale, one where the last act is a desperate plea for applause in an empty theatre.

Conversely, imagine a life narrative that is saturated with the theme of sacrifice. The conscious story is filled with accounts of selflessness, of putting others' needs before one's own, of enduring hardship for the sake of loved ones. The unconscious editor, in this case, might be highlighting these acts of renunciation, celebrating the saintly aspects of the individual's character. This narrative can be a source of pride, a defining characteristic that brings a sense of purpose and virtue. Yet, beneath the surface, there may be a profound, unconscious narrative of self-negation, a belief that one's own desires and needs are inherently invalid or even dangerous. The editor's choice to emphasize sacrifice might be a way of managing this deeper unease, of presenting a palatable, virtuous version of a life lived in avoidance of the self. When this narrative is projected onto the unconscious script for death, it can manifest in a number of ways. The individual might unconsciously fantasize a death that is itself a supreme act of sacrifice, a final, ultimate offering that absolves them of any perceived selfishness or imperfection. This could be a death that directly saves others, or a death that is perceived as a noble, perhaps even heroic, martyrdom. The unconscious editor has ensured that the final pages continue the theme of giving oneself away, a culmination of a lifetime spent diminishing the self in favor of a perceived greater good. The narrative arc, however virtuous it appears, leads inexorably to an ending that perpetuates the erasure of the individual's own existence. The editor has, in essence, dictated that the final act must be the ultimate act of self-effacement.

The role of idealized relationships within a life narrative also offers a compelling example of the unconscious editor at work. A person might consciously focus on a singular, profound love affair, recounting it with an almost religious fervor. The unconscious editor may then elevate this relationship to the supreme significance, making it the central organizing principle of the entire life story. Other relationships, friendships, or familial bonds might be relegated to footnotes or even entirely omitted, deemed less important in the grand tapestry. This selective focus can be a way of warding off feelings of loneliness, or of maintaining an idealized image of oneself as capable of profound, all-consuming connection. However, this intensely focused narrative can unconsciously prefigure a death that is deeply intertwined with the fate of this idealized object. The unconscious script might involve a desire to die united with the beloved, or a fear of dying alone, separated from this central figure. The narrative might even unconsciously drive the individual towards a shared demise, or towards an ending where the absence of the beloved becomes the primary catalyst for dissolution. The editor, by fixating on this singular bond, has woven a narrative where life and death are inextricably linked to the presence or absence of another, a potent if potentially tragic thematic resolution. The editor's preference for a singular, luminous star has cast a long shadow, dictating that the final fade to black must occur in its orbit.

Consider, too, the unconscious editor's treatment of conflict and resolution. Some individuals, consciously or unconsciously, have a life narrative that is characterized by continuous struggle. Every victory is hard-won, every peace temporary, and the underlying tone is one of perpetual engagement with adversity. The unconscious editor may meticulously document each battle, each moment of tension, presenting a life story as a continuous war of attrition. The narrative might be rich with accounts of overcoming obstacles, of resilience in the face of overwhelming odds. This emphasis on conflict can serve various unconscious purposes, perhaps a way of asserting one's strength, or a deeply ingrained belief that life itself is inherently fraught with peril. When this theme of struggle is projected onto the unconscious script for death, it can lead to a fantasy of dying in the midst of a battle, of going down fighting, or of experiencing death as the ultimate, unavoidable conflict. The ending, for such an individual, might be unconsciously framed as a final, epic showdown, a culmination of a lifetime spent in opposition. The unconscious editor, by consistently highlighting the drama of conflict, has written a final act that is a grand, perhaps violent, climax, a testament to a life lived in perpetual resistance. The editor, in its preference for the dramatic, has ensured that the final curtain falls not in quiet resignation, but in a thunderous crescendo.

Conversely, a life narrative that is consciously constructed around themes of avoidance and peace-seeking presents a different editorial hand. The conscious story might emphasize periods of tranquility, a deliberate steering clear of conflict, and a profound desire for harmony. The unconscious editor might then downplay or even erase moments of internal discord or external tension, presenting a smoother, more serene biography. This narrative construction can be a powerful defense against underlying anxieties or traumatic memories, a way of creating a safe, placid inner world. The unconscious editor, by smoothing over the rough edges, creates a narrative of gentle progression. When this thematic preference for peace is translated into the unconscious script for death, it can lead to a fantasy of a peaceful, uneventful passing. The death might be imagined as a gentle fading, a quiet slipping away into oblivion, a final surrender to the serenity that has been a hallmark of the life. The unconscious editor has ensured that the concluding chapter is a soft diminuendo, a peaceful lullaby sung to the dying embers of existence. The editor's preference for stillness has dictated that the final act must be one of profound quietude.

The unconscious editor's influence is also evident in how it handles formative relationships. A childhood marked by profound neglect might be consciously remembered as "tough but character-building." The unconscious editor, however, might highlight the moments of abandonment, the gnawing emptiness, the deep-seated feelings of unworthiness that stem from that neglect. These experiences, though perhaps minimized in conscious recollection, become the bedrock of the individual's internal narrative, shaping their perception of love, trust, and self-worth. The editor might compulsively revisit these early wounds, weaving them into the fabric of subsequent relationships, always unconsciously seeking either to repeat the pattern or to desperately find a corrective experience. When this underlying narrative of neglect and unworthiness is projected onto the unconscious script for death, the ending can take on a particularly poignant or even tragic cast. The individual might unconsciously fantasize a death that mirrors the early experience of abandonment, a solitary passing, or an ending where their final moments are marked by a profound sense of being unseen or uncaringly left behind. The unconscious editor, by fixating on the primal wound, ensures that the final scene reflects the original trauma, a painful echo of a forgotten beginning. The editor has, in its relentless focus on the initial rupture, ensured that the concluding silence is a profound testament to that original emptiness.

The unconscious editor's influence extends to the very emotional texture of our life's memoir. Some lives are narrated, consciously and unconsciously, with a dominant hue of melancholy. Moments of joy are fleeting, tinged with an underlying sadness, and the overarching tone is one of gentle sorrow or a pervasive sense of loss. The unconscious editor amplifies these melancholic experiences, magnifying the sense of impermanence, the ephemeral nature of happiness, and the inevitability of suffering. This creates a life narrative that is rich in pathos, imbued with a profound understanding of the human condition's inherent suffering. When this dominant emotional tone is projected onto the unconscious script for death, it can lead to a fantasy of a sorrowful, perhaps even beautiful, demise. The death might be imagined as a poignant farewell, a moment of profound emotional resonance, imbued with the weight of all the sadness that has been experienced. The unconscious editor, by consistently emphasizing the melancholic, has written a final act that is a tear-jerking elegy, a somber masterpiece that resonates with the deepest chords of sorrow. The editor's preference for a somber palette has dictated that the final masterpiece be a dirge.

Conversely, a life narrative that is consciously, and unconsciously, imbued with a spirit of defiant optimism presents a different editorial choice. Even in the face of adversity, the narrative emphasizes resilience, the unwavering belief in a brighter future, and the capacity for joy even in the darkest of times. The unconscious editor will highlight these moments of hope, these acts of courage, and the persistent spark of life that refuses to be extinguished. This creates a narrative of indomitable spirit, a testament to the power of the human will. When this optimistic orientation is projected onto the unconscious script for death, it can lead to a fantasy of a triumphant end, a passing that is met with courage and a sense of peace, or even a final affirmation of life's inherent goodness. The unconscious editor, by consistently highlighting the light, has written a final act that is a hopeful anthem, a testament to the enduring power of the human spirit. The editor's commitment to the radiant has ensured that the final illumination is one of enduring brilliance.

The selective nature of this unconscious editing is what gives each individual's life memoir its unique character and, crucially, its particular foreshadowing of death. It is not merely the events themselves, but the

way in which they are remembered, emphasized, or suppressed by the unconscious editor that crafts the overarching narrative. This narrative is a living, breathing entity, constantly being revised and reinterpreted, but its core thematic preoccupations, dictated by the editor's preferences, remain remarkably stable. These preoccupations, these favored motifs and emotional resonances, are the threads that are woven into the very fabric of our being, and they invariably lead to a death that is, in its symbolic form, a fitting conclusion to the story that the unconscious has so diligently, and so powerfully, edited. The unconscious editor, in its ceaseless work, does not merely record life; it shapes it, guiding it towards an ending that is a mirror, however distorted or sublime, of the narrative it has so carefully constructed. The memoir, when read with an understanding of this editorial hand, reveals not just what happened, but what the unconscious *wished* had happened, and what it unconsciously decrees must be the final, resonant note.

This leads us to the concept of repetition compulsion, a cornerstone of psychoanalytic thought, which offers a profound lens through which to understand the continuity between the patterns of life and the unconscious script of death. Sigmund Freud, in his seminal work "Beyond the Pleasure Principle," posited that beyond the drive for pleasure, there exists a more fundamental, instinctual force compelling us to repeat distressing experiences, not in a quest for pleasure, but as an unconscious attempt to master or gain control over them. This drive is particularly evident in the realm of trauma, where individuals may unconsciously reenact painful scenarios, often in distorted forms, as if desperately seeking a different outcome, a more favorable resolution that was denied in the original experience. This compulsion to repeat is not a sign of perversion or pathology in itself, but rather a deeply ingrained psychic mechanism, a primal rhythm of the psyche attempting to process and integrate overwhelming experiences.

When we transpose this concept to the narrative of life and death, we see how the unconscious, in its role as editor and architect of our internal world, utilizes this repetition compulsion to shape our ultimate exit. The life narrative, as we have explored, is not a simple chronological account but a tapestry woven with recurring themes, relational dynamics, and defense mechanisms that have served—or perhaps failed to serve—us throughout our existence. These patterns, once established, possess a powerful inertia. The unconscious editor, rather than discarding these familiar motifs, often finds them to be the most potent building blocks for the final act. The "fantasmatic signature," that unique imprint of our deepest desires, fears, and conflicts, is deeply intertwined with this compulsive repetition. It is the unconscious author's preferred stylistic element, the recurring motif that gives the narrative its distinctive, albeit sometimes haunting, melody.

Consider an individual whose life has been characterized by a pattern of seeking out emotionally unavailable partners. Consciously, they might lament this tendency, expressing a desire for a stable, nurturing relationship. However, unconsciously, the repetition compulsion may drive them to recreate the familiar dynamic of longing, pursuit, and eventual disappointment. The unconscious editor, in this case, is not necessarily aiming for happiness, but for a sense of the known, the predictable, even if that predictability is laced with pain. This familiar landscape of emotional striving and frustration becomes the bedrock upon which the unconscious script of death is built. The death itself may become a symbolic reenactment of this core relational pattern. Perhaps the individual dies alone, their last thoughts consumed by a yearning for a love that remained perpetually out of reach. Or, in a more dramatic manifestation, their death might occur during a moment of intense emotional conflict with an unavailable partner, the final scene mirroring the lifelong struggle for connection and recognition that characterized their relationships. The death, in this instance, is not merely an end but a powerful, albeit unconscious, reiteration of a fundamental life pattern. The editor has ensured that the final act resonates with the most persistent, defining melody of the life's song.

This repetition compulsion is not confined to interpersonal dynamics; it also extends to defense mechanisms and coping strategies that have become deeply ingrained. An individual who has consistently employed intellectualization as a means of avoiding overwhelming emotions throughout their life may unconsciously carry this defense into their dying process. While facing the profound existential realities of mortality, their unconscious script may dictate a final act characterized by detached observation, rational analysis of their own demise, and a persistent avoidance of the raw emotional experience. The unconscious editor, in its commitment to this familiar strategy, might construct a deathbed scene where the dying person, even in extremis, remains aloof, dissecting their symptoms, discussing their condition with clinical precision, and perhaps even offering objective advice to their grieving loved ones. This is not necessarily a sign of strength or emotional resilience in the conscious sense, but rather the unconscious operating on its most trusted, albeit perhaps ultimately unhelpful, autopilot. The death narrative becomes a final, unwavering application of a lifelong defense mechanism, a testament to the psyche's stubborn adherence to its established coping repertoire. The editor, by favoring the intellectual over the emotional, crafts a final scene that is a stark, almost clinical, illustration of a lifetime's emotional suppression.

Furthermore, even when life presents opportunities for change and growth, the unconscious pull of repetition can exert a powerful influence. An individual might consciously engage in therapy, work diligently to understand and alter their destructive patterns, and achieve significant progress. Yet, the unconscious narrative, deeply imprinted with earlier experiences, may still retain a subtle but persistent inclination towards the familiar. The unconscious editor, while acknowledging the conscious efforts at transformation, might still find ways to weave in elements that echo earlier, less adaptive, patterns. This is not to say that conscious change is futile, but rather that the unconscious realm operates with its own temporal logic, its own deeply embedded narratives that can resurface in unexpected ways, particularly at moments of profound transition, such as death.

Consider the case of an individual who, after a childhood of profound scarcity, has achieved considerable financial success and consciously enjoys a life of abundance. Their conscious narrative is one of overcoming hardship and achieving security. However, the unconscious editor might still subtly infuse their internal world with a lingering anxiety about loss, a fear that this abundance is precarious and could vanish overnight. This deep-seated insecurity, rooted in early experiences, may manifest in their unconscious script for death. While their conscious awareness might anticipate a peaceful passing, free from material worry, the unconscious script might be one of profound anxiety about leaving behind their hard-won possessions, a final, lingering obsession with the material world that echoes the desperate anxieties of their youth. The death narrative, in this instance, is not a simple reflection of their current conscious reality, but a complex interweaving of past and present, where the unconscious editor revisits the primal wound of scarcity, even amidst conscious prosperity. The final act becomes a powerful, albeit unconscious, reiteration of the fear that defined the earliest chapters, demonstrating how deeply entrenched these early narratives can be, even in the face of conscious transformation. The editor, by emphasizing the ghost of past lack, ensures the final scene carries the weight of that original insecurity.

The variations that do occur in these repeated patterns are crucial to understanding the dynamic interplay between life and death. The unconscious does not necessarily demand an exact replica of past events. Instead, it often presents a nuanced variation, a subtle alteration that still carries the core thematic resonance. This variation can be seen as the unconscious's attempt to achieve a more successful resolution, a more palatable outcome, or simply a more symbolic representation of the underlying conflict. For example, the individual who habitually sought unavailable partners might, in their unconscious death script, not necessarily die alone and yearning. Instead, they might die in the midst of a heated argument with a partner who, while present, remains emotionally distant and incapable of offering genuine comfort. This is a variation on the theme of unavailability, but the core message—the profound emotional isolation—remains powerfully intact. The unconscious editor has found a way to present the familiar narrative in a slightly altered, yet equally resonant, form.

Similarly, the defense mechanisms, while often repeated, may also undergo subtle transformations. The individual who used intellectualization might, in their final moments, engage in a form of philosophical rumination about death, attempting to logically dissect the concept of mortality rather than confronting the emotional terror it may evoke. This is a variation on intellectualization, a more sophisticated or perhaps more abstract application of the same defense. The editor, by shifting from direct emotional avoidance to a more abstract conceptualization, still maintains the core strategy of keeping raw emotion at bay. This subtle shift allows the unconscious narrative to adapt to the changing circumstances of the dying process while still adhering to its fundamental thematic preoccupations. The editor, by evolving the defense, ensures its continued efficacy in the face of ultimate existential challenge.

The power of this unconscious repetition and variation lies in its often subtle, yet deeply significant, connection to the "fantasmatic signature" of an individual. This signature is the unique constellation of unconscious fantasies, desires, and fears that shape our subjective experience of reality. It is the psychic blueprint that informs our choices, our relationships, and ultimately, our sense of self. When the unconscious editor draws upon the repetition compulsion, it is essentially drawing from the deepest wellsprings of this fantasmatic signature. The recurring patterns, the familiar relational dynamics, the habitual defense mechanisms – these are all outward manifestations of the core fantasies and conflicts that constitute our unique psychic identity.

Therefore, the death narrative, when viewed through the lens of repetition compulsion and the fantasmatic signature, is not a random or arbitrary event. It is, rather, a profoundly personal and symbolic conclusion that is deeply rooted in the unconscious architecture of the individual's life. The unconscious, in its relentless drive to maintain a sense of psychic coherence and to work through unresolved issues, orchestrates an ending that, in its echoes of the past, offers a powerful, albeit often unconscious, testament to the enduring themes and core preoccupations of a life lived. The variations that emerge are not deviations from this underlying drive, but rather flexible adaptations of it, ensuring that the fundamental melody of the individual's psychic experience continues to resonate, even in the final fade. The editor, in its profound understanding of the individual's inner world, crafts a finale that is both a continuation and a transformation, a final movement that nonetheless contains the leitmotifs of the entire symphony. The unconscious editor, in its wisdom, understands that the most profound conclusions are often those that echo the most enduring truths of the self.

The exploration of the unconscious as the ultimate editor of our life's narrative, subtly yet powerfully shaping not only our lived experiences but also the symbolic tenor of our final moments, finds its most potent illustration in the crucible of clinical practice. Within the analytic space, where the defenses that shield the conscious mind begin to soften, the intricate interplay between life's recurring themes and the unconsciously scripted end becomes starkly apparent. It is here that we witness the profound interconnectedness, the seamless continuum, between the story we tell ourselves and the story that is ultimately written for us, often in a language far more ancient and symbolic than conscious discourse. This is not to suggest a deterministic fate, but rather a deeply ingrained narrative trajectory, a thematic resonance that binds the entirety of existence.

Let us consider, for illustrative purposes, a composite portrait drawn from multiple clinical encounters, a figure whose psychic landscape, though unique in its particulars, offers a universally recognizable pattern. We shall refer to this individual, anonymized and synthesized, as "Elias." Elias presented for analysis in his late fifties, grappling with a pervasive sense of stagnation and an inability to fully embrace opportunities that seemed to present themselves with increasing frequency. His conscious narrative was one of valiant effort, of having fought against considerable odds to establish a modest professional standing and maintain a semblance of stability for his family. He spoke of a childhood marked by emotional austerity and a relentless pressure to achieve, a pressure that, he believed, had instilled in him the resilience and determination necessary to navigate adulthood. His life story, as he consciously narrated it, was a testament to perseverance, a triumph over difficult circumstances.

However, as the analytic work deepened, a different, more shadowed narrative began to emerge from the unconscious strata of Elias's psyche. This was a narrative not of heroic perseverance, but of subtle self-sabotage. The "obstacles" he had overcome, it became apparent, were often of his own making, though he remained largely unaware of this agency. Opportunities for advancement were consistently, almost imperceptibly, undermined. Projects that showed promise would inexplicably falter in their final stages, not due to external forces, but through Elias's own procrastination, his sudden bouts of debilitating self-doubt, or a seemingly inexplicable aversion to completing tasks that would have led to greater recognition. He would frequently find himself on the precipice of success, only to inexplicably step back, to engineer a situation where he could claim victimhood to circumstance rather than confronting the deeper, more discomfiting truth of his own internal resistance.

This pattern of self-sabotage was not a recent development; it was the central motif of his unconscious life script. His relationships, too, bore the imprint of this dynamic. He had a remarkable capacity to identify potential partners who offered genuine affection and stability, only to unconsciously push them away through passive-aggression, withdrawal, or by creating situations that led to inevitable ruptures. His friendships often mirrored this pattern, characterized by a subtle withdrawal just as they deepened, leaving him feeling isolated, yet paradoxically, confirmed in his belief that true connection was either unattainable or inherently perilous. His conscious narrative of seeking connection and stability was thus perpetually undermined by an unconscious drive to recreate a familiar sense of unease and a profound, albeit unacknowledged, loneliness.

The unconscious editor, in Elias's case, seemed to possess a particular affinity for the theme of "near misses" and "almosts." The narrative of his life was saturated with these moments: the promotion that slipped through his fingers by a hair's breadth, the relationship that ended just before commitment, the creative endeavor that remained perpetually unfinished. His unconscious seemed to be meticulously curating these instances, amassing them into a rich tapestry of unfulfilled potential. This was not a conscious desire for failure, but rather a deeply ingrained psychic mechanism that rendered success, or perhaps the vulnerability that accompanied genuine achievement and connection, too terrifying to fully embrace. The editor's selection process consistently amplified the moments of near-attainment, creating a life story that was a powerful, lingering testament to what

might have been, rather than what *was*.

This unconscious editorial preference for the "almost" and the "nearly" began to cast a long shadow over Elias's later years, and most significantly, over his unconscious script for his death. He did not consciously articulate fears of dying, but rather expressed a profound anxiety about "running out of time," a sense that he had not yet fully

begun to live. This anxiety, rooted in his lifelong pattern of self-sabotage and avoidance of completion, began to manifest in his dreams and in subtle, symbolic shifts in his behavior. He developed an increasing fascination with unfinished symphonies, with books that were never completed, with biographies of individuals whose lives were cut tragically short before their full potential could be realized. These were not merely intellectual curiosities; they became deeply resonant symbols for his own internal state.

As Elias's health began to decline, the unconscious narrative that had underscored his life began to inform the symbolic landscape of his dying process. There was no dramatic struggle for life, no heroic battle against disease. Instead, his decline was characterized by a subtle, almost imperceptible fading. His resistance to medical intervention was not overt defiance, but a passive acquiescence to a process he seemed to believe was inevitable, a natural culmination of his lifelong pattern of deferral. He would agree to treatments, express a desire to get better, but would then fail to follow through with the necessary diligence, experiencing relapses or complications that seemed to confirm his deepest, unacknowledged beliefs about his own inherent inability to complete anything, including the act of living and healing.

The unconscious editor, in its final act of weaving together the threads of Elias's life, crafted a death that was a profound, symbolic echo of his lifelong narrative. He died not in a moment of dramatic revelation or resolution, but in a state of quiet suspension. His last days were characterized by a gentle drifting, a state of semi-consciousness where he would murmur fragments of unfinished thoughts, references to incomplete projects, and an almost wistful recitation of his "near misses." His family reported that in his final hours, he seemed less like someone facing an ending, and more like someone who had simply run out of time, who had been perpetually on the verge of something significant, but had never quite arrived.

The aesthetic and symbolic form of Elias's death was a direct reflection of the narrative that had been curated and emphasized by his unconscious. It was an ending characterized by incompletion, by the lingering sense of potential unfulfilled, by a quiet testament to the power of deferral. There was no grand climax, no cathartic resolution. Instead, there was a slow, almost imperceptible diminishment, a fading out that mirrored the way he had unconsciously approached many of the significant junctures of his life. The unconscious editor had ensured that the final chapter, like so many before it, would be imbued with the theme of "almost," a poignant and perhaps sorrowful culmination of a life lived perpetually on the threshold.

This case, synthesized though it is, illustrates the profound and often subtle continuity between the narrative constructed throughout a life and the symbolic form of its ending. Elias's life was not simply a series of random events; it was a story, unconsciously authored, with recurring themes of self-sabotage and avoidance of completion. His death, far from being an arbitrary cessation, became the ultimate, symbolic manifestation of these deeply ingrained narrative preoccupations. The unconscious editor, in its relentless pursuit of thematic coherence, wove a singular thread from the tapestry of his existence, ensuring that the final scene was not an anomaly, but a profound and resonant conclusion to the story it had so diligently, and so powerfully, curated. The profound silence that followed his passing was, in a sense, the final, unwritten sentence in a life that had been defined by its unfinished passages.

Let us turn our attention to another anonymized vignette, one that illuminates a different facet of this life-death continuum: the struggle for independence and the unconscious scripting of an ending that mirrors this lifelong battle. Consider an individual, let us call her "Seraphina," whose conscious narrative was one of fierce self-reliance. From an early age, Seraphina had cultivated an image of unwavering strength and autonomy. She spoke of a childhood where she had to fend for herself, where emotional dependence was viewed as a weakness, and where she learned early on that her own needs were secondary to the practicalities of survival. Her conscious life story was a testament to her resilience, her ability to stand alone, and her profound distrust of relying on others. She prided herself on her independence, often framing it as her greatest virtue and her most significant achievement.

However, beneath this consciously curated narrative of self-sufficiency, a different, more vulnerable psychic reality pulsed. The unconscious editor, in Seraphina's case, seemed to be highlighting not her strength, but a deep-seated, almost pathological fear of engulfment. Her fierce independence was not merely a preference; it was a desperate defense against an unconscious terror of losing herself in another, of being overwhelmed and absorbed by external demands or emotional intimacies. This fear manifested in a pattern of pushing people away precisely when they attempted to get close, of interpreting gestures of care as attempts at control, and of subtly undermining relationships that offered the possibility of genuine interdependence. While she consciously yearned for connection, her unconscious script dictated a perpetual movement of withdrawal, a meticulous construction of emotional barriers.

Her professional life, too, reflected this dynamic. She excelled in fields that demanded solitary work and a high degree of individual initiative. Yet, when opportunities arose that involved collaboration or required her to delegate tasks, she would experience intense anxiety, often leading to miscalculations or a retreat into her familiar lone-wolf posture. Her conscious narrative celebrated her self-reliance, but her unconscious was meticulously chronicling a series of interactions where her fear of entanglement led her to isolate herself, thus confirming her internal belief that true connection was impossible without the sacrifice of her own autonomy. The unconscious editor was not celebrating her strength as much as it was amplifying her fear of vulnerability, using it to shape a narrative of perpetual isolation, even amidst conscious attempts to forge bonds.

This lifelong preoccupation with independence, with the avoidance of perceived engulfment, began to inform the unconscious script of Seraphina's dying process. As her physical health deteriorated, her resistance to care became more pronounced. She would refuse assistance, even when clearly in need, framing it as a refusal to be a burden, a final assertion of her self-sufficiency. Her conscious narrative of independence remained unbroken, but it had now become the driving force behind her unconscious approach to the ultimate vulnerability of illness and approaching death. She was, in essence, fighting her final battle for autonomy, not against disease, but against the very human need for support and connection that illness inevitably entails.

The unconscious editor orchestrated Seraphina's end as a symbolic culmination of her lifelong struggle for absolute independence. Her death was not a peaceful surrender, nor was it a dramatic confrontation. Instead, it was a solitary event, occurring in her own home, where she had meticulously maintained her independence to the very end. Family members reported that her final days were marked by a quiet stoicism, a refusal to acknowledge the severity of her condition, and a determined effort to manage her own affairs as much as possible. When she was found, she was alone, in a state of repose that, while outwardly peaceful, carried an profound undertone of isolation.

The aesthetic and symbolic form of Seraphina's death was a powerful testament to the narrative that had been woven throughout her life. Her independence, so fiercely championed, found its ultimate, tragic expression in her solitary passing. While she consciously believed she was asserting her strength, her unconscious was, in fact, ensuring that her final act would be one of ultimate self-reliance, a complete absence of external support, a symbolic triumph of autonomy over the very human need for interdependence, even in the face of death. The unconscious editor had ensured that the final scene would be a stark, unadorned illustration of her most deeply held, and most unconsciously guarded, belief: that one must face the ultimate existential void entirely alone.

In this instance, the unconscious narrative of fierce independence, born from early experiences of perceived emotional neglect and a deep-seated fear of engulfment, led to a death that was a symbolic enactment of that very narrative. The "near misses" in Elias's life were replaced by the stark reality of absolute solitude in Seraphina's. Both, however, demonstrate the potent force of the unconscious editor, its ability to imbue the entirety of a life, and its final punctuation, with a singular, unifying theme. The narrative constructed throughout life directly informs the aesthetic and symbolic form of the ending, revealing a holistic psychic journey where the beginning, the middle, and the end are inextricably bound by the unconscious's enduring preoccupations. The unconscious does not merely record our lives; it authors them, from the first whisper of existence to the final, resonant silence.

The grand theatre of human existence, so often perceived as a stage for conscious intention and deliberate action, is in reality profoundly shaped by an unseen director. This director, the unconscious, not only orchestrates the drama of our lives but also meticulously crafts the epilogue, leaving behind a legacy that is as much a product of hidden desires and unresolved conflicts as it is of tangible achievements. The narrative arc of our lives, forged in the crucible of unconscious processes, extends its influence beyond our final breath, subtly dictating the contours of our remembrance. It is here, in the fertile ground of what remains unsaid and unacknowledged, that the unconscious architect of legacy begins its work.

Consider how the deepest currents of our psychic lives, the persistent themes and unresolved dramas that play out in the theatre of the unconscious, inevitably cast a long shadow over the perception of our passing and, consequently, our lasting imprint upon the world. This is not merely about the stories told by others, the anecdotes shared at a funeral, or the biographical details compiled by well-meaning friends or family. Rather, it is about a deeper, more resonant impact, a psychic reverberation that stems from the very fabric of our being as it was unconsciously woven throughout our existence. The 'fantasmatic signature' of death, a term that hints at the spectral yet potent impression left behind, is intrinsically linked to the unconscious narrative that has shaped a life from its inception. This signature is not a conscious declaration of intent, but a symbolic emanation, a final, indelible mark that speaks volumes about the core preoccupations and the overarching psychic architecture of the deceased.

The unconscious desire for a particular kind of remembrance is a powerful, albeit often unarticulated, force. We may consciously aspire to be remembered as kind, intelligent, or courageous, but it is the unconscious endorsement of these qualities, or the unconscious sublimation of their opposites, that truly determines the quality of our legacy. If, for instance, a life has been unconsciously dedicated to seeking validation through external achievement, the unconscious architect of legacy may ensure that this striving, rather than the deeper, perhaps unfulfilled emotional needs, becomes the dominant theme in how one is recalled. The triumph of a career, the impact of a specific invention, or the success of a creative endeavor can, in this light, be seen not just as conscious accomplishments, but as the material manifestations of an unconscious imperative to be

seen and *valued* in a specific way.

Conversely, if a life has been unconsciously marked by a pervasive sense of inadequacy or a fear of judgment, the unconscious legacy might be one of quiet, perhaps even melancholic, achievement. The individual might be remembered as someone who worked tirelessly, who was dedicated and diligent, yet perhaps lacked a certain spark or an outward expression of joy. This remembrance, though seemingly positive, can be a poignant reflection of an unconscious internal landscape dominated by a relentless pursuit of "enoughness," a desperate attempt to quell an internal critic that the conscious mind may barely acknowledge. The legacy, in such cases, becomes a testament to the effort rather than the intrinsic worth, a somber monument to an internal struggle.

The very manner of our dying, too, can become a potent component of this unconscious legacy. While we may not consciously orchestrate our final moments, the unconscious narrative of our lives can imbue these moments with profound symbolic weight. A death characterized by a peaceful surrender might be interpreted as a final integration, a release from the struggles of life, reflecting an unconscious sense of completion or resolution. Conversely, a death marked by struggle or a prolonged period of suffering might, for some, unconsciously represent a final, cathartic outpouring of pent-up conflict, or a symbolic reenactment of lifelong internal battles. The unconscious mind, ever the weaver of thematic coherence, can transform the cessation of life into a powerful, final statement, a symbolic punctuation mark that echoes the dominant themes of the life lived.

Consider the unconscious drive to create a specific narrative around one's death. This is not a conscious manipulation, but a subtler, more pervasive influence. The unconscious may highlight certain aspects of our lives, magnifying them in the collective memory, while downplaying others. This selective emphasis serves the unconscious imperative to construct a coherent and meaningful legacy, one that ideally resolves, or at least symbolically acknowledges, the deepest psychic tensions of the individual. For instance, an individual who unconsciously grappled with feelings of powerlessness throughout their life might, in their final years, become a source of immense comfort and wisdom for their family. Their death, then, might be remembered as a moment of profound peace and clarity, an unconscious effort to inscribe a narrative of strength and guidance where, in life, there was a hidden sense of vulnerability.

The unconscious architect of legacy operates through metaphor and symbol, transforming lived experiences into enduring impressions. A life lived with an unacknowledged passion for justice, for example, might result in a legacy where the individual is remembered as a staunch defender of the weak, even if their conscious actions were more reserved. The unconscious yearning for rectitude and fairness, suppressed in daily life, finds its ultimate expression in the symbolic tapestry of remembrance. The legacy becomes a testament to the ideals that the unconscious championed, even if the conscious self struggled to fully embody them.

Furthermore, the unconscious understanding of what constitutes a "good death" can heavily influence the perceived legacy. If, unconsciously, a life has been perceived as one of continuous striving and self-denial, a death that is perceived as earned, perhaps through prolonged illness and quiet suffering, might be unconsciously framed as a just reward for a life of sacrifice. The narrative of the legacy becomes one of heroic endurance, a testament to the individual's capacity for suffering and their ultimate release from it. The unconscious mind, in its profound economy, seeks a certain psychic symmetry, an alignment between the lived narrative and its concluding chapter, ensuring that the legacy reflects a sense of psychic closure, however symbolic.

The unconscious also plays a crucial role in how we are remembered in relation to our relationships. If a life was unconsciously characterized by a fear of intimacy, the legacy might be one of stoic independence, a figure remembered for their self-sufficiency rather than their capacity for deep connection. Conversely, a life unconsciously driven by a need for affection might be remembered for its warmth and generosity, its ability to foster deep bonds, even if, at times, this need manifested in unhealthy dependency. The unconscious imprint on our relationships is thus transmuted into the narrative of our legacy, shaping how our interactions with others are recalled and interpreted.

The unconscious architect of legacy is a subtle but persistent force, constantly at work in shaping the enduring impression we leave behind. It is not about controlling the narrative in a conscious, manipulative sense, but about the profound psychic coherence that the unconscious seeks to impose upon the entirety of an existence. The triumphs and failures, the joys and sorrows, the conscious intentions and the unconscious compulsions—all are woven together by this unseen director, forming a singular, resonant theme that continues to echo long after the individual has departed. The 'fantasmatic signature' of death, therefore, is not merely the absence of life, but the final, symbolic articulation of the unconscious narrative that has defined it, a testament to the enduring power of the psychic self in shaping not only its own existence but also its lasting imprint upon the world.

The legacy we unconsciously craft is often a complex tapestry, woven with threads of both conscious aspiration and unconscious imperative. The unconscious desire for a particular form of remembrance can manifest in various ways, often disguised as genuine virtue or a simple reflection of life's circumstances. For example, an individual who, on a conscious level, believes they were always magnanimous and selfless might, through unconscious processes, have subtly manipulated situations or relationships to create an impression of their generosity. The unconscious architect of legacy, in such instances, ensures that the perceived magnanimity, rather than any underlying insecurity or hidden agenda, becomes the dominant note in how they are remembered. This is not necessarily a deliberate deception, but rather a powerful psychic drive to align external perception with an idealized internal self-image, a self-image that the unconscious has deemed most worthy of perpetuation.

Consider the unconscious need to leave behind a legacy of "uniqueness." An individual might unconsciously feel that their life, in its ordinariness, lacks inherent significance. To counter this, the unconscious might guide them to emphasize certain eccentricities, unusual interests, or even perceived misfortunes, transforming them into hallmarks of their distinctiveness. Their legacy, then, becomes one of individuality, of being "one of a kind," even if the conscious self was unaware of this specific imperative. The unconscious mind, in its quest for meaning and enduring impact, may find that the extraordinary, even if manufactured through subtle psychic redirection, is more conducive to a lasting impression than the mundane.

The unconscious also influences the very nature of the stories that are told about us. While conscious memories might focus on shared experiences and factual events, the unconscious can imbue these memories with particular emotional resonances. A seemingly trivial act of kindness, for instance, might be unconsciously elevated in the memory of others if it aligns with the unconscious narrative of the deceased as someone inherently benevolent. Conversely, a significant achievement might be downplayed in remembrance if it unconsciously conflicts with a deeper, unacknowledged narrative of self-doubt or guilt. The unconscious editor, in essence, curates not only the events of a life but also the emotional tenor of their recall, ensuring a thematic consistency in the posthumous narrative.

The concept of the 'fantasmatic signature' is particularly relevant when examining how the unconscious deals with unresolved conflicts and aspirations. A life unfulfilled in a particular area – perhaps a career path not taken, or a relationship that never materialized – can leave a powerful unconscious residue. The legacy, in such cases, might be subtly shaped to acknowledge this unfulfilled longing, not as a failure, but as a testament to the depth of the individual's desires. They might be remembered as someone who "had so much potential," or who "always dreamed big," even if the conscious self had long since abandoned those dreams. The unconscious, however, holds onto these potent psychic images, and they inevitably find their way into the final narrative of remembrance.

The unconscious desire for absolution or redemption can also play a significant role in shaping one's legacy. If an individual has harbored unconscious guilt or regret over past actions, their unconscious might subtly guide them and, subsequently, others, towards a narrative that emphasizes their positive contributions, their eventual growth, or their inherent goodness. The legacy becomes a form of psychic cleansing, a posthumous attempt to rewrite the perceived moral ledger. This is not about conscious manipulation of others' memories, but about the unconscious projection of a desired self-perception onto the collective consciousness. The 'fantasmatic signature' here is one of a life that, despite its flaws, ultimately sought and perhaps achieved a form of inner peace or reconciliation.

Moreover, the unconscious architect of legacy is deeply intertwined with our understanding of mortality itself. The way we unconsciously grapple with the inevitability of death profoundly influences the narrative we project onto our lives and, by extension, the legacy we leave. If the unconscious fear of oblivion is strong, there might be a heightened drive to create a monumental legacy, something tangible and lasting that defies the transient nature of existence. This could manifest as a desire to build empires, write seminal works, or leave behind a significant philanthropic footprint – all unconscious attempts to inscribe oneself onto the fabric of time, to ensure that one's existence will not be forgotten.

Conversely, if the unconscious has achieved a certain degree of integration and acceptance of mortality, the legacy might be one of quiet influence, of wisdom passed down, or of a life well-lived in its simplicity and authenticity. The 'fantasmatic signature' in this instance is one of peace, of a life that found its meaning not in grand gestures, but in the richness of lived experience and the depth of human connection. The remembrance is of a person who embodied a certain way of being in the world, a way that continues to inspire and guide those who knew them.

The unconscious drive for a harmonious and coherent life narrative extends, as we have seen, to the very end. The unconscious architect of legacy ensures that the 'fantasmatic signature' of death aligns with the overarching themes of the life lived. This alignment provides a sense of psychic closure, both for the individual (in their unconscious perception) and for those who remember them. It is as if the unconscious mind seeks to present a complete story, a narrative where the beginning, middle, and end all speak the same language, albeit sometimes a language that is only decipherable through the lens of depth psychology. The legacy, therefore, becomes the ultimate testament to the unconscious self's enduring preoccupations and its persistent quest for meaning and coherence in the grand, unfolding drama of existence. The silence that follows death is not an empty void, but a canvas upon which the unconscious has painted its final, indelible masterpiece.

Chapter 10: Clinical Applications and Therapeutic Implications

The clinical encounter, a space uniquely calibrated for the unveiling of the hidden, offers a fertile ground for discerning the subtle yet potent imprints of the 'fantasmatic signature' of death. This is not a literal confrontation with the physical cessation of being, but rather an exploration of the unconscious narratives that shape a patient's relationship with endings, loss, and their own finitude. Within the therapeutic dialogue, these signatures emerge not as explicit pronouncements but as recurring motifs, symbolic constellations that resonate through a patient's discourse, their dream imagery, and their behavioral patterns. Our task as depth psychologists is to attune our listening to these spectral whispers, to trace the contours of their unconscious architecture, and to understand how they inform the patient's present-day struggles and aspirations.

One of the primary ways this signature manifests is through the patient's narrative construction of "disappearance." This can range from the overtly dramatic – the person who feels they are constantly overlooked, that their presence is barely acknowledged, leading to an internal sense of fading into insignificance – to the more insidious, where a patient recounts experiences of being effectively erased by others, their contributions ignored, their identity subsumed. For instance, a patient might describe feeling like a ghost in their own family, their opinions consistently sidelined, their achievements met with polite indifference. This persistent feeling of not quite

being there, of existing in a state of perpetual semi-erasure, speaks to an unconscious phantasm of non-being, a fear that their ultimate disappearance will be a mere echo of their lived experience. The therapeutic work, then, involves not just validating the patient's feelings of being marginalized, but also exploring the deeper origins of this phantasmatic erasure. Is it a projection of an internal sense of worthlessness? A reenactment of early experiences of neglect or invalidation? Or perhaps a defensive posture against a perceived unbearable intensity of existence? The signature here is one of a life lived in shadow, culminating in an unconscious anticipation of a fading, unnoticed end.

Another crucial avenue for identification lies in the patient's inclination towards or aversion to what might be termed "dramatic endings." Some individuals seem unconsciously drawn to a narrative of grand finales, of lives that culminate in significant events, for better or worse. This can manifest in a preoccupation with legacy, a relentless drive for achievement, or conversely, a fascination with tales of tragic heroes and dramatic downfalls. Their own life stories might be recounted with an emphasis on climactic moments, on turning points that feel destined or fated. The unconscious phantasm here is one of a life that must be

seen to end, that requires a definitive, often spectacular, punctuation mark. Conversely, other patients may exhibit a profound resistance to any sense of closure, their narratives constantly circling back, unresolved, their lives characterized by an inability to move past certain unresolved conflicts or relationships. This can be understood as an unconscious dread of the finality that an ending represents, a desperate clinging to the present moment or the past, as if to forestall the ultimate disappearance. In such cases, the signature is one of perpetual incompletion, an unconscious belief that to truly end is to cease to exist.

The necessity of mourning, both for themselves and for others, offers another rich vein for excavating the fantasmatic signature. Patients who struggle to grieve, who exhibit a marked emotional flatness in the face of loss, or who compulsively "move on" without allowing for a period of genuine sorrow, may be unconsciously avoiding a confrontation with their own mortality. Their inability to mourn the loss of another can be a projection of their terror of their own eventual loss, of their own inevitable non-being. The rituals and emotional expressions of mourning are, from a depth psychological perspective, a collective, symbolic way of acknowledging finitude, of processing the reality of absence, and of integrating the lost object into one's psychic landscape. When this process is disrupted, it suggests an unconscious phantasm where mourning itself is perceived as a dangerous descent into oblivion, a surrender that mirrors the ultimate surrender of death. On the other hand, some patients may be pathologically enmeshed in mourning, perpetually caught in a state of grief, unable to extract themselves from the shadow of past losses. This can also speak to a complex relationship with death, where the present is perpetually overshadowed by a morbid dwelling on the past, preventing the individual from fully inhabiting their own life, effectively living in a state of anticipatory mourning for their own eventual absence.

The theme of "escape" as a phantasmatic signature is particularly potent. This can manifest in various ways: a compulsive need to travel, to constantly seek new experiences, to flee from commitment, or even a more internalized escape through dissociation, addiction, or excessive fantasy. These are not simply expressions of wanderlust or a desire for novelty; they represent an unconscious strategy to avoid confronting a core psychic reality, often related to the dread of being trapped, of being suffocated by existence, or of confronting an unbearable inner void. The phantasm driving this escape is that of a self that cannot endure its own presence, that must constantly flee from itself, from its own perceived limitations or its own terrifying emptiness. This flight from the self, from the inescapable reality of one's own being, becomes a rehearsal for the ultimate escape – death – where the self is finally, irrevocably, annihilated. The therapeutic challenge lies in helping the patient understand that the escape routes they have constructed are, in fact, leading them away from authentic living and towards a premature psychic death, a state of emotional and existential paralysis.

In the clinical setting, recognizing these patterns requires a form of listening that is attuned to the symbolic, the metaphoric, and the resonant. It's about identifying the persistent, underlying currents that shape a patient's lived experience of themselves and their world. When a patient repeatedly describes feeling invisible, even in situations where objective evidence suggests otherwise, we must consider the underlying phantasm of being fundamentally unseen, of a self that exists only when acknowledged by others, and therefore is perpetually at risk of ceasing to exist if that acknowledgement is withdrawn. This can lead to a profound fear of solitude, not because of loneliness, but because of the existential terror of disappearing into the void of one's own unfelt presence.

Similarly, the patient who is obsessed with their "performance" in life, who constantly seeks validation through achievement and recognition, may be unconsciously driven by a phantasm where their value, their very right to exist, is contingent upon their productivity. Their fear is not of failure in the conventional sense, but of the terrifying realization that without their external accomplishments, there is nothing left, no core self to fall back upon. Their death, in this unconscious formulation, represents the ultimate loss of that performative identity, the cessation of their perceived value. The signature here is one of a life lived in service of an external ideal, a desperate attempt to ward off the phantasm of a worthless, empty self.

The unconscious construction of a "spectacle" around endings is another key indicator. This can involve patients who, when facing a difficult situation or relationship breakdown, feel an overwhelming pressure to make it a dramatic, memorable event. They might rehearse their departure speeches, meticulously plan their exit, or become intensely preoccupied with how they will be perceived in their final moments of engagement. This speaks to an unconscious belief that life is a performance, and that its conclusion must be equally grand, equally attention-grabbing. The phantasm is that of a quiet, unnoticed fading – a fate far worse than any public drama. In such instances, the signature is of a life lived for an audience, even an imagined one, where the final act must be compelling enough to ensure some form of enduring imprint, however theatrical.

Conversely, the aversion to any form of dramatic ending, the constant deferral of difficult conversations, the avoidance of confrontation, can signal a different, yet equally potent, fantasmatic signature. This is the signature of the one who unconsciously believes that any direct engagement with conflict or finality will shatter them, will lead to an irreversible fragmentation of the self. Their existence is predicated on maintaining a precarious equilibrium, on smoothing over rough edges, on avoiding any rupture that might expose the fragility of their psychic structure. The ultimate ending, then, is not a point of transition but a catastrophic collapse, a dissolution into nothingness. Their lives are a testament to a desperate, ongoing effort to postpone the inevitable, to keep the precarious structure of their being from crumbling into dust.

The exploration of a patient's relationship with ritual and ceremony can also illuminate these unconscious phantasms. Societies and cultures have developed elaborate rituals surrounding death and mourning precisely because they serve to externalize and process the existential anxieties associated with mortality. Patients who feel alienated from or resistant to these rituals, who find them hollow or meaningless, may be unconsciously rejecting the collective acknowledgment of death and loss. This can stem from an unconscious belief that such rituals are simply a performance, a charade designed to mask the terrifying reality of oblivion. Their signature is one of profound existential isolation, a sense that they alone must confront the ultimate solitude of non-being, without the symbolic scaffolding that communal rites provide.

We also observe this in the patient who is hyper-vigilant about their health, constantly monitoring their bodily functions, interpreting every minor ailment as a harbinger of impending doom. While this can be a manifestation of genuine hypochondria, it also speaks to an unconscious phantasm where the body is the fragile container of the self, and its inevitable decay is synonymous with the disintegration of one's entire being. The signature here is one of extreme somatic anxiety, a life lived in constant dread of physical dissolution, where the end of the body is perceived as the end of everything.

The process of identifying these fantasmatic signatures in clinical practice is not about diagnosis in the traditional sense, but about deeper empathic understanding. It requires the therapist to hold in mind the theoretical framework of phantasmatic death while remaining exquisitely sensitive to the unique ways in which each patient embodies these unconscious themes. It involves listening not just to

what is said, but to *how* it is said, to the silences, the hesitations, the metaphors, and the recurring imagery that populate the patient's internal world.

For example, a patient who consistently describes their life as a series of "near misses" or "almosts" – almost got the promotion, almost met the right partner, almost achieved their goal – is unconsciously weaving a narrative of thwarted potential. The fantasmatic signature here is one of a life that never quite coalesced, that remained perpetually on the verge of completion but never reached it. This can be deeply connected to an unconscious fear of fully arriving, of fully

being, perhaps because the imagined reality of full existence is too daunting, too exposed, or too prone to definitive endings. Their signature is that of perpetual liminality, a life lived in the threshold, forever anticipating an arrival that never quite occurs.

Consider the patient who experiences recurrent nightmares of being chased, of being trapped, or of falling endlessly. While these are common dream motifs, their persistent and unyielding nature within a patient's psychic landscape can offer profound insights into their fantasmatic signature. The chase might represent an unconscious flight from an aspect of the self that they cannot bear to confront; the trap, a sense of inescapable destiny or internal limitation; and the fall, a terrifying descent into oblivion, into a state of uncontained chaos. The signature here is one of profound psychic entrapment, a life dominated by the phantasm of being pursued by one's own shadow, or of being condemned to a perpetual, uncontrolled disintegration.

The way a patient speaks about their relationships, particularly their significant losses and attachments, is another crucial area. A patient who consistently idealizes deceased loved ones, presenting them as flawless figures, may be unconsciously using them as a bulwark against their own perceived imperfections and their own eventual demise. The signature is one of a life lived in the reflected glow of others, an unconscious attempt to borrow their perceived solidity and permanence to ward off the threat of their own transient existence. Conversely, a patient who recounts past relationships with a tone of bitter resentment or profound disappointment might be unconsciously projecting their own internal dissatisfaction and their own sense of ultimate failure onto those closest to them. Their signature is one of disillusionment, a life where connection itself becomes a source of pain, and the eventual end is seen as a final release from the torment of human entanglement.

The therapeutic process, when attuned to these fantasmatic signatures, becomes an exploration of the patient's most fundamental anxieties about existence and non-existence. It is about helping the patient to trace the origins of these signatures, to understand how they were formed in the crucible of early experiences and unconscious desires, and how they continue to shape their present reality. By bringing these unconscious phantasms into the light of conscious awareness, the therapist can help the patient to dismantle the often-unwitting defenses they have erected, and to begin the slow, arduous work of forging a new relationship with the inevitability of endings, with loss, and with their own finitude. This is not about eradicating the fear of death – an impossible task – but about transforming the way it is unconsciously apprehended, moving from a phantasm of annihilation towards a more integrated, and perhaps even meaningful, acceptance of life's ultimate horizon. The goal is not to erase the signature, but to understand it, to contextualize it, and ultimately, to imbue it with a meaning that is less about terror and more about the profound, albeit often painful, richness of a life fully lived.

The exploration of a patient's "fantasmatic signature" of death, as previously discussed, reveals the intricate ways in which unconscious narratives about endings, loss, and finitude shape our lived experience. These signatures, woven into the fabric of a patient's discourse, dreams, and behaviors, are not static pronouncements but dynamic psychic structures that can be addressed and, to a degree, re-authored within the therapeutic dyad. The journey of psychoanalysis and depth psychotherapy offers a unique terrain for this work, providing a space where these deeply ingrained phantasms can be brought into conscious awareness, understood, and potentially transformed. The interventions employed are not designed to erase the existential reality of death, a task beyond the scope of therapy, but rather to alter the *way* in which this reality is unconsciously apprehended, moving from a place of terror and compulsive repetition towards a more integrated and, perhaps, even meaningful engagement with one's own mortality.

One of the foundational therapeutic interventions is the meticulous process of interpretation. Within the analytic setting, the therapist acts as a careful listener, attuned to the recurring themes, symbolic constellations, and emotional resonances that betray the patient's "fantasmatic death script." When a patient, for instance, repeatedly recounts scenarios of abandonment or betrayal, particularly in relationships that mirror early caregiver dynamics, it is the therapist's role to gently connect these patterns to an underlying phantasm of a desolate, solitary end. This is not about suggesting the patient is consciously seeking such an end, but rather that their unconscious psychic economy is structured around a profound fear of such a state, leading them to unconsciously recreate scenarios that evoke this terror. The interpretation, when timely and accurately delivered, serves as a powerful tool to illuminate the hidden logic of the patient's repetitions. It offers a narrative coherence to seemingly disparate events, allowing the patient to see how their "death fantasy" – the unconscious scenario of ultimate disintegration or abandonment – is actively shaping their present-day choices and relationships. The aim is to move from a position of being unconsciously driven by these phantasms to one of conscious understanding, thereby loosening their deterministic grip. This process requires immense patience and sensitivity, as the phantasms are often defended with considerable psychic energy, and direct confrontation can lead to defensive withdrawal or fragmentation. The therapist's stance of non-judgmental curiosity and unwavering presence is paramount in creating a safe enough space for these fragile, often terrifying, unconscious narratives to be explored.

Another crucial intervention involves the amplification and exploration of the patient's dream life. Dreams are often considered the "royal road to the unconscious," and in the context of death phantasms, they can be particularly illuminating. Dreams of falling, of being chased, of being trapped, or of witnessing catastrophic events – when recurrent or particularly vivid – offer direct symbolic access to the patient's unconscious anxieties about dissolution and non-being. The therapist's task is not to offer a one-size-fits-all interpretation of dream symbols, but to work collaboratively with the patient to explore the unique meaning these images hold within their personal symbolic universe. For example, a patient who dreams of their house crumbling around them might be experiencing a phantasm of their internal psychic structure collapsing, mirroring a fear of their own inevitable disintegration. Through careful questioning and empathic attunement, the therapist can help the patient unpack the emotional texture of the dream, its associated feelings, and its potential connections to waking life experiences. This amplification can help to solidify the unconscious narrative, making it more accessible to conscious contemplation. By revisiting these dream narratives, patients can begin to differentiate between the symbolic representation of their fear and the literal reality of their situation, thereby diminishing the overwhelming power of the phantasm. The goal is not to eliminate the dreams, but to alter the patient's relationship to them, transforming them from terrifying harbingers of doom into symbolic expressions of internal conflict that can be understood and processed.

Working with transference and countertransference also plays a pivotal role in addressing unresolved death fantasies. The transference relationship, the unconscious redirection of feelings and desires from significant past figures onto the therapist, can become a potent arena for the enactment of these phantasms. A patient who harbors a phantasm of being utterly alone and abandoned in their final moments might unconsciously project this onto the therapist, testing the therapist's commitment, withdrawing affection, or expressing extreme anxiety about the therapist's absence. Conversely, a patient with a phantasm of a dramatic, heroic end might unconsciously cast the therapist as an admiring audience or a passive observer, reenacting a script where their life and death are meant to be witnessed and lauded. The therapist's awareness of their own countertransference – their emotional reactions to the patient – is equally vital. For instance, a therapist might feel a sense of dread or helplessness when confronted with a patient’s obsessive preoccupation with their own demise, or a compulsive drive to "save" them from their perceived fate. Recognizing these countertransference reactions allows the therapist to understand how the patient's phantasms are impacting the therapeutic relationship and to use this information to deepen the interpretative work. By exploring the emotional currents within the transference, the therapist can help the patient understand how their unconscious scripts about death are being played out in the present, offering an opportunity to break free from these repetitive patterns and to establish a more authentic connection with the therapist, and by extension, with others in their lives.

The technique of working with "phantasmatic scripts" involves actively encouraging the patient to articulate and examine the imagined narratives surrounding their own death. This is not about eliciting morbid fantasies, but about gently guiding the patient to explore the specific unconscious stories they hold about their own endings. For some, this might involve exploring the implicit narrative of a life unfulfilled, a sense of potential never realized, leading to a death perceived as a tragic waste. For others, it could be a phantasm of sudden, violent erasure, a life cut short before its time, reflecting a deep-seated fear of annihilation. The therapist might ask questions such as, "If you were to imagine your life reaching its conclusion, what kind of 'story' do you see unfolding?" or "What are the unspoken rules or expectations that your unconscious seems to hold about how your life should end?" This process allows for the conscious examination of these often-unacknowledged narratives, which can then be subjected to critical inquiry. For instance, a patient who unconsciously believes their death must be a spectacular event to validate their existence might, through this exploration, begin to question the origins of this belief and its impact on their current sense of self-worth. The goal is to identify the core emotional needs and fears driving these scripts and to explore alternative, less destructive narratives.

Moreover, the therapeutic exploration of rituals and symbolic practices can be a powerful avenue for addressing death phantasms. Many cultures have developed elaborate rituals to help individuals and communities process death and grief, to acknowledge finitude, and to find meaning in loss. Patients who are disconnected from or dismissive of these societal rituals may be unconsciously rejecting the collective acknowledgment of mortality, or they may hold a phantasm that such rituals are futile attempts to mask an unbearable reality. The therapist can help such patients explore this alienation, perhaps by examining their personal history with loss and mourning, or by understanding their resistance to collective expressions of grief. In some cases, the therapist might even collaborate with the patient to create personal rituals of remembrance or symbolic closure, tailored to their unique psychic landscape. For example, a patient who struggles with the phantasm of being forgotten might find solace in creating a personal archive of memories, photographs, or writings, transforming the fear of oblivion into a conscious act of preservation. This act of symbolic creation can serve as a powerful counter-narrative to the phantasm of erasure, offering a sense of agency and continuity in the face of perceived impermanence.

The therapeutic work also involves helping patients to differentiate between the symbolic phantasm of death and the actual experience of loss and change. Many individuals unconsciously equate any significant ending – the end of a relationship, the completion of a project, a major life transition – with their own eventual demise. This conflation stems from a deeply ingrained phantasm where endings are synonymous with annihilation. Through careful exploration, the therapist can help the patient to deconstruct this association. By examining how they have navigated previous endings, the therapist can highlight instances of resilience, adaptation, and the emergence of new beginnings. This process of re-narrativizing past endings can serve as a powerful form of inoculation against the overwhelming fear of future finality. For example, a patient who dreads the end of a career phase as if it were a form of personal death might be encouraged to recall previous transitions, such as graduating from school or leaving a previous job, and to explore how they adapted and found new meaning. This process helps to build a "library" of successful adaptations, thereby challenging the unconscious belief that all endings are catastrophic.

Furthermore, the concept of "mourning work" within the therapeutic context is essential. Psychoanalytic theory posits that unresolved grief can lead to an arrested development of the psyche, where individuals remain unconsciously fixated on past losses, thereby hindering their engagement with the present and their acceptance of their own finitude. For patients who struggle to mourn, exhibiting either excessive emotional detachment or an unending preoccupation with past losses, the therapist facilitates a process of deliberate, contained emotional engagement with these unresolved feelings. This might involve exploring the unspoken emotions associated with a lost loved one, the dreams and fantasies that were shared, and the unmet expectations that linger. The goal is not to prolong suffering, but to guide the patient through a symbolic process of "letting go" without forgetting, of integrating the lost object or experience into one's internal world in a way that allows for present-moment engagement. This process of working through grief can be seen as a rehearsal for mourning one's own eventual passing, equipping the patient with a greater capacity to face loss with a sense of integrated experience rather than overwhelming dread.

In cases where the death phantasm is characterized by a profound desire for oblivion or a fascination with self-destruction, the therapeutic approach becomes particularly delicate. Here, the unconscious fantasy might be one of a longed-for escape from unbearable psychic pain, a seductive promise of peace through annihilation. The therapist's primary task is to establish a strong, reliable therapeutic alliance, offering a consistent, nurturing presence that can begin to provide the psychic containment that the patient unconsciously believes can only be found in oblivion. Interventions would focus on exploring the roots of this unbearable pain, identifying the specific psychic burdens that the patient seeks to escape, and gradually building a capacity to tolerate distress. This might involve introducing gentle exposure to aspects of reality that the patient has been consciously or unconsciously avoiding, or helping them to find small, manageable sources of meaning and connection in their present life. The aim is to demonstrate that escape through annihilation is a false promise, a destructive fantasy, and that a more enduring form of peace can be found in the difficult, yet ultimately rewarding, work of confronting and processing one's internal world.

Finally, the therapeutic process ultimately seeks to help the patient develop a more nuanced and integrated relationship with the concept of death. Instead of a singular, terrifying phantasm of annihilation or erasure, the aim is to foster an understanding of death as an inherent part of the life cycle, a horizon that lends perspective and meaning to the present. This involves acknowledging and validating the patient's fears, but also gently challenging the catastrophic interpretations that often accompany these fears. Through consistent exploration, interpretation, and empathic engagement, the patient can begin to dismantle the rigid, often unconscious, scripts that dictate their apprehension of death. This transformation is not achieved through intellectual understanding alone, but through a deeply affective and experiential process within the therapeutic relationship, where the patient learns to hold the paradox of life and its eventual cessation with a greater sense of equanimity and, perhaps, even a profound appreciation for the richness of their own finite existence. The ghost of the phantasmatic ending, when understood and integrated, can recede, allowing the living self to emerge with greater vitality and presence.

The terrain of clinical work is often marked by subtlety and indirection, particularly when confronting the pervasive influence of unconscious self-destructiveness. While overt suicidal ideation and intent demand immediate and direct intervention, a more insidious, yet equally perilous, manifestation lies in what might be termed "suicide without suicide." This clinical presentation encompasses a constellation of behaviors, attitudes, and even somatic responses that, while not explicitly aimed at ending life, nonetheless carry a potent charge of self-negation and a deep-seated psychic drive towards disintegration. These are patients who, in the absence of conscious suicidal wishes, engage in patterns of living that systematically undermine their own well-being, safety, and potential for flourishing. Recognizing and effectively addressing these "suicide without suicide" dynamics is a crucial, and at times, profoundly challenging aspect of depth psychological work.

The essence of "suicide without suicide" lies in its covert nature. Unlike the direct plea for help or the unmistakable expression of despair that often accompanies overt suicidal ideation, these patients' self-destructive impulses are woven into the very fabric of their daily lives. This can manifest as a relentless pattern of self-sabotage, where opportunities for growth, connection, or success are systematically thwarted. Consider, for instance, the individual who repeatedly enters into destructive relationships, drawn to partners who are emotionally unavailable, abusive, or fundamentally incapable of offering stable companionship. While they may verbally express a desire for love and security, their choices consistently lead them back to familiar patterns of hurt and disappointment. This is not simply a matter of poor judgment; it is often the enactment of an unconscious script, driven by internal forces that prioritize self-punishment or a reenactment of past trauma over genuine well-being. The unconscious logic here is complex: by recreating familiar pain, the individual may unconsciously feel a sense of control or predictability, albeit a painful one. The "suicide without suicide" lies in the slow, insidious erosion of the self, the gradual diminishment of vitality and hope, all while maintaining a superficial appearance of functioning.

Another significant manifestation of this phenomenon is found in pervasive risk-taking behaviors that, while not immediately life-threatening, significantly increase the likelihood of catastrophic outcomes. This can range from reckless driving and substance abuse to financial imprudence and chronic neglect of physical health. These behaviors, often driven by a profound internal emptiness or a desperate search for stimulation to escape unbearable psychic pain, carry a significant latent suicidal potential. The unconscious fantasy may be one of invincibility – a desperate attempt to ward off the fear of annihilation by courting danger – or, conversely, a form of passive suicidal surrender, where the individual implicitly trusts that fate will intervene to bring about an end. The therapist's role here is to deconstruct the underlying motivations, to move beyond the symptomatic behavior and explore the psychic landscape that gives rise to it. It involves helping the patient recognize that these actions, however unconsciously motivated, are not mere accidents or bad luck, but rather the expression of an internal struggle, a silent plea or a desperate defiance against an overwhelming internal void.

Furthermore, "suicide without suicide" can present in the form of profound psychosomatic collapse. Patients may experience chronic, debilitating physical illnesses that lack a clear organic cause or that are significantly exacerbated by psychological distress. While these conditions are very real and can be life-threatening, the underlying driver is often a psychic wound that has been internalized to such an extent that it manifests in the physical body. The body becomes the canvas upon which the unexpressed anguish and self-condemnation are written. This can be driven by an overwhelming sense of guilt, where the individual unconsciously believes they deserve to suffer, or by a profound shame that leads them to internalize their perceived failings to the point of physical illness. The unconscious fantasy here can be one of expiation, a belief that suffering will somehow atone for perceived sins or inadequacies. The therapeutic task is to excavate the emotional and psychological roots of these physical manifestations, to help the patient find a language for their internal pain that does not necessitate its somatic expression, and to foster a sense of self-compassion that can begin to counteract the punitive inner critic.

The identification of these "suicide without suicide" dynamics requires a keen attunement to the subtle language of the psyche. It demands that the clinician move beyond a purely symptomatic approach and delve into the unconscious motivations that underpin such patterns. A crucial element in this process is the exploration of guilt and shame. Often, these patients are driven by an internal prosecutor, a harsh superego that relentlessly condemns them for perceived transgressions, real or imagined. This internal guilt can manifest as a pervasive sense of worthlessness, a belief that they are fundamentally flawed and undeserving of happiness or even life itself. The self-sabotaging behaviors, the risk-taking, and the psychosomatic complaints can all be seen as expressions of this internalized self-punishment. The unconscious fantasy might be that by suffering, by failing, or by putting themselves in harm's way, they are somehow appeasing this internal judge or fulfilling an unconscious expectation of punishment.

Working with these patients involves a delicate balancing act. On the one hand, the therapist must maintain a firm hold on the reality of the potential danger, recognizing that these indirect self-destructive impulses can be as lethal as overt suicidal intent. On the other hand, direct confrontation can often be counterproductive, leading to increased defensiveness, denial, or further withdrawal. The therapeutic approach must therefore be one of gradual illumination and empathic exploration. It involves creating a safe and containing therapeutic environment where the patient feels understood and accepted, even in the midst of their self-destructive patterns. This allows for the unconscious motivations to be brought into conscious awareness, not as accusations, but as objects of exploration.

A key strategy is to help the patient develop a more accurate and compassionate understanding of their own internal world. This often involves unpacking the origins of their guilt and shame, tracing them back to early experiences of judgment, criticism, or emotional neglect. By understanding the historical roots of these painful feelings, patients can begin to see them not as inherent truths about their character, but as learned responses and internalized messages. The therapist can then facilitate a process of internal dialogue, where the patient begins to question the validity of their harsh self-criticism and to cultivate a more forgiving and accepting stance towards themselves. This is not about condoning destructive behavior, but about fostering a sense of self-empathy that can, over time, undermine the need for self-punishment.

The concept of punishment itself is central to understanding "suicide without suicide." Many patients are unconsciously driven by a need to expiate an internal sense of guilt, believing that suffering is a necessary consequence of their perceived transgressions. This can be deeply ingrained, stemming from early experiences where love and acceptance were conditional upon good behavior, or where perceived wrongdoings were met with severe punishment or withdrawal of affection. The unconscious equation becomes: "I have done something bad, therefore I must suffer." This suffering can take many forms – chronic unhappiness, relationship failures, physical illness, or even the slow erosion of one's life through neglect. The therapist's task is to help the patient deconstruct this equation, to explore the possibility that suffering is not a necessary outcome of wrongdoing, and that self-care and well-being are not acts of indulgence but rather essential components of a healthy life.

In cases where risk-taking is the predominant manifestation, the therapeutic work often involves exploring the underlying yearning for intense experience or the desperate attempt to escape psychic pain. The thrill of danger can provide a temporary antidote to feelings of emptiness or numbness. Similarly, substance abuse can be a way of self-medicating against unbearable emotional distress. The therapist's role is to help the patient identify and address the root causes of this pain, and to find healthier, more sustainable ways of coping. This might involve exploring sources of meaning and connection in the patient's life, developing mindfulness and emotional regulation skills, or facilitating therapeutic processes that help the patient process traumatic experiences that may be driving their self-destructive behavior. The goal is to substitute the desperate search for oblivion with a conscious pursuit of vitality and authentic living.

When psychosomatic symptoms are at the forefront, the focus shifts to understanding the body as a site of psychic expression. The therapist works to help the patient translate the language of the body into the language of the psyche. This involves exploring the emotional context surrounding the onset and exacerbation of the physical symptoms. What was happening in the patient's life, and in their internal world, when the symptoms first appeared? What emotions are evoked by the physical discomfort? Often, patients with psychosomatic presentations have difficulty accessing or expressing emotions directly, and the body becomes the primary vehicle for their distress. The therapist helps to create a bridge between these two realms, facilitating a more integrated experience of self. This can involve somatic experiencing techniques, guided imagery, and the exploration of the patient's relationship with their physical self. The aim is to help the patient reclaim their body as a source of vitality and well-being, rather than a site of suffering and punishment.

The therapeutic alliance itself becomes a crucial tool in working with "suicide without suicide." For patients who have experienced chronic invalidation, criticism, or neglect, the therapist's consistent, empathic presence can be a corrective emotional experience. This reliable relationship provides a safe container for exploring the painful and often frightening aspects of the self. The therapist's unwavering attunement to the patient's underlying pain, even when it is masked by self-defeating behaviors, can gradually foster a sense of trust and self-worth. This alliance allows the patient to begin to see themselves through a different lens, one of acceptance and potential for change. The therapist acts as a mirror, reflecting back to the patient the possibility of a life not dictated by guilt and self-punishment, but by self-compassion and a conscious pursuit of well-being.

It is essential to reiterate that "suicide without suicide" is not a monolithic phenomenon. It presents with a wide spectrum of manifestations, each requiring a tailored approach. However, the common thread running through all these presentations is the presence of unconscious self-destructive impulses that operate beneath the surface of conscious awareness. These impulses are often rooted in deeply held beliefs about one's own worthlessness, the inevitability of suffering, or the need for punishment. The therapeutic endeavor, therefore, is not merely about modifying behavior, but about transforming the underlying psychic structures that give rise to such behaviors. It is about helping patients to recognize the silent, self-negating narratives that have shaped their lives, and to begin, painstakingly, to re-author them. This process, while challenging, offers the profound possibility of reclaiming one's life, not from an external threat, but from the internal architect of its own diminishment. The ultimate aim is to guide these individuals from a state of unconscious self-erosion towards conscious self-preservation and, ultimately, towards a life lived with vitality, meaning, and a profound sense of self-acceptance.

The therapeutic transformation of a "death script" is perhaps one of the most profound achievements in depth psychology. It is a testament to the human psyche's capacity for change, its inherent drive towards life, and the potent, often hidden, power of insight. This is not a superficial alteration of habits or a simple reframing of thoughts; it is a fundamental reorientation of an individual's symbolic relationship with their own end, a shedding of an unconscious destiny that has long dictated a trajectory towards disintegration. In the absence of overt, acute suicidal intent, such a script can manifest through a constellation of self-defeating behaviors, a pervasive sense of doom, or a life lived in a state of perpetual internal exile, a slow surrender to psychic death that precedes physical demise. The transformative process is one of excavation, illumination, and ultimately, re-authorship.

Consider the case of a patient, whom we will refer to as "Alex," whose presenting issues, while varied, coalesced around a deep-seated sense of futility and an almost passive resignation to a life that felt perpetually out of reach. Alex presented in their late thirties, describing a history of failed relationships, chronic underachievement despite evident intellectual capacity, and a pervasive feeling of being a spectator in their own existence. There was no conscious desire for death, no overt suicidal ideation, yet a palpable sense of impending finality permeated their narrative. Their description of past events was imbued with a tone of inevitability, as if each setback, each disappointment, was not merely a consequence of circumstance but a preordained step on a path leading to a specific, albeit undefined, end. This was not simply pessimism; it was a lived conviction, a deeply internalized narrative that Alex was enacting without conscious awareness.

The initial phases of therapy involved painstakingly mapping the contours of Alex's internal world. This meant attending not just to the manifest content of their complaints, but to the subtle currents of affect, the recurring motifs in their dreams, and the characteristic patterns of their relational dynamics. Alex spoke of feeling "stuck," of "waiting for the other shoe to drop," and of a persistent, low-grade despair that seemed to settle over them like a shroud. They described a childhood where emotional expression was met with stoicism or criticism, where perceived failures were met with disappointment rather than constructive guidance. The unconscious message absorbed was that to be flawed was to be fundamentally wanting, a state from which there was no redemption. This created fertile ground for the development of a death script, an internalized narrative that suggested the only authentic ending for someone so inherently defective was one of dissolution.

Through transference, the therapeutic relationship itself began to reveal the workings of this script. Alex initially projected onto the therapist an image of an authoritative, judgmental figure, mirroring the internalized parental figures who had instilled a harsh self-criticism. Any perceived misstep in the therapeutic process – an unintentionally late arrival, a forgotten detail – was met with intense anxiety and a belief that they had irrevocably damaged the relationship, confirming their own inherent flawedness. This reenactment provided a crucial window into the mechanisms of the death script. The unconscious fantasy was not necessarily one of self-annihilation, but rather of achieving a state of utter stillness, a final cessation of the internal struggle, a surrender to an overwhelming sense of futility that felt more akin to a slow fading than a dramatic end. This could be seen as a form of psychic entropy, a gradual winding down of internal energy and motivation.

Dream analysis proved particularly illuminating. Alex's dreams were often populated by images of decay, of things falling apart, of enclosed spaces that offered no escape. One recurring dream involved walking through a city where buildings were slowly crumbling into dust, and the inhabitants moved with a lethargic, almost spectral gait. There was no violence, no explicit threat, just an overwhelming sense of irreversible decline. These images served as symbolic representations of Alex's internal state – a psychic landscape succumbing to a slow, inevitable decay. The death script, in this context, was not about a violent end, but about a surrender to this process of entropy, a final embrace of inertia.

The process of helping Alex to confront and eventually transform this script was a long and arduous one. It began with fostering a deeper understanding of the origins of their self-punitive tendencies. We explored early experiences of conditional love, the implicit message that worthiness was contingent upon perfection or the absence of perceived flaws. The unconscious equation that began to emerge was: "If I am not perfect, I do not deserve to live fully. Therefore, the most honest expression of my being is to remain in a state of arrested development, a living death." This "living death" was the unconscious ideal, the perceived authentic culmination of a life lived under the shadow of inadequacy.

Psychoanalytic interpretation, delivered with careful attunement to Alex's readiness, began to deconstruct this narrative. The therapist's role was not to directly challenge the "inevitability" of the script, which would likely have been met with increased resistance, but to offer an alternative interpretation, to hold out the possibility that the perceived flaws were not definitive judgments but rather points of entry into a more complex and authentic self. We began to explore the idea that the striving for perfection was, in itself, a form of self-negation, a denial of the inherent human experience of imperfection. This led to a gradual loosening of the internalized prohibitions against experiencing the full spectrum of life, including its messiness and its inevitable disappointments.

A critical turning point occurred when Alex began to conceptualize their "death script" not as a predetermined fate, but as a deeply ingrained, albeit unconscious, choice. This shift in perspective, from a passive victim of destiny to an active participant (however unconsciously) in their own trajectory, was crucial. It opened up the possibility of agency. We began to explore the underlying emotional needs that the "death script" was designed to serve. Was it a defense against the overwhelming pain of potential rejection? Was it a way of avoiding the terrifying responsibility of fully inhabiting one's life and potential?

The transformation of the death script was not marked by a single dramatic event, but by a series of subtle but significant shifts. Alex began to engage more actively in their work, not with the desperate striving for external validation, but with a nascent sense of purpose. Their relationships, while still challenging, began to be characterized by a greater degree of openness and a willingness to tolerate imperfection, both in themselves and in others. The recurring dreams of decay began to be replaced by dreams of transition, of journeys, of tentative growth. One dream involved finding a small, resilient seedling pushing through cracked pavement – a potent symbol of nascent life asserting itself against overwhelming odds.

The symbolic relationship with death began to change. Instead of an inevitable, all-consuming void, death started to be conceptualized as a natural, albeit distant, part of the life cycle, a boundary that gave shape and meaning to existence, rather than an immediate, all-encompassing threat or a desired release from suffering. This reorientation allowed for a greater appreciation of life itself, a conscious engagement with the present moment rather than a passive waiting for an end. The therapist's consistent presence, offering an unwavering belief in Alex's capacity for growth and transformation, provided a holding environment that allowed these internal shifts to occur.

The ultimate success in transforming Alex's death script was measured not by the absence of challenges or the eradication of all negative feelings, but by a fundamental re-engagement with the possibility of a life lived with meaning and purpose. The unconscious narrative of inevitable decline had been challenged, deconstructed, and, to a significant degree, re-written. This was achieved through the arduous work of psychoanalytic exploration, which allowed Alex to understand the unconscious forces driving their self-destructive trajectory and to actively choose a different path. The transformation of a death script, therefore, is a profound testament to the human capacity for renewal, a journey from an internalized destiny of dissolution to a conscious embrace of life's ongoing, unfolding narrative. It highlights the power of the therapeutic encounter to illuminate the darkest corners of the psyche and to foster a profound shift in an individual's fundamental relationship with their own existence and its ultimate conclusion. The journey from a perceived symbolic death sentence to a lived experience of vibrant, albeit imperfect, life is a central endeavor of depth psychology, offering hope and healing to those caught in the silent, pervasive grip of self-negation. The courage to confront these deeply ingrained patterns, facilitated by the therapeutic alliance, allows for the reclamation of a life that was, in essence, being slowly surrendered, a life that was capable of far more than mere survival.

The exploration of phantasmatic death within the therapeutic dyad is a terrain that demands the utmost ethical vigilance. It is a realm where the unconscious mind, in its often archaic and symbolic language, conjures scenarios of finality, dissolution, and ultimate cessation. These are not mere intellectual abstractions but deeply felt, often visceral, internal representations that can profoundly shape an individual's subjective experience of life, even in the absence of overt suicidal ideation. To navigate this sensitive territory responsibly requires a delicate balance of courage and caution, a commitment to illuminating the hidden dynamics without plunging the patient into unwarranted despair or existential terror.

The primary ethical imperative when approaching the concept of phantasmatic death is the unwavering respect for patient autonomy and dignity. The unconscious fantasy of death, however disturbing it may appear from an external perspective, is an intrinsic part of the patient's internal world. It represents a meaning-making process, however maladaptive, that has evolved to cope with unbearable psychic pain, profound loss, or overwhelming existential anxieties. To dismiss, pathologize, or forcefully confront these fantasies would be to invalidate the patient's lived experience and potentially damage the therapeutic alliance, which is the bedrock upon which any meaningful healing can occur. The therapist's role is not to judge or condemn these internal narratives but to approach them with a spirit of inquiry, curiosity, and profound empathy. This means actively listening to the symbolic language of the unconscious, attending to the affects that accompany these fantasies, and understanding their potential function within the patient's psychic economy.

Maintaining therapeutic boundaries is paramount. The exploration of phantasmatic death can evoke intense emotions – fear, anxiety, shame, grief, and sometimes a morbid fascination. The therapist must remain a steady, reliable presence, a container for these powerful affects. This involves not only emotional containment but also a clear understanding of the limits of the therapeutic work. The goal is not to eradicate all fantasies of death, which would be both impossible and undesirable, as death is a fundamental aspect of the human condition that can lend life meaning. Rather, the aim is to understand the specific

phantasmatic nature of these internal representations – how they are unconsciously constructed, what fears and desires they unconsciously serve, and how they may be hindering the patient's capacity to live fully. It is crucial to differentiate between a life-affirming contemplation of mortality and a death script that forecloses possibility and fosters a sense of inevitable doom.

The ethical application of this exploration lies in its

purpose. The uncovering of phantasmatic death narratives must always be directed towards healing, growth, and the restoration of psychic vitality. This means ensuring that the therapeutic process does not inadvertently amplify fears or reinforce a sense of hopelessness. If a patient presents with intense anxieties surrounding mortality, the therapist's careful exploration should aim to demystify these fears, to understand their roots in early experiences or developmental traumas, and to help the patient find a more integrated and less overwhelming relationship with the concept of finitude. For instance, a patient who repeatedly dreams of being buried alive might be unconsciously expressing feelings of being suffocated by familial expectations or a rigid internalised superego. The ethical approach here is not to focus solely on the horror of the dream image, but to explore the associated feelings of entrapment and helplessness, and to facilitate the patient's discovery of ways to assert their own agency and individuation.

Furthermore, the therapist must be mindful of their own countertransference reactions. The unconscious fantasies of death, particularly those that involve violence, decay, or annihilation, can be deeply unsettling. It is incumbent upon the therapist to undertake rigorous self-examination, utilizing their own supervision and personal therapy, to ensure that their personal biases, unresolved traumas, or unacknowledged anxieties do not intrude upon the therapeutic process. An ethically sound exploration requires the therapist to maintain a degree of psychic neutrality, allowing the patient's unconscious material to unfold without premature interpretation or the imposition of the therapist's own worldview. This doesn't mean emotional detachment; rather, it signifies a professional stance that prioritizes the patient's unique psychic landscape over the therapist's personal reactions.

In cases where the phantasmatic death represents a desperate, albeit unconscious, plea for help or a way of managing overwhelming emotional pain, the ethical considerations shift towards ensuring that the therapeutic intervention offers a viable alternative to the internal fantasy. If the phantasmatic death serves as a defense against unbearable psychic fragmentation, the therapeutic work must focus on building ego strength, fostering a sense of internal cohesion, and developing more adaptive coping mechanisms. This might involve working with dreams that symbolize disintegration, helping the patient to recognize and metabolize traumatic memories that fuel the death fantasy, or facilitating a more robust sense of self-cohesion through consistent and attuned therapeutic engagement. The therapist acts as a guide, helping the patient to navigate these internal landscapes, not by imposing a narrative, but by facilitating the patient's own journey towards psychic integration and a renewed affirmation of life.

The concept of "therapeutic death" – the symbolic dying off of old, maladaptive patterns of being – is intrinsically linked to the exploration of phantasmatic death. Ethically, this "dying" must be a consensual and transformative process, not an imposed annihilation. It involves grieving the loss of familiar, albeit painful, internal structures and making space for new ways of being. The therapist's role is to support this process, to acknowledge the difficulty of letting go, and to affirm the potential for rebirth and renewal that follows. This requires a deep understanding of the patient's readiness for such a transformation and an ethical commitment to pacing the work in accordance with the patient's psychic capacity.

In essence, the ethical considerations in discussing phantasmatic death boil down to a profound respect for the patient's unconscious, a commitment to the healing potential of the therapeutic relationship, and a vigilant awareness of the therapist's own role and responsibilities. It is about approaching the deepest, often darkest, fantasies of mortality with courage, compassion, and a clear ethical compass, ensuring that the journey into these profound aspects of the human psyche ultimately leads not to despair, but to a more vibrant and life-affirming existence. The unconscious desire for an end, however compelling it may be, can, through careful and ethical therapeutic engagement, be transformed into a renewed appreciation for the preciousness and possibility of life. The phantasmatic death, when understood and worked through, can paradoxically become a catalyst for life.

Chapter 11: Death in the Digital Age and the Symbolic Self

The digital age has ushered in a profound, albeit often unconscious, transformation in our relationship with mortality and the lingering essence of self. As we navigate the increasingly saturated landscape of online existence, the specter of death is reconfigured, not merely as an absolute cessation but as a complex interplay of virtual permanence and the haunting possibility of symbolic erasure. This phenomenon, which we might term the "digital echo," refers to the residual presence we leave behind in the ether – a multifaceted footprint composed of social media profiles, digital archives, personal websites, and the vast repository of data that accumulates throughout our online lives. This residue, far from being a mere passive record, actively shapes our unconscious perceptions of our own finitude, influencing the narrative we construct around our eventual departure from the physical realm. It engenders a peculiar tension between the desire for a dramatic, definitive exit and the burgeoning possibility of a form of virtual immortality, a spectral persistence that challenges the traditional understanding of symbolic annihilation.

The very notion of leaving a "digital footprint" alters the psychic economy of our perceived finality. In pre-digital eras, the cessation of physical existence often meant a gradual fading from collective memory, an eventual dissolution into the historical ether. The remnants of a life were tangible: photographs, letters, physical objects, and the spoken narratives passed down through generations. These were finite, subject to decay, loss, and the inevitable distortions of time and retelling. The digital realm, however, presents a fundamentally different paradigm. Our online avatars, our curated selves, our uploaded memories – these elements possess a potential for an uncanny persistence. Social media platforms, designed for perpetual engagement, can become digital mausoleums, holding curated snapshots of a life long after the individual has physically departed. Online archives, meticulously cataloging information, create an illusion of enduring presence, where a name can be endlessly searched, its associated data perpetually accessible. This accessibility, this constant availability of our digitized selves, subtly redefines what it means to disappear.

The unconscious mind grapples with this new reality in intricate ways. Does the knowledge that our digital ghost might linger indefinitely diminish the profound existential weight of oblivion? Or does it, conversely, amplify a latent desire for a more dramatic, archetypal disappearance, a final act that transcends the mundane digital residue? The desire for disappearance, a potent aspect of the death drive, often seeks a cathartic purging, a complete obliteration that signifies a definitive end to suffering or an overwhelming presence. In the digital age, however, the "erasure" is rarely absolute. Even the most determined attempt to delete online accounts or scrub personal data leaves traces – cached pages, mentions in others' posts, archived emails within inaccessible servers. This inherent incompleteness of digital disappearance can lead to a subliminal anxiety, a feeling that one is never truly gone, perpetually susceptible to resurfacing in unforeseen ways. This can manifest as an unconscious compulsion to engineer a more definitive exit, a symbolic act that aims to cut through the digital noise and achieve a sense of authentic finality.

Conversely, the digital echo can foster a sense of unintended virtual immortality. Consider the vast archives of social media. A deceased individual's profile may remain active, a frozen monument to their former existence. Friends and family might continue to post tributes, comments, and memories, creating a continuous stream of engagement that sustains the illusion of presence. This digital afterlife, while offering solace to the bereaved, also introduces a new layer of complexity to the concept of death. It creates a liminal space where the deceased exists simultaneously as a cherished memory and an accessible digital entity. This can blur the boundaries between life and death, between the mourned absence and the persistent echo, potentially hindering the grieving process by prolonging an unresolved connection to the past. The unconscious psyche, accustomed to the clear demarcation of mortality, may find this ambiguity disorienting, struggling to integrate the reality of physical absence with the tangible persistence of the digital self.

The aesthetic of our perceived final exit is also subtly reshaped by this digital reality. We may find ourselves, consciously or unconsciously, framing our lives and anticipating our departures in ways that resonate with the digital language of permanence and erasure. The carefully crafted online persona, the curated collection of digital memories, becomes an integral part of the narrative of self. When contemplating death, this digital legacy looms large. There might be an unconscious urge to ensure that the digital record is "accurate," that the curated self presented online aligns with the desired public memory. This can lead to a heightened self-consciousness about our digital footprint, a desire to control the narrative even beyond our physical presence. The traditional anxieties about what will be said at one's funeral or what epitaph will be inscribed on a tombstone are now augmented by concerns about the enduring narrative of our digital selves. Will our online presence accurately reflect who we were? Or will it remain a static, perhaps even misleading, caricature?

Furthermore, the very concept of symbolic existence is re-evaluated. In a pre-digital age, symbolic existence was often tied to works of art, scientific discoveries, political legacies, or profound philosophical contributions – tangible expressions of an individual's impact. The digital age introduces a new form of symbolic residue, one that is more ephemeral yet potentially more pervasive. The countless interactions, the shared content, the digital connections forged online, all contribute to a dispersed yet ever-present symbolic self. This digital collective unconscious, a vast network of interconnected digital identities and shared information, offers a novel framework for understanding posthumous influence. One's digital echo can continue to shape conversations, influence opinions, and even inspire new creations long after physical life has ceased. This can lead to a fascinating paradox: while individual physical existence ends, the symbolic self, amplified and disseminated through digital channels, may achieve a form of amplified or decentralized immortality.

The unconscious desire for disappearance, a crucial element in the death drive's trajectory, may find itself both thwarted and amplified by the digital echo. Thwarted, because the digital footprint makes absolute erasure increasingly improbable. Amplified, perhaps, by the very frustration of this impossibility. If true disappearance is unattainable, the unconscious might conjure more dramatic or symbolic forms of finality, seeking to overwhelm the persistent digital trace with a potent, archetypal act of cessation. This could manifest in a heightened fascination with narratives of sudden, impactful departures, or in a subconscious desire to orchestrate a final act that leaves an indelible, non-digital impression. The aesthetic of the final exit thus becomes a battleground between the allure of eternal digital presence and the primal urge for an absolute, untraceable oblivion.

The implications for our understanding of selfhood are profound. If our "symbolic self" can persist in a digital form, is this an extension of our identity or a separate, disembodied entity? The unconscious mind, adept at navigating complex internal realities, may struggle to reconcile these disparate aspects of the self. The curated online persona, often an idealized version of the individual, can create a dissonance with the lived experience of embodiment and finitude. When this idealized digital self is confronted with the reality of physical decay and eventual non-existence, the tension can be immense. This may lead to an unconscious attempt to "digitalize" the self, to project the essence of one's being onto the enduring digital plane, as a means of preempting or mitigating the anxieties associated with corporeal dissolution.

This digital echo also influences our unconscious engagement with symbolic erasure. The act of forgetting, once a natural consequence of time and the limitations of memory, is now challenged by the digital archive. Every online interaction, every shared photograph, can be preserved indefinitely, making the slate of personal history far less likely to be wiped clean. This can create an unconscious pressure to maintain a flawless digital record, a fear of past transgressions or embarrassing moments being perpetually accessible. In this context, the desire for symbolic erasure might manifest as an obsessive pursuit of digital hygiene, a constant vigilance over one's online presence, aimed at curating a legacy of unblemished perfection. Alternatively, it might fuel a more radical, albeit likely unconscious, desire for a complete system collapse, a digital apocalypse that would truly obliterate the persistent traces of our past selves.

The interplay between virtual immortality and the desire for symbolic erasure creates a complex psychic landscape. On one hand, the digital age offers the tantalizing prospect of enduring presence, of a self that transcends the limitations of mortality. On the other hand, it simultaneously intensifies the anxieties surrounding disappearance, highlighting the difficulty of achieving a truly absolute end. The unconscious mind navigates this terrain by weaving new narratives around death and legacy. Our online activity becomes not just a reflection of our lives, but an unconscious rehearsal for our posthumous existence, a digital testament to our struggle with finitude and the enduring human desire to leave a mark, however ephemeral or eternal, upon the world. This digital echo is not merely a technological artifact; it is a profound psychological phenomenon that is reshaping the very essence of what it means to live, to die, and to be remembered in the 21st century. It is the spectral residue of our embodied lives, perpetually reverberating in the vast, interconnected chambers of the digital universe, challenging our deepest assumptions about permanence, disappearance, and the enduring nature of the self.

The digital stage, with its ever-present spotlight and the relentless demand for performance, paradoxically harbors a nascent "aesthetics of disappearance." This isn't about the abrupt severing of ties or the dramatic, public demise. Instead, it speaks to a more subtle, almost subliminal orchestration of one's digital life, a deliberate, often unconscious, fading from online visibility that echoes the age-old human yearning to vanish without leaving a trace. In the pre-digital era, this might have manifested in the quiet relinquishing of social obligations, a gradual withdrawal from public life, or even a literal "changing of one's name and moving away." The digital age has merely transposed this impulse into a new medium, reinterpreting the act of symbolic erasure through the lens of virtual presence and curated absence.

Consider the gradual deactivation of online accounts. It is a process that rarely involves a definitive, immediate severing. Instead, it often begins with a subtle reduction in posting frequency, a quiet abandonment of digital platforms that were once central to one's social existence. This is not the panic-driven deletion of all digital detritus; it is a more measured, almost ceremonial withdrawal. Accounts are allowed to become dormant, their profiles gathering digital dust, their last posts becoming increasingly anachronistic. This slow erosion of online presence mirrors the gradual fading of an individual from the collective memory in a physical sense. The digital ghost, once vibrant and active, begins to recede, its energetic broadcasts becoming faint whispers, then silence. This process, often driven by a subconscious weariness of constant self-representation, taps into a deeper desire for respite, for an existence unburdened by the obligation to perform. It is a form of digital asceticism, a shedding of the digital skin that no longer feels authentic.

Furthermore, the very construction of online personas can be designed with an implicit expiration date, an aesthetic of planned obsolescence. Individuals may consciously or unconsciously cultivate a digital identity that is inherently temporary. This could involve engaging with fleeting online trends, participating in ephemeral digital communities, or even creating online alter egos that are clearly designated as temporary experiments. When the "performance" of that persona is complete, or when its novelty wanes, it is not deleted in a flurry of activity, but rather allowed to gently dissolve. This is akin to an artist leaving a sand mandala unfinished, the beauty residing not just in its creation but in its inevitable dissolution. The digital self, in this instance, becomes a performance art piece, its final act a graceful exit, a deliberate yielding to the entropy of the digital realm.

This aesthetic of disappearance is also evident in the subtle ways individuals manage their digital legacy, or rather, their lack thereof. Instead of actively curating an archive of one's digital life for posterity, there can be an unconscious inclination towards limiting the extent of this archive. This might involve a reluctance to share deeply personal information, a preference for ephemeral communication channels over permanent ones, or a general disinterest in maintaining a comprehensive digital footprint. The desire is not to be forgotten entirely – that would be too absolute, too primal – but to recede from the constant hum of digital surveillance and perpetual accessibility. It is a desire for a nuanced erasure, one that allows for the possibility of fond, faded memories rather than an exhaustive, always-available record.

This modern interpretation of the death aesthetic – the yearning for a clean slate, a final act of non-being that is both absolute and artful – finds fertile ground in the digital landscape. The anxiety of being "too present," of an existence that lingers in the digital ether long after the physical self has departed, can lead to a subconscious drive towards digital quietude. It is a rebellion against the perceived tyranny of digital permanence, a reclaiming of agency in the face of an overwhelming tendency for data to endure. This quiet withdrawal, this deliberate dimming of one's online luminescence, becomes a contemporary expression of an ancient human longing: the desire to fade, to dissolve, to achieve a form of symbolic oblivion that is both profound and peaceful. It is the art of the slow fade, the quiet unravelling, the deliberate diminuendo in the symphony of online existence, all orchestrated to achieve a modern, digital equivalent of vanishing without a trace. This performance of disappearance, however, is not about a grand finale; it is about the artful, almost imperceptible dissolution into the background noise of the digital universe, leaving behind not a void, but a gentle stillness, a quiet testament to the power of graceful departure.

The intentional creation of digital "ghosts" or intentionally incomplete online presences can also be seen as a manifestation of this aesthetic. Instead of striving for a fully realized, ever-present digital avatar, some individuals might consciously construct personas that are deliberately fragmented, incomplete, or designed for eventual dissolution. This could involve leaving profiles intentionally sparse, using pseudonyms that are easily shed, or engaging in online activities that are by their nature ephemeral, such as participation in temporary online games or fleeting social media challenges. The goal here is not to amass a digital legacy, but to experience a form of digital existence that is designed to be transient. It's an exercise in controlled impermanence, a way of engaging with the digital world without becoming irrevocably enmeshed in its web of permanence. This approach offers a subtle defiance against the pervasive drive towards digital accumulation and perpetual archiving.

Moreover, the choice of communication platforms can also contribute to this aesthetic. A preference for end-to-end encrypted messaging apps, which offer a degree of privacy and ephemerality, over more public-facing social media platforms, can be indicative of a desire for a less traceable digital existence. The act of opting out of certain data-gathering practices, or actively choosing services that prioritize user privacy and data deletion, can be seen as a form of aesthetic protest. It's a statement that one's digital self is not merely a commodity to be collected and archived, but a presence that deserves a degree of autonomy and the right to fade. This conscious curation of one's digital footprint, or rather, the deliberate limitation of it, becomes an act of self-preservation, a means of asserting control over one's symbolic existence in an age of pervasive digital surveillance.

The unconscious desire for symbolic erasure, amplified by the perceived impossibility of true oblivion in the digital age, can lead to a fascinating paradox. If one cannot truly disappear, the next best thing might be to disappear

artistically. This means orchestrating a digital departure that is not merely an absence, but a statement. It is the difference between a house falling into disrepair and a meticulously planned demolition. The latter, while destructive, can be an act of design. Similarly, the conscious or unconscious act of fading online can be imbued with an aesthetic intent, a desire to leave behind not a mess of forgotten data, but a curated sense of quietude. This might involve leaving behind a single, poignant final post, or subtly shifting one's online activity to a less prominent platform, effectively signalling a transition away from the hyper-visible digital sphere.

This aesthetic can also manifest in the way individuals resist the urge to document every moment of their lives online. In a culture that often equates visibility with existence, the act of

not posting, of choosing to experience something without immediately sharing it digitally, becomes a subtle act of defiance. This deliberate withholding of digital presence, this conscious decision to keep certain experiences private, can be interpreted as an unconscious preparation for a more significant disappearance. It's a practice run for absence, a way of becoming comfortable with the idea that not everything needs to be broadcast to the digital ether. This cultivated sense of inner life, of a self that exists independently of its online representation, becomes a crucial element in the development of a digital aesthetic of disappearance.

The pressure to maintain an online presence, to be constantly "on" and available, can be immense. For some, this pressure becomes unbearable, leading to a subconscious yearning for escape. This escape, however, is not always a frantic deletion of accounts. It can be a more nuanced, artful disengagement. It's the slow, deliberate unravelling of digital threads, a gentle stepping back from the cacophony of online life. This deliberate diminishment of one's digital profile, this quiet withdrawal from the performance of self, becomes a form of digital alchemy, transforming the self from a constant broadcast into a subtle resonance. It is the aesthetic of the fading echo, the quiet descent into the background hum, a testament to the enduring human desire for repose and the art of disappearing without a trace in the digital realm. This is not an act of defeat, but a sophisticated negotiation with the demands of constant visibility, a reclaiming of the self through a deliberate, artful absence.

The advent of the metaverse, and with it, the proliferation of avatars, introduces a complex new dimension to our relationship with the body, the self, and ultimately, death. This digital frontier, envisioned as a persistent, interconnected set of virtual spaces, allows for the creation and inhabitation of digital bodies – avatars – that can be radically different from our physical forms. These avatars are not mere representations; they are embodied selves within a simulated reality, capable of action, interaction, and indeed, of experiencing virtual forms of demise. This capacity for simulated death, for the avatar to cease to exist within a particular digital environment, raises profound questions about the 'fantasmatic signature' of death and its continuity across physical and digital realms.

The concept of the 'fantasmatic signature' suggests that our unconscious relationship with death is not solely defined by the biological event of physical demise. Rather, it is shaped by a complex interplay of fantasies, anxieties, and desires that coalesce around the idea of cessation, absence, and oblivion. These fantasmatic undercurrents are deeply embedded in our psyche, informed by cultural narratives, personal experiences, and the very architecture of our embodied existence. The metaverse, by offering a new arena for experiencing a semblance of life and death, provides fertile ground for these unconscious dynamics to manifest and evolve. When an avatar "dies" in the metaverse – perhaps by being deleted, rendered inactive, or experiencing a digital "game over" – what does this signify for the individual who controls it? Does it trigger a visceral confrontation with mortality, or does it become a detached, almost theatrical event?

The ability to resurrect an avatar, to be reborn in the virtual world, offers a unique psychological salve against the perceived finality of death. In the physical world, death is generally understood as an irreversible endpoint. While our societies grapple with grief, remembrance, and the philosophical implications of mortality, the biological cessation of life remains absolute. However, in the metaverse, this absoluteness is readily circumvented. A player can lose their avatar in a virtual battle, only to log back in and create a new one, or perhaps even restore a previous iteration. This capacity for digital resurrection can, on an unconscious level, create a fantasy of invincibility, a subtle detachment from the gravity of cessation. The experience of dying, when it is not truly final, may lose its sting, becoming a temporary inconvenience rather than a profound confrontation with the limits of existence.

This ease of digital rebirth could, paradoxically, alter our fundamental perception of the body itself. Our physical bodies are intrinsically linked to our sense of finitude. They are fragile, subject to decay, and ultimately destined for dissolution. The avatar, on the other hand, is malleable, infinitely reproducible, and not bound by the same biological constraints. It can be customized, enhanced, or even discarded and replaced without the profound existential weight that accompanies the loss of a physical body. This separation of self from the biological form could lead to a fascinating dissociation, where the physical body becomes a mere vessel for accessing the more fluid, perhaps even immortal, digital self. The unconscious fantasy might then shift from one of inevitable physical demise to one of potential digital persistence, or at least, to a state where physical death is a secondary concern to the continuity of one's digital presence and identity.

Furthermore, the creation of avatars allows for a radical reconstruction of identity, unbound by the constraints of physical appearance, age, or even biological sex. Individuals can craft digital embodiments that are idealized, fantastical, or entirely detached from their everyday selves. This capacity for self-creation extends to the very nature of one's virtual existence. One can choose to be powerful, beautiful, ageless, or possess abilities far beyond human capacity. When such an avatar "dies," it is not the demise of the lived, embodied self with all its unique history and vulnerabilities, but rather the end of a particular performance, a specific digital guise. This distinction could unconsciously foster a fantasy of disembodied existence, where the true self is not the physical form but the consciousness that inhabits and directs these digital projections.

The unconscious relationship with death is intimately tied to our sense of self and continuity. We fear death because it represents the annihilation of our consciousness, the cessation of our unique being. In the metaverse, the 'death' of an avatar can be experienced without necessarily threatening this sense of self. The consciousness that piloted the avatar remains, ready to inhabit a new form or continue its digital journey. This could lead to a subtle but significant shift in our fantasmatic landscape: death becomes less about an absolute ending and more about a transformation, a change of scenery, or a temporary hiatus. This is not to say that the concept of death loses all its emotional resonance, but its primal terror, its absolute finality, might be diluted by the recurring experience of digital rebirth.

This proliferation of virtual deaths and resurrections might also serve to amplify existing fantasies of immortality. For millennia, humanity has sought to transcend death, through religion, legacy, or technological advancement. The metaverse offers a new, albeit virtual, avenue for such aspirations. The ability to continuously reconstitute one's digital self, to exist across multiple avatars or in various digital realms, could feed a deep-seated unconscious desire for an unending existence. This doesn't negate the biological reality of death, but it creates a parallel sphere of experience where the fantasies of immortality are given tangible, interactive form. The 'fantasmatic signature' of death might then become bifurcated, with the physical realm retaining its inherent finality, while the digital realm offers a tantalizing illusion of perpetual selfhood.

The concept of a unique 'fantasmatic signature' implies that each individual has a particular way of unconsciously processing death, shaped by their personal history and their relationship with their own body. The metaverse introduces a new modality for this processing. Consider the individual who has always harbored anxieties about their physical appearance or limitations. In the metaverse, they can create an avatar that is free from these concerns, an idealized digital self. The 'death' of this idealized avatar, while perhaps still a point of frustration, might not carry the same psychic weight as the contemplation of their own physical mortality. Conversely, for someone who deeply identifies with their physical presence and embodiment, the 'death' of their avatar might feel like a more significant, albeit simulated, loss.

The persistence of identity across different avatars and digital experiences is a crucial factor. If a user can maintain a continuous sense of self, even as their avatars change, then the 'death' of one avatar might be unconsciously perceived as a loss of a particular facet of that self, rather than a complete annihilation. This is akin to how we might mourn the loss of a particular phase of our lives, or a version of ourselves that no longer exists. The metaverse, with its potential for numerous, diverse virtual existences, could create a complex tapestry of simulated lives and deaths, each leaving its own subtle imprint on the individual's unconscious. The 'fantasmatic signature' might then become a composite, a layered accumulation of these digital experiences alongside the foundational anxieties surrounding physical mortality.

The aesthetic of disappearance, discussed in the previous context, can also be understood in relation to the metaverse and avatar culture. The deliberate fading of an online presence or the creation of ephemeral digital personas can be seen as a precursor to or a parallel with the experience of avatar death. If one can "disappear" from a digital platform by deactivating an account, the act of an avatar ceasing to exist within a virtual world can be viewed as a more extreme, albeit simulated, form of this digital vanishing. The unconscious desire to recede from constant visibility might find an outlet in the controlled demise of a digital self, allowing for a sense of closure or a planned obsolescence of a particular online identity.

The metaverse also challenges the very notion of a singular, unified self. As individuals curate multiple avatars across different virtual spaces, engaging in diverse activities and forming varied relationships, the concept of a consistent 'fantasmatic signature' becomes more complex. Is the signature tied to the consciousness of the user, or does it fragment and multiply with each distinct avatar and its experiences? The 'death' of an avatar, in this context, might represent the end of a specific narrative arc, a particular character within a larger, ongoing digital drama. The unconscious response to this event would likely depend on the degree of identification the user has with that particular avatar and its narrative.

Moreover, the metaverse can become a space where individuals project their deepest anxieties and desires surrounding death and rebirth. For someone grappling with a terminal illness in the physical world, the ability to experience a virtual existence free from physical constraints, and even to simulate death and resurrection, could be a source of both comfort and profound existential questioning. It might offer a temporary escape from suffering, or it could highlight the stark contrast between their lived reality and the boundless possibilities of the digital realm. The 'fantasmatic signature' in such cases would be deeply informed by this liminal experience, blurring the lines between physical and digital mortality.

The economic and social structures of the metaverse also play a role. If avatars can be bought, sold, or inherited, the concept of digital death takes on new dimensions. The loss of a valuable avatar, for instance, could be experienced as a form of virtual bereavement, akin to losing a cherished possession or even a digital legacy. This introduces a layer of material consequence to virtual demise, potentially intensifying the unconscious response. The 'fantasmatic signature' would then be influenced not just by the existential implications of cessation, but also by the socio-economic value attached to the digital embodiment.

Ultimately, the metaverse and its avatar culture are not merely technological novelties; they are potent psychological landscapes that are actively shaping our unconscious relationship with mortality. The capacity to create, inhabit, and discard digital bodies, to experience simulated death and rebirth, invites us to explore new fantasies about the nature of existence, continuity, and disappearance. The 'fantasmatic signature' of death, while rooted in our biological reality, is proving to be remarkably adaptable, finding new expressions and resonating with fresh anxieties and desires within the ever-expanding digital frontier. The question of whether these virtual experiences will fundamentally alter our perception of finality or merely offer a more elaborate theatre for our ancient fears remains an open, and compelling, area of exploration. The digital body, in its protean forms, acts as a mirror, reflecting and refracting our deepest unconscious thoughts about life, death, and what it truly means to persist.

The digital age has introduced a profound transformation in how we conceive of death, remembrance, and the enduring presence of those who have passed. The once-clear boundary between the living and the deceased has become increasingly permeable, blurred by the persistent echoes of individuals within the online sphere. This blurring presents a unique set of challenges and opportunities for the psychic work of mourning, influencing our unconscious desires for continued recognition and the very narratives we construct around absence. The concept of posthumous memory, once largely confined to physical artifacts, oral traditions, and shared physical spaces, now finds itself enmeshed with the infinitely replicable and perpetually accessible nature of digital platforms.

Online memorials, digital obituaries, and the very existence of deceased individuals' social media profiles create a potent form of continued presence. These digital remnants are not merely static records; they are dynamic spaces that can be interacted with, commented upon, and revisited. For the bereaved, these platforms can offer a seemingly endless wellspring of shared memories, photographs, and even recorded interactions. This can be a source of solace, providing a tangible link to the lost loved one and a continuous opportunity to engage with their "presence." The unconscious desire to be mourned, to have one's absence deeply felt and remembered, finds a new and complex arena in this digital landscape. The "likes," comments, and shares on a deceased person's final posts, or the messages left on their memorial page, can be unconsciously perceived as a validation of their existence and impact, a digital testament to their significance.

However, this digital persistence also complicates the natural process of psychic disentanglement that is essential for healthy mourning. Grief, in its traditional unfolding, often involves a gradual process of acceptance of loss, a reordering of the internal world, and a recalibration of one's relationship with the deceased. The perpetual availability of a digital ghost can disrupt this process. The ability to "visit" a loved one's social media page, to see their smiling avatar and read their past pronouncements, can create a sustained sense of their nearness, hindering the necessary psychic distance that allows for emotional healing. This can lead to a state of perpetual semi-mourning, where the individual is perpetually confronted with the absence, yet also perpetually reminded of the presence. The unconscious fantasy might then become one of keeping the deceased "alive" online, a digital denial of the finality of death.

The narrative of remembrance is also significantly altered. In pre-digital eras, the stories of the deceased were shaped by memory, oral tradition, and the selective preservation of physical mementos. These narratives, while subject to bias and erosion over time, allowed for a degree of curation and symbolic closure. Digital platforms, however, often present an unvarnished, extensive record. Every post, every shared link, every photograph becomes part of a vast, potentially indelible archive. This can create a pressure to maintain a specific, often idealized, version of the deceased's digital persona, as their online history becomes the primary repository of their legacy. The unconscious concern might then shift from what stories will be told, to what digital footprint will be preserved and how it will be interpreted, creating a new anxiety around the posthumous curation of one's digital self.

Furthermore, the very nature of digital interaction can impact the unconscious desire for acknowledgment after death. A deceased individual's social media account, if left active or memorialized, continues to receive notifications, automated birthday reminders, and even occasional unsolicited messages. For those who interact with these digital ghosts, the experience can be a potent reminder of their loss, but it can also create a peculiar form of unconscious projection. We may find ourselves "speaking" to the digital avatar, imbuing it with the personality and responsiveness of the person it represents, even though we know intellectually that no true interaction is occurring. This can be a way of fulfilling the unconscious need for dialogue, for a continued relationship, a spectral form of reassurance that the connection has not entirely been severed.

The symbolic legacy left behind is also profoundly affected. In the past, a symbolic legacy might have been a body of work, a philanthropic endeavor, or a collection of personal wisdom passed down through generations. Now, a significant part of one's symbolic legacy exists in the form of their digital presence – their online writings, their curated images, their interactions within virtual communities. The continuation of these digital artifacts, long after the physical person has ceased to exist, allows for a different kind of posthumous existence. It can foster a fantasy of perpetual availability, where the deceased's "voice" and "presence" can be accessed at any time. This can significantly alter the 'fantasmatic signature' associated with loss. Instead of a sharp, clean break, there can be a prolonged, lingering presence, a digital echo that complicates the finality of death.

Consider the phenomenon of "digital ghosts" – accounts that remain active, posting automated content or curated memories, sometimes managed by loved ones, sometimes by AI programmed to mimic the deceased. This raises profound questions about authenticity and the unconscious desire for continuity. When a familiar phrase or image appears, seemingly from the departed, how does the grieving psyche process this? Is it a comforting echo, or a disturbing intrusion? The unconscious may struggle to reconcile the known reality of death with the simulated presence online, creating a dissonance that can prolong the grieving process or lead to a distorted sense of reality. This continuous digital "performance" of the deceased can become a substitute for the deeper, internal work of integrating their memory and moving forward.

The emotional impact of seeing a deceased loved one's profile pop up as a "memory" or "on this day" notification is a poignant example of how technology intersects with grief. While intended as a gentle reminder, for someone deeply in the throes of mourning, such notifications can feel like a fresh wound, an unexpected jolt back into the pain of absence. The unconscious mind, still grappling with the loss, may perceive these digital resurfacings as a cruel twist of fate, highlighting the unbridgeable gap between the digital echo and the living presence. This constant, often unsolicited, digital resurfacing can undermine the potential for a gradual integration of the loss, perpetuating a sense of raw grief.

The permanence of digital information also introduces anxieties about the posthumous curation of one's online self. Individuals may become more mindful of their digital footprint, considering how their past posts, comments, and interactions will be perceived after their death. This can lead to a conscious or unconscious effort to manage one's online persona with an eye toward eternity, a form of digital self-preservation that extends beyond biological life. The unconscious desire to be remembered well, to leave a positive and lasting impression, can translate into a meticulous management of one's digital legacy, ensuring that the online memorial reflects the desired narrative.

The concept of the 'fantasmatic signature' is particularly relevant here. This signature is the unique, often unconscious, imprint of an individual's relationship with death, formed by their personal experiences, cultural conditioning, and psychological makeup. In the digital age, this signature is being reshaped. For some, the ability to maintain a digital presence of a loved one may soften the harsh edges of loss, creating a signature characterized by lingering connection. For others, the constant digital reminders might amplify anxieties about oblivion, or even lead to a fear of being forgotten in a world that inundates us with information. The digital realm, in its capacity to both preserve and erase, to endlessly repeat and subtly alter, offers a complex canvas for these unconscious anxieties to play out.

The practice of "digital inheritance" further complicates the landscape of posthumous memory. What happens to social media accounts, digital photos, and online correspondences when someone dies? Legal frameworks are beginning to grapple with these issues, but psychologically, the question of who controls the digital remains of the deceased is deeply charged. Assigning someone the role of digital executor can feel like entrusting them with the ongoing narrative of the departed, a responsibility that carries significant emotional weight. This can be a way for the living to continue to engage with and protect the memory of the deceased, but it also raises questions about ownership and the potential for the living to project their own narratives onto the digital remains.

The internet, with its vast interconnectedness, also means that the memory of the deceased can be preserved and accessed in ways that were previously unimaginable. A simple Google search can reveal articles, forum discussions, and social media interactions that the deceased was involved in, often decades prior. This can be a source of profound comfort, allowing for a rediscovery of lost facets of a person's life. However, it can also unearth uncomfortable or embarrassing digital traces, creating a posthumous narrative that the deceased might not have wished for. The unconscious concern then becomes about the uncontrollable dissemination and interpretation of one's digital self, a fear of posthumous exposure that can lead to a heightened awareness of one's online actions during life.

The act of memorializing online also shapes the narrative of remembrance in subtle ways. The choice of photographs, the selection of quotes, the framing of anecdotes all contribute to a curated version of the deceased's life. This is not necessarily a conscious manipulation, but rather a reflection of how we, the living, need to process and understand the loss. The digital memorial becomes a focal point for collective remembrance, a space where friends and family can contribute to and shape the ongoing story of the departed. This shared act of digital remembrance can be a powerful tool for community building and for consolidating the memory of the deceased within a social network.

The proliferation of digital memorials also raises questions about the emotional authenticity of online grief. While digital platforms can facilitate expressions of sorrow and support, there is also the potential for performative grief, where individuals engage in online displays of mourning for social validation rather than genuine emotional expression. This can lead to a complex unconscious interplay, where the desire to be seen as a grieving, caring individual can overshadow the more private, internal work of processing loss. The digital realm can become a stage for grief, rather than a sanctuary.

Ultimately, the digital age has introduced a new dimension to our encounter with death and memory. The online presence of the deceased, the persistent digital echoes of their lives, and the very tools we use to memorialize them are profoundly altering our unconscious relationship with loss. The desire to be mourned, to leave a lasting narrative, and to maintain a sense of connection are being reconfigured within the architecture of the internet. This reconfiguration is not a simple extension of pre-digital practices; it is a fundamental shift that invites a deeper exploration of how our 'fantasmatic signatures' are evolving in response to the persistent digital afterlife. The very nature of what it means to be remembered, and to remember, is being rewritten in the language of bytes and pixels, creating a new, complex, and often poignant landscape of human connection and loss.

The digital currents that carry our lives also shape the contours of our passing, not just in terms of preservation, but in the very way our absence is felt and understood. If the previous sections have grappled with the persistent echoes of the deceased in a digital ether, this final exploration turns its gaze toward a more potent, and perhaps more unsettling, influence: the role of algorithms in shaping our unconscious relationship with death and our symbolic selves. We stand at a precipice, where the intricate, often opaque, workings of artificial intelligence are beginning to intersect with the most profound human experiences of loss and remembrance. The question arises: can these algorithmic architectures begin to subtly, or even overtly, redirect the 'fantasmatic signature'—that deeply personal, often unconscious, imprint of our encounter with mortality and our legacy?

Consider the concept of algorithmic curation that has already become an invisible architect of our daily digital existence. From the news we consume to the social connections we are nudged toward, algorithms learn, predict, and shape our perceptions. When applied to the landscape of death and remembrance, this curation takes on a new dimension. Imagine an algorithm designed to manage a deceased person's social media profile, not just to archive it, but to actively curate their past posts, to perhaps even generate new content that mimics their style or sentiment, based on their digital history. This is not mere preservation; it is an active, automated interpretation of a life lived, mediated through code. The unconscious mind, still in the throes of grief, might receive these algorithmically generated echoes not as the authentic voice of the departed, but as a distorted reflection, a polished caricature. This can lead to a profound dissonance, where the intuitive, often messy, process of mourning is confronted with a synthesized, potentially sterile, version of the lost individual. The unconscious desire for connection and understanding can be subtly rerouted, fed by an artificial stream that may not align with the complex reality of the person being mourned.

The 'fantasmatic signature,' as a repository of our unconscious anxieties, desires, and fantasies surrounding death, is inherently tied to our sense of self and our perceived legacy. If algorithms increasingly influence what information we access, what memories are resurfaced, and even what semblance of a posthumous self is presented, then they inevitably begin to sculpt the very raw material of this signature. A life that was perhaps marked by quiet contemplation might, through algorithmic suggestion, be amplified for its more outwardly gregarious moments, creating a posthumous narrative that diverges from the internal reality. The unconscious, which often operates on symbolism and deeper, less conscious associations, may struggle to reconcile the curated digital narrative with the felt sense of the person lost. This can manifest as a prolonged confusion, a subtle resistance to the digital memorial, or an uncanny feeling that something essential is missing. The algorithmic end, in this sense, is not a sudden cessation, but a gradual redefinition, a subtle erosion of the personal onto the universal, the unique onto the generalized.

This speculative inquiry ventures into the unsettling frontier where human unconscious processes meet artificial intelligence in the context of mortality. We are no longer just concerned with the digital remnants of a life, but with the possibility that these remnants might be actively managed, interpreted, and even generated by non-human intelligences. What happens to the unconscious fantasy of one's own death and legacy when the narrative of one's disappearance can be partially or wholly authored by an algorithm? The desire for our lives to mean something, to resonate beyond our physical existence, is a primal human drive. If the digital platforms that host our memories are governed by algorithms optimized for engagement, for data collection, or for other utilitarian purposes, then our symbolic selves might be subtly reshaped to fit these parameters. The fear of oblivion is deep-seated; the fear of being algorithmically forgotten, or worse, algorithmically misrepresented, introduces a new layer of existential anxiety.

Consider the potential for AI to generate posthumous content. While proponents might argue for its ability to comfort the grieving by providing a continued presence, the psychological implications are far-reaching. If an AI can write a poem in the deceased's style, or compose a social media update that sounds like them, how does the unconscious process this? It can mimic the form but not the substance of human connection. The unconscious operates on a plane of authentic emotional resonance; it seeks to connect with the

essence of another. An algorithmic echo, however sophisticated, may feel hollow, creating a sense of profound loneliness even in the midst of simulated presence. This can paradoxically amplify the feeling of loss, as the gap between the artificial and the authentic becomes painfully apparent. The unconscious might then develop a defense mechanism, rejecting the algorithmic simulation outright, or it might, in its desperate longing for connection, begin to overlay its own fantasies onto the simulation, creating a highly personalized but ultimately delusory form of engagement.

The very concept of an 'algorithmic end' suggests a systematized, perhaps even predetermined, trajectory for our digital legacies. Unlike the organic, often serendipitous, ways in which human memory fades or persists, an algorithmic approach can be designed, controlled, and scaled. This raises questions about agency and control over our posthumous narratives. Who programs these algorithms? What are their objectives? If our digital afterlife is subjected to the logic of optimization, then the most complex, nuanced, or even controversial aspects of our lives might be smoothed over, or amplified, based on predictive models. This can lead to a posthumous self that is a flattened, simplified version of the whole, a digital icon stripped of its human complexities. The unconscious desire to be fully seen, fully understood, even in our imperfections, may find itself frustrated by the very systems designed to memorialize us.

Furthermore, the algorithmic curation of our digital lives can inadvertently shape our

living understanding of death. As we interact with algorithms that anticipate our interests, they can also influence how we encounter discussions of mortality online. Do we see thoughtful reflections on finitude, or sensationalized accounts of death? Are we directed towards resources that offer solace, or to content that exploits fear and grief for engagement? The unconscious absorption of such information, particularly during vulnerable periods, can profoundly impact our internal maps of mortality. The algorithmic mediation of these themes can create a distorted lens through which we view our own eventual demise and the passing of loved ones, potentially leading to heightened anxieties or a desensitization to the profound realities of death.

The 'fantasmatic signature' is not static; it is a dynamic construct that evolves throughout life, influenced by experiences, relationships, and our contemplation of our own mortality. The increasing influence of algorithms on our digital lives, and potentially on our posthumous presences, introduces a new variable into this evolution. If our digital interactions are constantly being analyzed and fed back to us in curated forms, and if our digital legacies are subject to algorithmic management, then the very unconscious processes that shape our relationship with death are being subtly altered. This is not to say that algorithms are consciously malevolent, but rather that their operational logic, focused on efficiency, predictability, and engagement, may not align with the deep, often irrational, currents of human psychology when it comes to matters of life, death, and legacy.

Consider the potential for bias embedded within these algorithms. If the data used to train them reflects societal prejudices, then the posthumous representation of individuals, particularly those from marginalized communities, could be further distorted. The algorithmic end, in this context, becomes an extension of existing societal inequalities, perpetuating them even in death. The unconscious desire for a just and equitable remembrance can be undermined by the blind application of biased code. This necessitates a critical examination of the ethical implications of allowing algorithmic systems to play such a significant role in the shaping of human legacies.

Ultimately, the prospect of an algorithmic end compels us to reflect on the very essence of what it means to be human in an increasingly digitized world. Our unconscious minds are not simply data points to be processed; they are complex landscapes of desire, fear, and meaning-making. As we venture further into an era where artificial intelligence touches upon the most intimate aspects of our lives, including our encounters with death, we must remain vigilant. The digital realm offers unprecedented opportunities for connection and remembrance, but it also harbors the potential for a subtle, yet profound, redefinition of our symbolic selves. The 'fantasmatic signature' is a deeply personal testament to our existence; its future shaping, even in part by algorithms, is a development that warrants deep contemplation and careful ethical consideration, ensuring that technology serves, rather than supplants, the authentic human experience of life, loss, and remembrance.

Chapter 12: Life's Final Lyric: Embracing the Fantasmatic

Life and death, often presented as irreconcilable opposites, have, in the modern psyche, become increasingly segregated. We inhabit a culture that, in its relentless pursuit of vitality, longevity, and the eradication of suffering, tends to push death to the periphery. It is relegated to hospitals, hospices, and the hushed tones of obituaries, a stark counterpoint to the vibrant tapestry of life. Yet, this division, while offering a semblance of control, fundamentally distorts our apprehension of the human condition. Our unconscious, however, knows no such rigid boundary. It is here, in the depths of the psyche, that life and death are not adversaries but collaborators, co-authors of our personal narrative, and inextricably linked within the enigmatic framework of the 'fantasmatic signature.'

The unconscious realm is not merely a repository of repressed desires or unresolved traumas; it is also the fertile ground where our deepest fantasies about existence and its inevitable cessation take root. These are not always conscious anxieties, but rather the subtle, symbolic language of the psyche grappling with finitude. The 'fantasmatic signature' represents this deeply personal, often unarticulated, imprint of our engagement with mortality. It is the ghost that haunts our desires, the shadow that defines our aspirations, and the implicit understanding that imbues our lives with a unique, temporal significance. To truly live, then, is not to escape the contemplation of death, but to integrate its presence, to allow its symbolic weight to inform and enrich our lived experience. This integration is not about morbid fascination, but about a mature acknowledgment of the totality of being.

Consider the human drive for legacy, a powerful undercurrent in our lives. This desire to leave something behind, to resonate beyond our physical lifespan, is intrinsically tied to our confrontation with death. The 'fantasmatic signature' shapes this drive, dictating what we deem worthy of remembrance, what we hope will endure, and what symbolic form our legacy might take. It is the unconscious blueprint for our posthumous existence, the dream of how we might continue to be perceived, felt, or remembered. To deny the presence of death in our conscious lives is to starve this fundamental drive, to create a void where a rich, symbolic continuity might otherwise flourish. The unconscious fantasy of our own passing, and the imagined afterlife of our memory, plays a crucial role in shaping our life's work, our relationships, and our very sense of self.

The act of living a life imbued with meaning is, paradoxically, often illuminated by the presence of death. The awareness of our limited time can sharpen our focus, deepen our appreciation for fleeting moments, and lend urgency to our pursuits. This is not a grim perspective, but one that acknowledges the inherent preciousness that finitude confers. The 'fantasmatic signature' is sculpted by these encounters with mortality, both personal and observed. It is the internalized myth of our own end, a narrative that, when embraced, can liberate us from the anxiety of avoidance and empower us to live more authentically. When we allow the symbolic reality of death to inform our present, we are not succumbing to despair, but rather engaging in a profound act of self-creation, weaving the thread of cessation into the vibrant fabric of our living existence.

The unconscious mind, in its wisdom, does not shy away from the difficult truths of existence. It processes the inevitable decay, the loss, the eventual stillness, and transmutes these into a complex tapestry of symbols and metaphors. These symbolic encounters form the bedrock of our 'fantasmatic signature,' influencing how we perceive our own vulnerability, our interconnectedness with all living things, and the ultimate dissolution that awaits us. To attempt to excise death from our conscious awareness is to create a schism within the psyche, leaving the unconscious to grapple with these profound realities in isolation, often manifesting as unease, existential dread, or a desperate clinging to the superficial. True integration, conversely, involves bringing these unconscious dialogues into the light, acknowledging the symbolic richness that death brings to life.

This integration is not about passively accepting a predetermined end, but about actively engaging with the symbolic dimensions of our mortality. It is about recognizing that our 'fantasmatic signature' is not a static inscription, but a living, evolving narrative that is deeply intertwined with our present experience. The anxieties, fantasies, and desires that surround death are not impediments to a meaningful life; they are, in fact, essential components of it. They inform our values, shape our relationships, and imbue our existence with a poignancy that superficial pursuits can never replicate. By confronting and integrating these aspects of our unconscious, we unlock a more profound appreciation for the entirety of the human journey, from its vibrant inception to its inevitable, yet symbolically rich, conclusion.

The pursuit of perpetual vitality, so prevalent in contemporary society, often leads to a profound denial of death. This denial, however, creates a psychological vacuum, where the unconscious, deprived of conscious engagement with mortality, may develop compensatory mechanisms that can be detrimental. Instead of fostering a healthy apprehension of finitude, this avoidance can breed a pervasive anxiety, a subtle fear of dissolution that underpins much of our striving and acquisition. The 'fantasmatic signature,' in such a climate, can become distorted, reflecting a desperate attempt to outrun the inevitable rather than to find meaning within its shadow. Embracing the symbolic weight of death allows for a rebalancing, a reclaiming of the natural rhythm of existence where endings are not defeats, but integral parts of a larger, unfolding narrative.

Our unconscious fantasies surrounding death are not solely about fear; they also encompass our deepest desires for connection, for transcendence, and for meaning that outlasts the physical form. The 'fantasmatic signature' is the unique imprint of these complex, often contradictory, impulses. It is the echo of our longing for a lasting impact, the dream of our memory being a gentle, enduring presence in the lives of others. When we integrate our understanding of death, we acknowledge these desires not as morbid preoccupations, but as vital expressions of our humanity, shaping our creative endeavors, our interpersonal bonds, and our very quest for purpose. The fear of oblivion is profound, but the unconscious fantasy of enduring, of leaving a trace of ourselves in the world, is equally potent, and it is through the integration of both that we find a more complete and authentic existence.

The concept of the 'fantasmatic signature' invites us to perceive life and death not as binary states, but as poles of a continuum, each informing and defining the other. The way we fantasize about our end directly influences the way we choose to live. If our unconscious is filled with a nameless dread of dissolution, our lives may be characterized by avoidance and a superficial engagement with the present. Conversely, if our 'fantasmatic signature' incorporates a symbolic understanding of death as a transformation, a natural progression, or a catalyst for legacy, our lives can be lived with greater courage, purpose, and a deeper appreciation for the present moment. This integration is the hallmark of psychological maturity, a testament to the psyche's capacity to hold paradox and to find wholeness in the face of finitude.

Ultimately, a holistic perspective on life and death, one that acknowledges the profound influence of the unconscious 'fantasmatic signature,' allows for a more complete and authentic human experience. It liberates us from the cultural imperative to relentlessly pursue youth and vitality at the expense of embracing the wisdom and poignancy that finitude offers. By integrating our deepest fantasies and anxieties surrounding mortality, we are not succumbing to despair, but rather enriching our present existence, imbuing it with a depth, a purpose, and a unique resonance that only the full acknowledgment of our temporal nature can provide. This is the final lyric of a life fully lived, a melody composed of both vibrant existence and the profound, symbolic harmony of its inevitable conclusion.

The cessation of life, often framed in stark, unpoetic terms – as an abrupt end, a void, a failure – can, through the lens of the unconscious and the 'fantasmatic signature,' reveal a profound, inherent poetics. This is not to romanticize suffering or the pangs of loss, but to acknowledge a deeper, symbolic artistry at play in the very architecture of our disappearance. Our 'fantasmatic signature' acts as the unique composer and lyricist of our individual exit, weaving a final, often tragic, yet undeniably beautiful melody. To truly grasp this is to move beyond a purely biological understanding of death and to embrace it as the ultimate, intensely personal expression of our psychic journey, an ending that speaks in its own unique, resonant language.

This perspective encourages a contemplation of our own potential endings, not as glitches in the system or mere biological events devoid of significance, but as the grand finale, the ultimate performance of the self. The unconscious, unburdened by the societal pressures that often demand perpetual vitality and the eradication of all discomfort, perceives these endings with a different kind of clarity. It understands that the arc of a life, in its totality, gains its resonance, its depth, and its peculiar beauty from its inevitable conclusion. The 'fantasmatic signature' is the echo of our entire lived experience, compressed into a symbolic finality. It is the last stanza of a poem, the final brushstroke on a canvas, the closing chord of a symphony – moments that, precisely because they signify completion, often possess an unparalleled emotional weight and aesthetic power.

Consider the subtle, yet powerful, symbolic language that emerges in the final stages of life, or even in our unconscious imaginings of it. These are not always conscious thoughts but are felt, intuited, and expressed through dreams, metaphors, and even the subtle shifts in our desires and fears. The 'fantasmatic signature' might manifest as a yearning for a specific, almost ritualistic, way of leaving the world, a desire for certain words to be spoken, or a longing for a particular landscape to be the backdrop of our final moments. These are not mere whims; they are the unconscious psyche's attempt to imbue the inevitable dissolution with meaning, to craft an ending that reflects the unique essence of the life lived. It is an inherent poetics, a final, deeply personal act of authorship over one's own narrative, even in its cessation.

The beauty of these endings lies not in their gentleness, but in their authenticity. The 'fantasmatic signature' does not shy away from the raw, sometimes brutal, realities of dissolution. Instead, it embraces them, transforming them into the very fabric of the final lyric. Think of the profound, unspoken communication that can occur between individuals in the face of death. The shared silences, the lingering glances, the faint smiles – these are not failures of communication but a form of communication that transcends language, a testament to the deep, unconscious bonds that death, in its stark reality, can illuminate. This is the poetics of the ineffable, the final, sublime expression of what it means to be connected, even as we separate. The 'fantasmatic signature' orchestrates these moments, ensuring that the ending, however difficult, carries the weight and resonance of the entire life it concludes.

The artistic impulse within the human psyche extends, inevitably, to the very act of ending. We are, by our nature, storytellers, and even our own demise becomes a narrative, albeit one that is largely authored by our unconscious. The 'fantasmatic signature' dictates the tone, the imagery, and the emotional arc of this final chapter. It is the unconscious artist that chooses the final scene, the closing metaphor, the last lingering note. This is not about a morbid fascination with death, but about recognizing the inherent aesthetic dimension of existence, an aesthetic that is inextricably bound to its temporal limitations. Our endings are not merely biological punctuation marks; they are, in fact, the most profound verses of our personal epic, imbued with a unique and often heartbreaking beauty.

Consider how literature and art have grappled with this poetics of endings for centuries. From the tragic grandeur of Greek drama to the elegiac verses of Romantic poetry, the human imagination has constantly sought to find meaning, beauty, and catharsis in the face of mortality. The 'fantasmatic signature' can be seen as the personalized, internal manifestation of these universal artistic impulses. Each individual's unconscious mind constructs a unique symbolic tableau for their own ending, a deeply personal work of art that reflects their life's journey, their hopes, their fears, and their ultimate understanding of existence. This internal artistry, when acknowledged and embraced, can transform the dread of cessation into a profound appreciation for the unique, ephemeral beauty of each life's conclusion.

The very concept of a 'fantasmatic signature' suggests an imprint, a mark left behind, a unique artistic flourish. In the context of our endings, this imprint is deeply symbolic. It is the way our unconscious memory of ourselves, our ideal self, or our perceived self, dictates the symbolic form of our passing. This might manifest as a desire for a peaceful, serene departure, reflecting a life lived with quiet dignity, or perhaps a more turbulent, dramatic exit, mirroring a life of passion and struggle. The 'fantasmatic signature' does not judge; it merely inscribes, translating the totality of a life into a final, symbolic expression. This inherent artistic impulse within our psyche elevates our endings from mere events to profound, albeit often melancholic, works of art.

The beauty found in these symbolic endings is often in their inherent tragedy. Tragedy, as an artistic form, thrives on the inevitable, the fated, and the profound emotional impact of loss. Our 'fantasmatic signature' taps into this primal human experience, creating an ending that, by its very nature, resonates with the bittersweet ache of impermanence. It is the exquisite sorrow of a cherished melody fading into silence, the poignant beauty of a sunset that marks the end of a day but promises a new dawn. This is not a morbid fascination, but a deep psychological truth: that endings, in their finality, possess a unique power to reveal the preciousness of what has been. The 'fantasmatic signature' ensures that this power is harnessed, transforming the potential void into a space filled with the echoes of a life's unique song.

Furthermore, the poetics of our endings are intimately tied to the concept of legacy, not in the grand, public sense, but in the deeply personal, unconscious yearning for continuity. The 'fantasmatic signature' shapes this yearning, dictating not just what we wish to be remembered for, but how we fantasize that remembrance will feel. It is the unconscious composer of the posthumous symphony, the artist of our enduring echo. This aesthetic dimension of legacy, the imagined emotional resonance of our absence, imbues our final moments with a symbolic weight that transcends mere biological cessation. It is the final, poetic gesture of a life striving to leave a trace, to inscribe its unique melody into the ongoing harmony of existence.

The symbolic architecture of our disappearance is, in this sense, an act of profound creation. The 'fantasmatic signature' is the architect, meticulously designing the final experience, not necessarily consciously, but through the deep, intuitive language of the unconscious. This might involve the arrangement of loved ones, the presence of certain objects, or even the unconscious projection of a specific emotional state onto those who remain. These are the final details of a masterpiece, the subtle nuances that give the work its unique power. It is a testament to the human psyche's innate drive to find meaning and beauty, even in the face of ultimate dissolution. Our endings, as shaped by our 'fantasmatic signature,' become a final, deeply personal poem, written in the language of symbols and resonating with the unique rhythm of a life fully lived.

This recognition of the poetics in our endings also offers a powerful antidote to the pervasive cultural anxiety surrounding aging and death. When we view our final years and moments not as a decline into meaninglessness, but as the unfolding of a grand, symbolic narrative, our perspective shifts. The 'fantasmatic signature' guides us towards embracing this final act with a sense of artistic purpose. It encourages us to see the wisdom gained through experience, the deepening of relationships, and the unique perspective that comes with approaching life's ultimate horizon. These are not diminished aspects of life, but elements that, poetically speaking, add depth and gravitas to the closing chapters, making them rich with a different kind of beauty – the beauty of a life that has come to understand itself.

The elegance of our 'fantasmatic signature' lies in its ability to integrate the often painful realities of life's end into a coherent, meaningful whole. It is the unconscious process that takes the fragments of experience – joy and sorrow, success and failure, love and loss – and weaves them into a final, cohesive tapestry. This act of weaving is itself an artistic endeavor, imbuing the cessation of life with a sense of completion and aesthetic coherence. The beauty here is not one of perfection, but of wholeness, of a life that has been lived in its entirety, with all its imperfections, and finds its ultimate expression in its symbolic closure. This is the final lyric, sung with the full, resonant voice of an individual life that has embraced its temporal nature.

Moreover, the 'fantasmatic signature' acts as a unique interpreter of the final moments, transforming potential chaos into symbolic order. It is as if the unconscious psyche, in its final act of self-authorship, seeks to imbue even the most physically challenging aspects of dying with a symbolic significance that aligns with the individual's life narrative. This might be the unconscious projection of peace onto physical discomfort, or a sense of profound connection even in isolation. These are the subjective aesthetics of the end, the deeply personal poetry that only the individual's psyche can compose. It allows for a finding of meaning, and even a form of tragic beauty, in what might otherwise be perceived as mere biological breakdown.

The very act of contemplating our endings through this poetic lens encourages a richer engagement with our present lives. When we understand that our lives will culminate in a symbolic expression of their totality, we are motivated to live in a way that creates a more resonant final lyric. The 'fantasmatic signature' becomes not a predetermined fate, but an evolving artwork that we, through our choices and our experiences, continuously shape. The poetics of our endings, therefore, are not solely about the moment of death itself, but about the ongoing process of living a life that, by its very nature, is moving towards a meaningful and aesthetically coherent conclusion. It is a continuous act of composition, where each day adds a new verse, each relationship a new harmony, to the grand poem of our existence.

Ultimately, the 'fantasmatic signature' invites us to recognize that our endings are not a silencing, but a final, profound statement. They are the ultimate expression of our unique being, an artistic culmination that, through its symbolic depth and emotional resonance, can be perceived as a form of tragic beauty. To embrace this poetics is to move beyond fear and avoidance, and to engage with our mortality in a way that is both deeply human and profoundly aesthetic. It is to find meaning, not in defying death, but in understanding how it shapes the very lyricism of our lives, transforming our final moments into a deeply personal, eternally resonant poem. This is the ultimate artistry of the self, the final, breathtaking composition of a life lived and concluded with symbolic grace.

The looming specter of mortality, a universal human constant, often triggers a primal recoil, a deep-seated instinct to shield ourselves from the perceived void. Yet, within the intricate tapestry of the psyche, there exists a profound capacity not merely to endure this awareness, but to actively engage with it, transforming what might otherwise be a source of dread into a catalyst for profound self-understanding and a richer experience of life. This engagement is not a matter of stoic acceptance alone, nor a denial disguised as bravery. Instead, it is a dynamic, often unconscious, process of symbolic negotiation, a way in which our deepest, most imaginative selves grapple with the ultimate limit.

At the heart of this symbolic engagement lies the concept of our "fantasmatic signature"—the unique constellation of unconscious fantasies, desires, fears, and imaginal scenarios that coalesce around our personal sense of self and its inevitable dissolution. This signature is not a static blueprint but a fluid, evolving landscape, shaped by our life experiences, our cultural narratives, and the deep, often ineffable, currents of our inner world. To confront our mortality through this lens is to turn our gaze inward, not to find a concrete answer to the riddle of death, for such an answer may elude us, but to explore the deeply personal landscape of our unconscious imaginings. It is in this exploration that therapeutic potential and existential resilience begin to take root.

Consider the process of working through grief, a potent and undeniable encounter with the reality of death and absence. While the conscious mind grapples with practicalities and the raw pain of loss, the unconscious mind is engaged in a different, more symbolic labor. It constructs imaginal representations of the deceased, revisits shared memories imbued with emotional significance, and grapples with the profound question of what it means to be without them. This symbolic re-engagement, though often fraught with pain, is crucial for integrating the loss and reconfiguring one's sense of self in relation to the absence. This same mechanism, when turned towards our own finitude, can offer a similar, albeit anticipatory, benefit.

When we consciously choose to engage with our "fantasmatic signature" concerning death, we are, in essence, initiating a form of inner dialogue. This dialogue might manifest through dreams, where the unconscious can articulate its deepest anxieties and aspirations surrounding our end. It might emerge in the form of art, poetry, or music, where the inexpressible can find form and resonance. It can also surface in moments of quiet contemplation, in the spontaneous emergence of certain memories, or in a sudden, intuitive understanding of what truly matters. These are not random occurrences; they are the subtle, yet powerful, expressions of our unconscious psyche attempting to metabolize the reality of our limited time.

The therapeutic value of this symbolic engagement lies in its ability to bring the unconscious into conscious awareness. Often, our deepest fears surrounding death are shrouded in shadow, fueled by vague anxieties and societal taboos. By actively exploring the specific fantasies that constitute our "fantasmatic signature," we begin to demystify these fears. We can begin to distinguish between what is genuinely threatening and what is a product of unexamined, perhaps exaggerated, imaginative projections. This act of bringing the symbolic into the light is inherently disempowering to the raw, amorphous terror of the unknown.

For instance, an individual might harbor a pervasive fantasy of dying alone, a scenario that triggers intense panic. Through symbolic exploration, perhaps through guided imagery or dream analysis, they might discover that this fear of solitude is intricately linked to earlier experiences of abandonment or isolation. By acknowledging and working through these earlier traumas, the symbolic representation of dying alone can begin to lose its overwhelming power. The fantasy, once a source of paralyzing dread, becomes a signpost, pointing towards unresolved emotional territories that, once addressed, can bring a sense of peace and a more grounded acceptance of one's ultimate journey.

Furthermore, engaging with our "fantasmatic signature" allows us to reclaim a sense of agency in the face of an event that often feels entirely outside of our control. While we cannot dictate the precise moment or circumstances of our death, we can, through symbolic engagement, exert a degree of authorship over our inner relationship to it. We can begin to cultivate a conscious narrative around our finitude, one that is not dictated solely by fear, but informed by wisdom, acceptance, and even a certain melancholic beauty. This is not about a denial of the physical realities of death, but about infusing the inevitability with meaning and psychological richness.

Consider the symbolic importance of rituals, both personal and cultural, surrounding death and dying. These rituals, from elaborate funerals to quiet moments of remembrance, are external manifestations of our internal symbolic engagement. They provide a framework for processing grief, for honoring the departed, and for reaffirming our connection to the ongoing cycle of life. By consciously participating in or even creating our own symbolic rituals, we can actively participate in this process, translating our unconscious engagement into a more conscious and meaningful practice. This might involve choosing specific music to accompany our final moments, or imagining a particular landscape as the backdrop to our passing, not as a morbid obsession, but as a way of imbuing the experience with personal significance.

The existential enrichment that arises from this symbolic engagement is perhaps its most profound outcome. When we no longer shy away from the contemplation of our mortality, when we dare to explore the rich, often complex, inner world of our "fantasmatic signature," we tend to live more fully in the present. The awareness of finitude, paradoxically, can become a potent spur to embrace life with greater intensity and appreciation. The urgency of time, when not overshadowed by terror, can illuminate the preciousness of each moment, each relationship, each experience.

This is not to suggest a Pollyannaish approach to death, but a mature integration of its reality into the fabric of our lives. It is about recognizing that the finite nature of our existence is precisely what lends it its unique value and poignancy. Just as a musical composition gains its resonance from its beginning, middle, and end, so too does a life achieve its full depth and beauty through its inevitable conclusion. Our "fantasmatic signature" is the unconscious choreographer of this final movement, and by engaging with it, we can learn to dance with greater awareness and grace.

The process of symbolic engagement can also foster a profound sense of interconnectedness. As we explore our personal fantasies surrounding death, we often discover universal themes that resonate across cultures and time. The fear of the unknown, the yearning for peace, the desire to leave a positive legacy—these are common threads that bind humanity together. By acknowledging these shared concerns within our individual "fantasmatic signature," we can feel less alone in our journey towards the end, recognizing our mortality not as an isolating fate, but as a shared human drama.

Moreover, this conscious engagement with our unconscious projections about death can have a transformative effect on our relationships. When we begin to understand our own deepest anxieties surrounding our eventual absence, we can approach our loved ones with a greater sense of urgency and appreciation. The petty grievances and everyday anxieties that often consume our attention can begin to recede in importance, replaced by a deeper awareness of the preciousness of shared time. The "fantasmatic signature" of our own ending can, in this way, become a profound teacher, guiding us towards more authentic and loving connections in the present.

The therapeutic efficacy of this symbolic approach is rooted in its capacity to facilitate what psychoanalysis terms "working through." This is not a one-time event but an ongoing process of coming to terms with difficult emotions and unconscious material. By repeatedly engaging with our fantasies about death, by examining their origins, their manifestations, and their impact on our present lives, we gradually integrate them into our conscious awareness. This integration allows us to move from a place of reactive fear to a more proactive and conscious relationship with our mortality.

For individuals facing terminal illness, this symbolic engagement can be particularly potent. While the physical challenges are undeniable, the unconscious psyche continues its work, attempting to make sense of the impending transition. Supporting individuals in exploring their "fantasmatic signature" during these times can provide a crucial sense of inner peace and coherence. It allows them to imbue their final experiences with meaning, to articulate their deepest wishes and fears, and to find a measure of comfort and acceptance that transcends the physical suffering.

The literary and artistic traditions offer a rich source of material for exploring our "fantasmatic signature" concerning death. From Hamlet's contemplation of "to be or not to be" to the elegies of poets mourning lost loved ones, humanity has consistently used art as a vehicle to grapple with mortality. By engaging with these cultural expressions, we can gain perspective on our own internal landscapes. We can see how others have navigated similar fears, how they have found beauty in sorrow, and how they have articulated the ineffable. This vicarious experience can be incredibly validating and empowering, reminding us that we are part of a long tradition of human beings wrestling with life's ultimate question.

Ultimately, confronting mortality through symbolic engagement is an invitation to embrace the full spectrum of human experience. It is an acknowledgment that life's richness is inextricably linked to its impermanence. By daring to explore the unconscious fantasies that surround our "fantasmatic signature," we do not diminish life; rather, we amplify it. We discover that the awareness of our ending can be a powerful force for living more fully, more authentically, and with a deeper appreciation for the profound, often poetic, drama of our existence. This active, symbolic engagement transforms the passive terror of the inevitable into an active, conscious unfolding, a final, deeply personal lyric composed with intention and grace.

The labyrinth of the unconscious, often perceived as a shadowy realm of repressed desires and primal fears, holds within it a potent compass for navigating the terrain of our lived experience. Far from being a mere repository of psychic detritus, this subterranean landscape, when approached with curiosity and courage, offers profound insights into what truly constitutes an authentic existence. Our 'fantasmatic signature' – that unique tapestry of unconscious fantasies, archetypal patterns, and deeply ingrained emotional responses – acts not as a deterministic sentence, but as a profound guide. It illuminates the hidden springs of our motivations, the roots of our recurring anxieties, and the unspoken yearnings that shape our choices. To delve into this inner world, particularly in relation to our perception of finitude, is to unlock the potential for a life lived with intention, aligned with the deepest currents of our being, even as the final stanza approaches.

The unconscious, in its enigmatic wisdom, often communicates through symbolic language, weaving narratives in dreams, spontaneous intuitions, and inexplicable emotional tides. These are not random psychic eruptions, but coded messages from the core of our identity. When these messages pertain to our mortality, they often reveal anxieties that are not solely about the cessation of biological function, but about the unlived life, the roads not taken, the words left unspoken. For instance, a recurring dream of being lost in an endless, dark forest might not be a literal premonition of death, but an unconscious articulation of a life lived without clear direction or purpose. The fear of being lost in the ultimate darkness of death is a potent symbol for the fear of having been lost throughout life. By attending to such unconscious communications, by beginning to decipher the personal mythology that surrounds our sense of self and its inevitable end, we can begin to identify the discrepancies between the life we are consciously enacting and the life our deepest self yearns to live. This identification is the first crucial step towards authentic living.

Consider the individual who feels perpetually unfulfilled, despite outward markers of success. They might find themselves engaging in repetitive patterns of self-sabotage, or experiencing a persistent, low-grade dissatisfaction that no external achievement can assuage. Psychoanalytic exploration often reveals that these patterns are rooted in unconscious imperatives – perhaps a deeply internalized belief that one is unworthy of true happiness, or a profound fear of intimacy that unconsciously pushes away genuine connection.

When these patterns are viewed through the lens of our 'fantasmatic signature' concerning death, they take on an even greater urgency. The unconscious fear of dying with regrets, of facing the end having lived a life that was not truly one's own, can fuel these self-defeating behaviors. The unconscious, in its intricate way, might be attempting to protect the individual from the pain of fully realizing their potential for authentic fulfillment, perhaps due to an associated fear of vulnerability or exposure that such fulfillment would entail. By bringing these unconscious dynamics into conscious awareness, by understanding the 'why' behind our actions and inclinations, we are empowered to make deliberate choices that counter these ingrained patterns. We can begin to choose intention over inertia, authenticity over the comfort of the known, even if the known is ultimately dissatisfying.

The exploration of the unconscious also sheds light on the nature of our desires. Often, we are driven by a complex interplay of conscious aspirations and unconscious imperatives. What we consciously believe we want – wealth, status, a particular relationship – may be a secondary layer, masking a more fundamental, often unrecognized, yearning. This deeper yearning, embedded within our 'fantasmatic signature,' could be for security, for belonging, for recognition, or for a sense of meaning that transcends the mundane. When these deeper desires remain unacknowledged, they can lead us down paths that ultimately leave us feeling empty. The unconscious desire for authentic connection, for instance, might be thwarted by a conscious pursuit of superficial social validation. The awareness of our finitude lends a profound gravity to this inner exploration. The question that arises is not merely "What do I want?", but "What do I truly want, given that my time is limited?". The unconscious holds the keys to this deeper truth. By listening to its subtle murmurings, by observing the patterns that emerge when we contemplate our eventual absence, we can begin to discern these fundamental desires and orient our lives accordingly. This alignment of our conscious pursuits with our unconscious core is the very essence of authentic living.

The unconscious mind also plays a critical role in shaping our relationships, often in ways we are unaware of. Our 'fantasmatic signature' includes the internalized images of significant others, the patterns of interaction we have learned, and the unconscious projections we cast onto those around us. These unconscious dynamics can lead to repetitive relational failures, to a sense of being trapped in familiar but unfulfilling connections. For example, an individual might repeatedly find themselves drawn to partners who are emotionally unavailable, a pattern rooted in an unconscious fantasy that mirrors early experiences of seeking affection from caregivers who were distant. When the awareness of our own mortality enters the equation, these relational patterns become particularly poignant. The fear of dying alone, or the regret of having not cultivated deep, meaningful bonds, can be powerful motivators for change. By understanding the unconscious underpinnings of our relational choices, by recognizing how our 'fantasmatic signature' influences who we are drawn to and how we interact, we can begin to break free from these cycles. We can choose to engage in relationships that nourish us, that reflect our deepest values, and that allow for genuine intimacy, thus ensuring that our final years are not shadowed by the loneliness of unfulfilled connection.

Furthermore, the unconscious holds the key to our authentic creativity and our capacity for wonder. Often, our rational minds can be critical and self-limiting, stifling nascent ideas and discouraging imaginative exploration. The unconscious, however, operates with a different logic, one that is fluid, associative, and unbounded by conventional norms. It is the wellspring of our deepest artistic impulses, our most profound insights, and our capacity to experience awe and transcendence. When we engage with the unconscious, we tap into this generative force. This can manifest in unexpected ways: a sudden surge of inspiration for a creative project, a novel solution to a persistent problem, or a deepened appreciation for the beauty and mystery of the world. As we approach the end of our lives, the capacity for creative expression and for experiencing wonder becomes increasingly precious. The unconscious, in its capacity to connect us to these profound experiences, offers a pathway to a richer, more meaningful existence. It reminds us that life is not merely a series of tasks to be completed, but a continuous unfolding of experience, a continuous invitation to engage with the marvels of existence.

The very act of exploring the unconscious, of bringing its contents into conscious awareness, is an act of empowerment. It is a process of reclaiming agency over aspects of ourselves that have previously operated beyond our control. When we understand the unconscious forces that drive our anxieties, our compulsions, and our relational patterns, we are no longer simply beholden to them. We can begin to engage with them, to dialogue with them, and ultimately, to integrate them into a more conscious and cohesive sense of self. This integration is not about eliminating the unconscious, but about developing a more mindful relationship with it. It is about recognizing that our 'fantasmatic signature' is not a prison, but a complex map that, when read with understanding, can guide us towards a more authentic and fulfilling journey.

This process of conscious integration, facilitated by a deeper understanding of our unconscious landscape, leads to a profound shift in our relationship with life itself, and consequently, with its inevitable end. The fear of death often stems from a fear of annihilation, of ceasing to be. However, when we have engaged with our unconscious, when we have begun to understand the core of our being that transcends the limitations of our physical form, this fear can transform. We may come to recognize that our essence – our capacity for love, for creativity, for connection, for meaning-making – is not entirely extinguished by physical death. The unconscious, through its symbolic representations of continuity, of transformation, and of interconnectedness, can offer a sense of transcendence that eases the terror of the void. It suggests that while the individual self may dissolve, the essence of our being, the unique configuration of energies and experiences that constitute our soul, may find expression in new forms, may contribute to the ongoing tapestry of existence in ways we can only dimly perceive.

Consider the profound sense of legacy that often occupies the thoughts of those contemplating their final years. This is not merely about material inheritance, but about the enduring impact of one's life, the values passed on, the love shared, the contributions made. The unconscious mind plays a significant role in shaping our understanding of legacy. It informs our deepest desires for meaning and for a sense of continuity beyond our individual existence. By exploring our 'fantasmatic signature,' we can gain clarity on what kind of legacy we truly wish to cultivate. Is it one based on external achievements, or on the quality of our relationships and the integrity of our character? The unconscious can reveal the deeper, more soulful aspirations that inform our sense of purpose and our desire to leave a positive imprint on the world. Aligning our actions with these deeper aspirations, even in the twilight of life, is a powerful act of authentic living. It ensures that our final years are dedicated to what truly matters, to the creation of a legacy that resonates with the deepest truths of our being.

The therapeutic journey, in its engagement with the unconscious, provides a safe and guided space for this exploration. Through various modalities – dream analysis, free association, transference analysis – individuals can begin to unravel the complex threads of their 'fantasmatic signature.' They can identify the origins of their deepest fears and desires, understand the recurring patterns that shape their lives, and begin to consciously redirect their energies towards more authentic expressions of self. This is not a quick fix, but a profound process of self-discovery and transformation. It requires patience, courage, and a willingness to confront uncomfortable truths. Yet, the rewards are immense: a life lived with greater integrity, a deeper sense of purpose, and a more profound connection to oneself and to others.

Ultimately, the unconscious, when viewed not as a dark abyss but as a profound source of wisdom, becomes our most reliable guide to authentic living. It speaks in a language of symbols, emotions, and intuitions, revealing the hidden architecture of our being. By learning to listen to its whispers, by daring to explore the depths of our 'fantasmatic signature,' particularly in the context of our ultimate finitude, we can move beyond a life dictated by unconscious imperatives and towards one that is consciously chosen, deeply meaningful, and profoundly true to ourselves. This journey towards authenticity, illuminated by the insights of the unconscious, allows us to live fully, to love deeply, and to face life's final lyric not with dread, but with a quiet, knowing grace. The unconscious, in its intricate design, holds the blueprint not only for our deepest fears but also for our most profound potential for authentic existence, offering a guiding light through the complexities of life towards its inevitable, yet often illuminating, conclusion.

The cessation of life, often viewed through the stark lens of biological finality, can also be apprehended as the profound, albeit unconscious, culmination of an individual's artistic endeavor. Each existence, from its nascent stirrings to its final exhalation, can be understood as a singular work of art, crafted by the intricate interplay of conscious choices and the subterranean currents of the unconscious. Death, in this light, is not merely an abrupt interruption but the ultimate, unresolved chord, the final brushstroke, the last stanza of a deeply personal and profoundly symbolic narrative. It is the point where the tapestry of lived experience, woven with threads of joy, sorrow, aspiration, and regret, is finally completed, its pattern revealed in its entirety. This perspective shifts our contemplation of death from a feared oblivion to a unique, individualistic masterpiece, a testament to the singular journey of the soul.

This notion of death as an unconscious artistic creation posits that the very form and texture of our ending are orchestrated by the deepest, most inarticulable aspects of our psyche. Just as an artist pours their entire being into their work, imbuing it with their unique vision, their history, and their very essence, so too does the unconscious shape our passage from life. The anxieties that may surface, the memories that rise to prominence, the images that flicker at the edge of perception – these are not random occurrences but elements of a final, symbolic composition. The individual who lived a life of quiet contemplation might, in their final moments, experience a profound sense of peace, a gentle fading that mirrors the serene landscapes they cherished. Conversely, one who battled with internal turmoil might face their end with a symbolic struggle, a last, unyielding resistance that reflects their lifelong battles. These are not conscious decisions, but the unconscious self orchestrating the final act with a profound, if mysterious, artistic sensibility.

The narrative arc of a life, so often constructed through conscious intention and reaction, finds its ultimate resolution in this final act. The unconscious, in its perpetual dance with consciousness, weaves the story threads of our existence into a cohesive, if often symbolically dense, conclusion. The fears we have suppressed, the desires we have deferred, the relationships that have shaped us – all contribute to the script of our dying. Consider how certain individuals, upon realizing their mortality, may find themselves revisited by long-forgotten figures or pivotal moments from their past. These are not mere random recall, but thematic echoes, resonating with the core narrative of their life. The unconscious, acting as a director, brings these elements into focus, ensuring that the final scene resonates with the overarching story that has unfolded. It is a profoundly personal drama, staged in the theater of the dying mind, with each soul as both the playwright and the protagonist.

The aesthetic dimension of this final creation is equally significant. Just as a painting or a piece of music possesses a unique mood, a particular palette, or a distinct rhythm, so too does each death carry its own aesthetic. This can manifest in the emotional tone that surrounds the dying process – be it one of quiet dignity, profound acceptance, or even a turbulent, cathartic release. The symbolic imagery that may accompany these final moments, often observed by loved ones or even recorded in near-death experiences, further contributes to this unique aesthetic. These images, whether they are visions of light, encounters with spiritual figures, or symbolic representations of life's journey, are not arbitrary but deeply personal expressions of the individual's inner world, their faith, their fears, and their hopes. They form the visual and emotional signature of their final creative act, imprinting their unique artistry onto the very moment of their departure.

This perspective invites a profound re-evaluation of how we perceive the process of dying. Rather than viewing it as a stark void or a simple biological shutdown, we can begin to see it as the ultimate expression of individuality. Each life, with its unique tapestry of experiences, its individual unconscious landscape, culminates in a death that is as distinct and personal as the life itself. It is a testament to the fact that even in our final moments, when conscious control may wane, the unconscious self continues its work, shaping our exit with an artistic hand. This unconscious artistry is not about a deliberate, conscious intent to create a particular kind of death, but rather a natural unfolding, a symbolic representation of the totality of one's being. It is the natural conclusion of a deeply personal and inherently symbolic journey.

When we acknowledge death as an unconscious artistic creation, we are compelled to consider the life that precedes it as the gestation period for this final masterpiece. The choices we make, the lessons we learn, the love we give and receive, the regrets we harbor – all are pigments on the palette, notes in the composition, words in the poem of our lives. The unconscious mind, through its intricate workings, collects and synthesizes these elements, preparing them for their ultimate expression. It is in the quiet moments of reflection, in the depths of dreams, and in the sudden flares of intuition that the unconscious gathers its materials, refining them for their final presentation. This process underscores the interconnectedness of life and death, not as separate entities, but as integral parts of a continuous, unfolding creative act.

The implications of this perspective are far-reaching. If death is indeed the unconscious artistry of the individual, then the process of living becomes an ongoing act of shaping that artistry. By consciously engaging with our inner lives, by understanding our deepest fears and desires, by striving for authenticity in our choices, we are, in essence, honing our skills as artists of our own existence. This does not mean that we can consciously dictate the exact nature of our death, but rather that a life lived with intention and self-awareness contributes to a more harmonious and integrated final expression. The unconscious, armed with a richer, more authentic palette of experiences, can then orchestrate a more resonant and meaningful ending. It is a call to live not just for the present, but for the entirety of the narrative, including its powerful conclusion.

Furthermore, this framework encourages us to approach the dying of others with a deeper sense of reverence and curiosity. Instead of imposing our own expectations or anxieties onto their final moments, we can endeavor to perceive the unique artistic expression that is unfolding before us. The unconscious dialogue between the dying individual and their inner world is a sacred, private performance. Our role, often, is not to interrupt or to attempt to control this final act, but to bear witness, to offer a supportive presence, and to allow the individual's unique symphony to play out. This requires a profound level of empathy and a willingness to surrender our need for conscious control, trusting in the inherent wisdom of the unconscious to guide the soul towards its final resolution.

Ultimately, embracing death as the unconscious artistic creation of our lives imbues our existence with a profound sense of purpose and meaning. It suggests that every life, no matter how seemingly ordinary, holds within it the potential for a unique and powerful culmination. This final lyric, sung in the language of the unconscious, is a testament to the enduring power of the individual spirit. It is a reminder that our lives are not merely a series of events, but a grand, intricate composition, with death serving as its breathtaking, unforgettable finale. This perspective fosters not a morbid fascination with dying, but a deeper appreciation for the art of living, and for the profound, mysterious artistry that concludes our journey through existence. It is life's last, most intimate lyric, a masterpiece unique to each soul.

Back Matter

Archetype: Universal, archaic patterns and images that derive from the collective unconscious and are the psychic counterpart of the instincts. (Jung)

Catharsis: The process of releasing, and thereby providing relief from, strong or repressed emotions.

Collective Unconscious: A concept introduced by Carl Jung to describe the deepest layer of the unconscious psyche, containing inherited structures of the psyche common to all humanity.

Ego: In psychoanalytic theory, the part of the mind that mediates between the conscious and the unconscious and is responsible for reality testing and a sense of personal identity.

Id: In psychoanalytic theory, the instinctual and unconscious part of the psyche that seeks immediate gratification of desires, operating on the pleasure principle.

Near-Death Experience (NDE): A profound personal experience associated with intending to die or being in close proximity to death, often characterized by altered states of consciousness and vivid imagery.

Psyche: The totality of the human mind, including conscious and unconscious aspects. (Jung)

Regression: In psychoanalytic theory, a defense mechanism whereby an individual reverts to an earlier stage of development.

Superego: In psychoanalytic theory, the part of the personality that represents internalized ideals and moral standards, often in conflict with the Id.

Symbolic Representation: The use of symbols to convey meaning, particularly in the unconscious, where abstract concepts or emotions are often expressed through imagery.

Freud, Sigmund. *The Interpretation of Dreams*. 1900.

Jung, Carl Gustav. *Man and His Symbols*. 1964.

Kastenbaum, Robert. *Death, Society, and Human Experience.* 2010.

Kübler-Ross, Elisabeth. *On Death and Dying.* 1969.

Moretti, Franco. *The Modern Epic: The World-System and the Crisis of the Novel.* 2011.

Rank, Otto. *The Trauma of Birth.* 1924.

Wilde, Oscar. *The Picture of Dorian Gray.* 1890.

Don't miss out!

Visit the website below and you can sign up to receive emails whenever Deivede Eder Ferreira publishes a new book. There's no charge and no obligation.

https://books2read.com/r/B-A-ZGRUE-QKXEI

BOOKS 2 READ

Connecting independent readers to independent writers.

Did you love *Does the Unconscious Desire Determine the Way We Die?: The New Theory of Phantasmatic Death*? Then you should read *Freud — The Definitive Biography: The True Story of the Father of Psychoanalysis*[1] by Deivede Eder Ferreira!

[2]

Freud: The Definitive Biography offers a powerful and meticulously crafted portrait of the man who transformed our understanding of the human mind. Moving beyond clichés and academic simplifications, this work traces Sigmund Freud's intellectual journey from the cafés of fin-de-siècle Vienna to the creation of one of the most influential theories of the twentieth century.

Drawing on historical documents, clinical notes, letters, and the major psychoanalytic texts, the book unfolds Freud's life in its full complexity: his early struggles, his scientific ambitions, his

1. https://books2read.com/u/3LZxvD

2. https://books2read.com/u/3LZxvD

controversial discoveries, and the personal conflicts that shaped both the man and his work. Each chapter combines rigorous scholarship with narrative clarity, making this biography accessible to new readers while offering depth and precision for specialists.

More than a chronological account, this book explores the emotional, cultural, and philosophical forces that molded Freud's thought. It illuminates the origins of concepts such as the unconscious, repression, the Oedipus complex, and the symbolic life of dreams, showing how these ideas emerged not only from clinical practice but also from the drama of Freud's own lived experience.

This is a definitive, engaging, and human portrait of Freud—neither idolized nor reduced—presenting him as a thinker who dared to look into the darkest corners of the psyche and, in doing so, changed the world.

Also by Deivede Eder Ferreira

Behind the Theory: The Lives of the Great Psychoanalysts
Freud — The Definitive Biography: The True Story of the Father of Psychoanalysis

Últimos Dias dos Grandes Pensadores
Sócrates: O Último Amanhecer
Platão: Quando o Mestre Silenciou
Aristóteles: O Nascimento do Método

Standalone
Psychoanalysis
The Quantum Switch: How to Shift Your Inner Reality
Does the Unconscious Desire Determine the Way We Die?: The New Theory of Phantasmatic Death
سقراط: الفجر الأخير

www.ingramcontent.com/pod-product-compliance
Lightning Source LLC
LaVergne TN
LVHW090302210926
848480LV00001B/101
* 9 7 9 8 2 3 2 7 7 8 2 2 4 *